Florida's B.E.S.T.

Standards for MATH

Grade 7

with CalcChat® and CalcView®

B.E.S.T. Test Prep and Practice Workbook

- Review & Refresh
- Self-Assessments
- B.E.S.T. Test Prep
- Post-Course Test
- Correlation to Florida's B.E.S.T. Standards
- Evidence-Based Scale Worksheets

Big Ideas Learning™

Erie, Pennsylvania

Printed in the United States

ISBN 13: 978-1-64727-848-9

89—25

Contents

About the B.E.S.T. Test Prep and Practice Workbook vii

Chapter 1 Exponents and Rational Numbers

1.1 Exponents 1
1.2 Product of Powers Property 3
1.3 Quotient of Powers Property 5
1.4 Rational Numbers 7
1.5 Rational Numbers and Exponents 9
Chapter Self-Assessment 11
B.E.S.T. Test Prep 13

Chapter 2 Operations with Rational Numbers

2.1 Adding Rational Numbers 17
2.2 Subtracting Rational Numbers 19
2.3 Converting between Fractions and Decimals 21
2.4 Multiplying Rational Numbers 23
2.5 Dividing Rational Numbers 25
2.6 Using Rational Number Operations 27
Chapter Self-Assessment 29
B.E.S.T. Test Prep 31

Contents

Chapter 3 Expressions, Equations, and Inequalities

3.1 Algebraic Expressions 35

3.2 Adding and Subtracting Linear Expressions 37

3.3 Writing Equivalent Expressions 39

3.4 Solving One-Step Equations 41

3.5 Solving Two-Step Equations 43

3.6 Writing and Graphing Inequalities 45

3.7 Solving Inequalities Using Addition or Subtraction 47

3.8 Solving Inequalities Using Multiplication or Division 49

Chapter Self-Assessment 51

B.E.S.T. Test Prep 53

Chapter 4 Ratios and Proportions

4.1 Ratios and Ratio Tables 57

4.2 Graphing Ratio Relationships 59

4.3 Rates and Unit Rates 61

4.4 Converting Measures between Systems 63

4.5 Identifying Proportional Relationships 65

4.6 Writing and Solving Proportions 67

4.7 Using Graphs of Proportional Relationships 69

4.8 Scale Drawings 71

Chapter Self-Assessment 73

B.E.S.T. Test Prep 75

Contents

Chapter 5 Percents

5.1 Fractions, Decimals, and Percents 79
5.2 The Percent Proportion 81
5.3 The Percent Equation 83
5.4 Percents of Increase and Decrease 85
5.5 Discounts and Markups 87
5.6 Simple Interest 89
Chapter Self-Assessment 91
B.E.S.T. Test Prep 93

Chapter 6 Probability and Data Displays

6.1 Probability 97
6.2 Experimental and Theoretical Probability 99
6.3 Circle Graphs 101
6.4 Choosing a Data Display 103
Chapter Self-Assessment 105
B.E.S.T. Test Prep 107

Chapter 7 Statistics

7.1 Measures of Center and Variation 111
7.2 Choosing Appropriate Measures 113
7.3 Samples and Populations 115
7.4 Comparing Populations 117
Chapter Self-Assessment 119
B.E.S.T. Test Prep 121

Contents

Chapter 8 Area, Surface Area, and Volume

8.1 Areas of Parallelograms 125

8.2 Areas of Trapezoids and Other Polygons 127

8.3 Circles and Circumference 129

8.4 Areas of Circles 131

8.5 Perimeters and Areas of Composite Figures 133

8.6 Surface Areas of Cylinders 135

8.7 Volumes of Cylinders 137

Chapter Self-Assessment 139

B.E.S.T. Test Prep 141

Post-Course Test 145

Correlation to Florida's B.E.S.T. Standards 155

Evidence-Based Scale Worksheets

Number Sense and Operations 157

Algebraic Reasoning 167

Geometric Reasoning 191

Data Analysis and Probability 207

About the B.E.S.T. Test Prep and Practice Workbook

Review & Refresh

Use the Review & Refresh exercises to practice the key concepts taught in each section as well as practice prior skills to improve retention.

Self-Assessments

Use the self-assessments provided for every section and chapter to rate your understanding of the learning targets and success criteria.

B.E.S.T. Test Prep

Use the cumulative test provided for each chapter to prepare for standardized test questions, including multiple choice, multi-select, and gridded response.

Post-Course Test

Use the Post-Course Test to measure your understanding of all content within this course. This assessment is designed to prepare you for standardized test questions, including multiple choice, multi-select, and gridded response.

Correlation to Florida's B.E.S.T. Standards

Use the correlation to see the standard(s) addressed by each item in the B.E.S.T. Test Prep and Post-Course Test.

Evidence-Based Scale Worksheets

Use the Evidence-Based Scale Worksheets to monitor your learning of Florida's B.E.S.T. Standards. Each worksheet focuses on one benchmark, and is broken down into four leveled targets, or mini-goals, to help you measure whether you have achieved the learning.

Name_______________________________ Date__________

Lesson 1.1

Review & Refresh

Write the product using exponents.

1. $7 \cdot 7 \cdot 7 \cdot 7 \cdot 7 \cdot 7 \cdot 7$

2. $6 \cdot 6 \cdot 6 \cdot 3 \cdot 3 \cdot 3 \cdot 3$

3. On a flash drive, 800 megabytes out of 1000 megabytes are used. Write the amount occupied as a percent.

4. You have piano lessons every 7 days, swimming lessons every 2 days, and chores every 6 days. You did all three things today. When will you have all 3 activities again?

Evaluate the expression.

5. 13^2

6. -4^4

7. -10^2

8. 1^8

9. A container holds 500 fluid ounces of water. Each glass holds $6\frac{1}{5}$ fluid ounces.

a. How many glasses are filled?

b. How many fluid ounces are left over?

10. You have given away 48 toy cars. You have 94 remaining. Write and solve an equation to find the number of toy cars you started with.

11. The expenses E (in millions of dollars) of a company are represented by the equation $E = 0.1x^2 + 1$ where x is the number of years after opening.

a. What are the expenses for year 1?

b. What is the difference in expenses between year 3 and year 4?

Name ________________________________ Date __________

Lesson 1.1 Review & Refresh (continued)

Evaluate the expression.

12. $7 + 4 \cdot 3^2$

13. $15^2 - 10^2 \div 5$

14. $\frac{1}{2}(8^2 - 24)$

15. $-5^3 - 20 \div 10$

16. $-6(16 - 4^3)$

17. $-5 + 12^2 \div 6 + 20$

18. You have 1000 cards. You sell them in packs of 5.

a. Write the expression that represents the number of cards remaining after p packs are sold.

b. How many cards are left after selling 38 packs?

19. The ratio of two numbers is 3 : 7. What are the numbers if their sum is 90?

20. A flag is in the shape of a triangle with a base of 24 feet and a height of 18 feet. What is the area of the triangle?

Lesson 1.1 Self-Assessment

Use the scale to rate your understanding of the learning target and the success criteria.

1 I don't understand yet. | 2 I can do it with help. | 3 I can do it on my own. | 4 I can teach someone else.

	Rating	Date
1.1 Exponents		
Learning Target: Use exponents to write and evaluate expressions.	1 2 3 4	
I can explain what an exponent is.	1 2 3 4	
I can evaluate expressions involving powers.	1 2 3 4	
I can use exponents to solve real-life problems.	1 2 3 4	

Name ______________________________ Date ________

Lesson 1.2 Review & Refresh

Simplify the expression. Write your answer as a power.

1. $7^4 \cdot 7^6$ **2.** $9^7 \cdot 9$ **3.** $(3^8)^3$

Write the product using exponents.

4. $4 \cdot 4 \cdot 4 \cdot 4 \cdot 4 \cdot 4 \cdot 4 \cdot 4$ **5.** $9 \cdot 9 \cdot 8 \cdot 8 \cdot 8 \cdot 8$

6. You buy \$14 in produce from a farmer's market. This is one-fourth of the money in your wallet. Write and solve an equation to find the amount in your wallet.

7. The area of a bedroom is 120 square feet. The smallest dimension of the room is no less than 8 feet. What are the possible dimensions for the room?

Simplify the expression. Write your answer as a product of powers.

8. $(7 \cdot 5)^2$ **9.** $(3 \cdot 8)^6$ **10.** $(9 \cdot 4)^3$

11. To rent a bicycle, the cost is \$12 per hour plus a \$20 fee.

a. Write the expression that represents the cost of renting the bicycle for h hours.

b. What is the cost for 4 hours?

12. The number of bacteria in a colony, B, after t hours is represented by the equation, $B = 25(3)^t$.

a. How many bacteria are there after 6 hours?

b. How many bacteria are there after half a day?

Name ______________________________________ Date __________

Lesson 1.2 Review & Refresh (continued)

Evaluate the expression.

13. 15^2 **14.** -5^3 **15.** 7^3 **16.** 2^7

17. A new housing development has 3^4 houses built. A new apartment complex has 9 times as many apartments. How many apartments does the complex have?

18. The table shows the quiz scores for 15 students.

16	17	18	20	18
17	18	19	15	20
16	17	18	20	15

a. What is the mean score?

b. What is the median score?

c. What is the mode score?

19. A car is purchased for $18,000 with a 10% sales tax. What is the amount of the sales tax?

Lesson 1.2 Self-Assessment

Use the scale to rate your understanding of the learning target and the success criteria.

1 I don't understand yet. 2 I can do it with help. 3 I can do it on my own. 4 I can teach someone else.

	Rating	Date
1.2 Product of Powers Property		
Learning Target: Generate equivalent expressions involving product of powers.	1 2 3 4	
I can find products of powers that have the same base.	1 2 3 4	
I can find powers of powers.	1 2 3 4	
I can find powers of products.	1 2 3 4	

Name ______________________________ Date __________

Lesson 1.3 Review & Refresh

Simplify the expression. Write your answer as a power.

1. $\frac{15^4}{15^2}$

2. $\frac{60^7}{60^3}$

3. $\frac{28^{18}}{28^9}$

4. $8^{12} \cdot 8^3$

5. $6^{10} \cdot 6^5$

6. $(1^{15})^4$

7. $\frac{6^{14}}{6^5 \cdot 6^3}$

8. $\frac{8^{20} \cdot 8^4}{8^7}$

9. $\frac{4^5 \cdot 4^2}{4^3 \cdot 4}$

10. The number of views, V, for a video, h hours after it is released is represented by the equation, $V = 8(2)^h$.

a. How many views are there after 10 hours?

b. How many views are there after 1 day?

11. You have $5\frac{5}{6}$ cups of sugar. One recipe used $1\frac{1}{2}$ cups. Another recipe needs $2\frac{1}{4}$ cups. How much sugar is remaining?

12. A copier copies 112 pages in 3.5 minutes.

a. How many pages can be copied in $\frac{1}{4}$ of an hour?

b. How long does it take to copy 800 pages?

Write the product using exponents.

13. $5 \cdot 5 \cdot 5 \cdot 5 \cdot 6 \cdot 6$

14. $2 \cdot 2 \cdot 7 \cdot 7 \cdot 7 \cdot 7 \cdot 7$

Name ______________________________ Date __________

Lesson 1.3 Review & Refresh (continued)

15. A cube has a side length of 11 centimeters.

a. Write the volume as a power.

b. What is the actual volume?

16. The point differentiation for a basketball team in its first games was –5, 7, 12, –4, –13, and 3 points.

a. How many games were won or lost?

b. List the point differential in order from least to greatest.

17. The volume of a box is 2^7 cubic inches. The box fits in a shipping container with a volume of $3^3 \cdot 2^{10}$ cubic inches. How many boxes can fit in the crate?

Evaluate the expression.

18. -14^2 **19.** 9^3 **20.** -12^2 **21.** 3^6

Lesson 1.3 Self-Assessment

Use the scale to rate your understanding of the learning target and the success criteria.

1 I don't understand yet. 2 I can do it with help. 3 I can do it on my own. 4 I can teach someone else.

	Rating	Date
1.3 Quotient of Powers Property		
Learning Target: Generate equivalent expressions involving quotient of powers.	1 2 3 4	
I can find quotient of powers that have the same base.	1 2 3 4	
I can simplify expressions using the Quotient of Powers Property.	1 2 3 4	
I can solve real-life problems involving quotients of powers.	1 2 3 4	

Name ____________________ Date ________

Lesson 1.4 Review & Refresh

Find the absolute value.

1. $|0|$

2. $\left|-\frac{2}{3}\right|$

3. $|-5.4|$

4. $\left|3\frac{7}{8}\right|$

Evaluate the expression.

5. $8 - 7 \cdot 4^2$

6. $\frac{3}{4}(8 + 4^2)$

7. $(-8 + 10 - 3^3) \div 5$

8. You are 6.5 feet above sea level. Your friend is diving 8.5 feet below sea level. Who is closer to sea level? Explain.

9. A device has 2^4 gigabytes of storage. You want to upgrade to a new device that has 2^9 gigabytes. How many times greater is the storage of the new device?

Simplify the expression. Write your answer as a power.

10. $\frac{6^8}{6^5}$

11. $\frac{10^{15}}{10^4 \cdot 10^7}$

12. $\frac{7^2 \cdot 7^5}{7} \cdot \frac{7^2}{7^3}$

13. $(6^2)^3$

14. $8^5 \cdot 8^7$

15. $(9^5)^4$

Complete the statement using <, >, or =.

16. 8 ____ $|-7|$

17. $|9|$ ____ $|-9|$

18. $|-4.9|$ ____ 4.8

19. $|0.9|$ ____ $\left|-\frac{8}{9}\right|$

20. $\left|-1\frac{3}{4}\right|$ ____ $|1.75|$

21. -7.5 ____ $-|7.3|$

Name ____________________ Date __________

Lesson 1.4 Review & Refresh (continued)

22. A stack of logs is kept beside a house. The number of logs ℓ in each row can be represented by the equation $\ell = 2^{n-1}$ where n is the row.

a. How many logs are there in the 8th row?

b. How many logs in total are there in 5 rows?

Order the values from least to greatest.

23. $-7, |-4|, 5, -3, |8|$

24. $\frac{1}{4}, -\frac{1}{8}, \left|-\frac{1}{6}\right|, -\frac{1}{10}, \left|\frac{1}{3}\right|$

25. One group has raised 10^4 dollars. Another group has raised 10^2 times more dollars. How many dollars were raised by the second group?

Simplify the expression. Write your answer as a product of powers.

26. $(3 \cdot 10)^3$

27. $(7 \cdot 4)^2$

28. $(11 \cdot 5)^5$

Lesson 1.4 Self-Assessment

Use the scale to rate your understanding of the learning target and the success criteria.

1 I don't understand yet. 2 I can do it with help. 3 I can do it on my own. 4 I can teach someone else.

	Rating	Date
1.4 Rational Numbers		
Learning Target: Understand how to compare rational numbers.	1 2 3 4	
I can graph rational numbers on a number line.	1 2 3 4	
I can find the absolute value of a rational number.	1 2 3 4	
I can use a number line to compare rational numbers.	1 2 3 4	

Name ______________________________ Date ________

Lesson 1.5

Review & Refresh

1. A cube has a side length of $\frac{2}{3}$ inch.

a. Write an expression involving a power that represents the surface area of the cube.

b. Write an expression involving a power that represents the volume of the cube.

2. There are 5 players in a game. Their point totals are shown in the table.

a. Order the point totals from least to greatest.

Player	1	2	3	4	5
Points	−50	100	0	−150	50

b. What is the point differential between the highest and lowest scores?

3. The area of your property in a rural area is 10^5 square feet. Your friend's property is $2 \cdot 10^6$ square feet. How many times greater is the area of your friend's property?

Simplify the expression. Write your answer as a power.

4. $\frac{5^{18}}{5^{16}}$

5. $\frac{9^{15}}{9^3 \cdot 9^5}$

6. $\frac{5^8 \cdot 5^4}{5^2 \cdot 5^6}$

7. $(3^8)^5$

8. $4^{12} \cdot 4^4$

9. $8^{10} \cdot 8^{10}$

Write the product using exponents.

10. $0.4 \cdot 0.4 \cdot 0.4 \cdot 0.4$

11. $\left(-\frac{1}{2}\right) \cdot \left(-\frac{1}{2}\right) \cdot \left(-\frac{1}{2}\right)$

Evaluate the expression.

12. $(0.8)^2$

13. $(-0.3)^4$

14. $-\left(\frac{1}{2}\right)^4$

15. $\left(\frac{3}{8}\right)^2$

Name ______________________________ Date __________

Lesson 1.5 Review & Refresh (continued)

Find the absolute value.

16. $|4|$ **17.** $|-7|$ **18.** $\left|-7\frac{1}{2}\right|$ **19.** $|18.4|$

Simplify the expression. Write your answer as a product of powers.

20. $(1 \cdot 8)^7$ **21.** $(10 \cdot 2)^5$ **22.** $(8 \cdot 6)^4$

Complete the statement using <, >, or =.

23. $|-4|$ ____ $|-5|$ **24.** $|-6|$ ____ 0 **25.** $|3.3|$ ____ $|-3.5|$

26. $-\left|-2\frac{2}{3}\right|$ ____ $-\left|2\frac{2}{3}\right|$ **27.** $\left|\frac{7}{10}\right|$ ____ $\left|-\frac{3}{4}\right|$ **28.** -8.8 ____ $-|8.9|$

Simplify the expression. Write your answer as a power.

29. $0.4^4 \cdot 0.4$ **30.** $\frac{7.2^{10}}{7.2^7}$ **31.** $(1.5^4)^6$

Lesson 1.5 Self-Assessment

Use the scale to rate your understanding of the learning target and the success criteria.

1 I don't understand yet. 2 I can do it with help. 3 I can do it on my own. 4 I can teach someone else.

	Rating	Date
1.5 Rational Numbers and Exponents		
Learning Target: Generate equivalent expressions involving powers with rational number bases.	1 2 3 4	
I can write products and evaluate expressions involving powers.	1 2 3 4	
I can simplify expressions involving powers.	1 2 3 4	
I can solve real-life problems involving powers.	1 2 3 4	

Name ______________________ Date ________

Chapter 1 Chapter Self-Assessment

Use the scale to rate your understanding of the learning target and the success criteria.

1 I don't understand yet. | 2 I can do it with help. | 3 I can do it on my own. | 4 I can teach someone else.

	Rating	Date
Chapter 1 Exponents and Rational Numbers		
Learning Target: Understand exponents and rational numbers.	1 2 3 4	
I can evaluate a power.	1 2 3 4	
I can evaluate expressions involving whole number bases.	1 2 3 4	
I can evaluate expressions involving rational number bases.	1 2 3 4	
I can solve real-life problems involving powers.	1 2 3 4	
1.1 Exponents		
Learning Target: Use exponents to write and evaluate expressions.	1 2 3 4	
I can explain what an exponent is.	1 2 3 4	
I can evaluate expressions involving powers.	1 2 3 4	
I can use exponents to solve real-life problems.	1 2 3 4	
1.2 Product of Powers Property		
Learning Target: Generate equivalent expressions involving products of powers.	1 2 3 4	
I can find products of powers that have the same base.	1 2 3 4	
I can find powers of powers.	1 2 3 4	
I can find powers of products.	1 2 3 4	

Name ______________________________ Date __________

Chapter 1

Chapter Self-Assessment (continued)

	Rating	Date
1.3 Quotient of Powers Property		
Learning Target: Generate equivalent expressions involving quotients of powers.	1 2 3 4	
I can find quotients of powers that have the same base.	1 2 3 4	
I can simplify expressions using the Quotient of Powers Property.	1 2 3 4	
I can solve real-life problems involving quotients of powers.	1 2 3 4	
1.4 Rational Numbers		
Learning Target: Understand how to compare rational numbers.	1 2 3 4	
I can graph rational numbers on a number line.	1 2 3 4	
I can find the absolute value of a rational number.	1 2 3 4	
I can use a number line to compare rational numbers.	1 2 3 4	
1.5 Rational Numbers and Exponents		
Learning Target: Generate equivalent expressions involving powers with rational number bases.	1 2 3 4	
I can write products and evaluate expressions involving powers.	1 2 3 4	
I can simplify expressions involving powers.	1 2 3 4	
I can solve real-life problems involving powers.	1 2 3 4	

Name________________________________ Date__________

Chapter 1 B.E.S.T. Test Prep

1. What power is equivalent to $3.5 \cdot 3.5 \cdot 3.5 \cdot 3.5 \cdot 3.5$?

Ⓐ 3.5^4

Ⓑ 3.5^5

Ⓒ $4^{3.5}$

Ⓓ $5^{3.5}$

2. Determine if the comparison is true or false.

	True	False
$\lvert -4 \rvert < 3$	Ⓐ	Ⓑ
$8 > \lvert -8 \rvert$	Ⓒ	Ⓓ
$\lvert -10 \rvert > 0$	Ⓔ	Ⓕ

3. A waitress makes \$8.40 per hour. She works 7.5 hours in one day. She also earns \$93.40 in tips. How much does she earn for the day?

Ⓐ \$109.30

Ⓑ \$116.80

Ⓒ \$154.20

Ⓓ \$156.40

4. What is the value of $-3(-2^4 + 30)$?

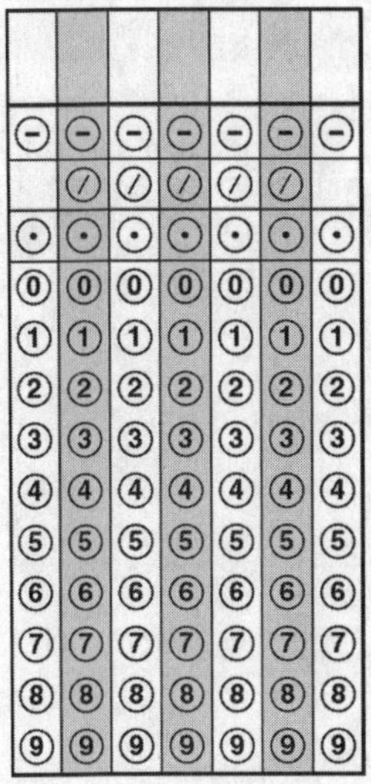

5. What is the value of $(14^2 - 13^2) \div (-3)$?

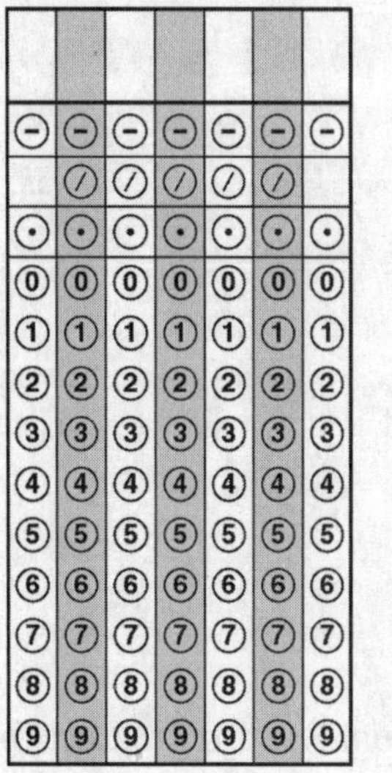

6. The cost of expenses, C, in millions of dollars of a company x years after opening is represented by the equation $C = 0.2x^2 + 5$. How much was the expense between years 3 and 4?

Ⓐ \$1,400,000

Ⓑ \$6,800,000

Ⓒ \$8,200,000

Ⓓ \$15,000,000

Name ______________________________ Date __________

Chapter 1 B.E.S.T. Test Prep (continued)

7. Which expressions are rewritten correctly?

Ⓐ $6^4 \cdot 6^7 = 6^{28}$

Ⓑ $(3^7)^9 = 3^{63}$

Ⓒ $(2 \cdot 5)^3 = 2^3 \cdot 5^3$

Ⓓ $\left(\frac{1}{2}\right)^4 \left(\frac{1}{2}\right)^8 = \left(\frac{1}{2}\right)^{32}$

Ⓔ $1.1^0 \cdot 1.1^9 = 0$

Ⓕ $\left(\left(\frac{2}{5}\right)^2\right)^8 = \left(\frac{2}{5}\right)^{16}$

8. Which expressions are rewritten correctly?

Ⓐ $\frac{3^7}{3^3} = 3^4$

Ⓑ $\frac{7^{15}}{7^4 \cdot 7^5} = 7^5$

Ⓒ $\frac{8^3 \cdot 8}{8^6} = 8^2$

Ⓓ $\frac{4.3^9}{4.3^2} = 4.3^7$

Ⓔ $\frac{1.1^{11}}{1.1 \cdot 1.1^8} = 1.1^2$

Ⓕ $\frac{0.8^9 \cdot 0.8^9}{0.8^3} = 0.8^{15}$

9. A plant is 40 inches tall. During the summer, the plant grows by 35%. What is the amount of growth in inches?

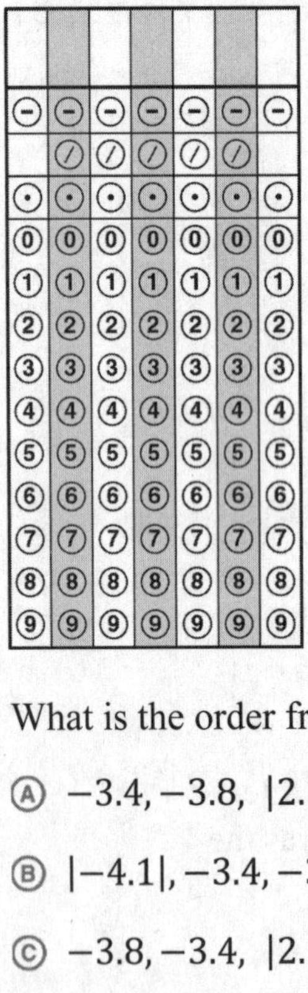

10. A storage container has these dimensions: 8 inches by 8 inches by 6 inches. What is its volume in cubic inches?

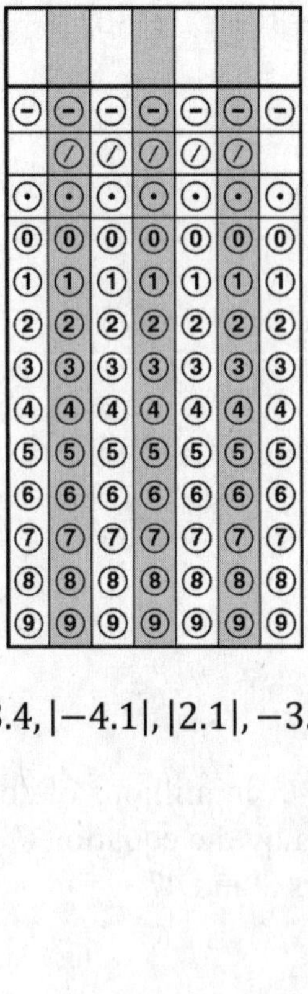

11. What is the order from least to greatest for $-3.4, |-4.1|, |2.1|, -3.8, 2.7$?

Ⓐ $-3.4, -3.8, |2.1|, 2.7, |-4.1|$

Ⓑ $|-4.1|, -3.4, -3.8, |2.1|, 2.7$

Ⓒ $-3.8, -3.4, |2.1|, 2.7, |-4.1|$

Ⓓ $|-4.1|, -3.8, -3.4, |2.1|, 2.7,$

Name____________________ Date__________

Chapter 1 B.E.S.T. Test Prep (continued)

12. There are 128 grams of a substance.
Every hour the product reduces by $\left(\frac{1}{2}\right)$. The expression for the amount left after 2 hours is [Ⓐ 2^4 / Ⓑ 2^5 / Ⓒ 2^6]. There is [Ⓐ 0.5 / Ⓑ 0.25 / Ⓒ 0.125] gram left after 8 hours.

13. The length of the side of a cube is 1.2^3 inches long. What is the volume of the cube?

Ⓐ 1.2^5 cubic inches

Ⓑ 1.2^6 cubic inches

Ⓒ 1.2^8 cubic inches

Ⓓ 1.2^9 cubic inches

14. An office has $3 \cdot 4^4$ employees. The employees are shared equally between 4 buildings. How many employees are in each building?

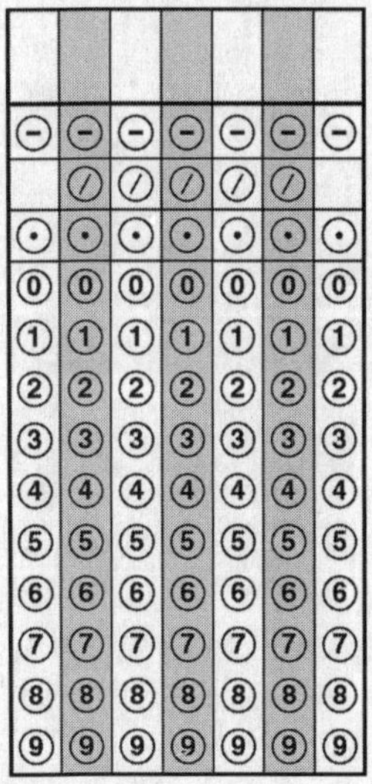

15. One megabyte of cellphone space is 2^{20} bytes. One app takes up 4^3 megabytes of storage space. How many bytes of storage space does the app use?

Ⓐ 4096 bytes

Ⓑ 8192 bytes

Ⓒ 16,384 bytes

Ⓓ 32,768 bytes

16. For every tile played in a game, you score 8 points. For every tile drawn, you lose 5 points. What is your score if you play 6 tiles and draw 12 tiles?

Ⓐ −18 points

Ⓑ −12 points

Ⓒ 48 points

Ⓓ 66 points

Name ______________________________ Date __________

Chapter 1 B.E.S.T. Test Prep (continued)

17. What is the value of -6^4?

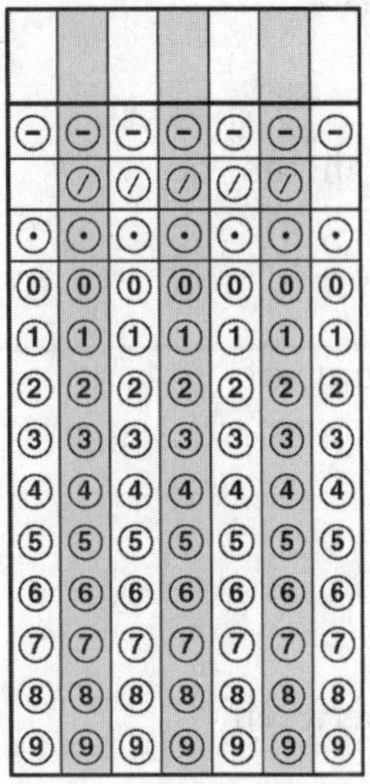

18. What is the value of $|-1.9|$?

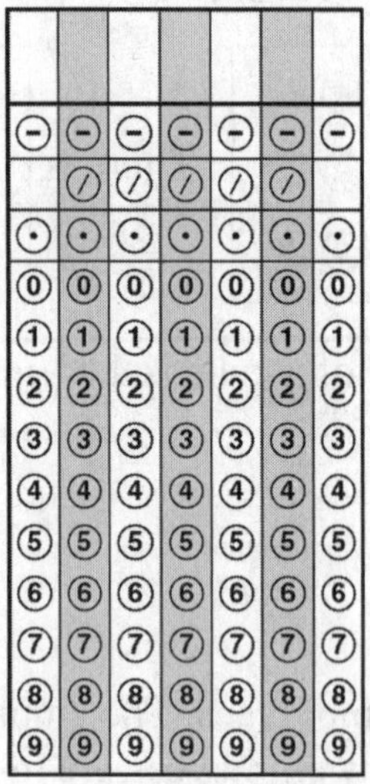

19. This question has **two** parts.

Four of your friends are diving below sea level.

Part A

Which depth represents the furthest from sea level?

Ⓐ −78 feet

Ⓑ −72 feet

Ⓒ −68 feet

Ⓓ −62 feet

Part B

What is the greatest difference in depth between the divers?

Ⓐ 4 feet

Ⓑ 10 feet

Ⓒ 8 feet

Ⓓ 16 feet

20. In a football game, a team lost 8 yards on first down, gained 7 yards on the second down, and gained 7 yards on the third down. What was the net gain or loss for the team?

Ⓐ −6 yards

Ⓑ −1 yard

Ⓒ 1 yard

Ⓓ 6 yards

Name____ Date__________

Lesson 2.1

Review & Refresh

Simplify the expression. Write your answer as a power.

1. $\frac{40^{16}}{40^{10}}$ **2.** $0.7^0 \cdot 0.7^9$ **3.** $\frac{11^5 \times 11^7}{11^4}$

4. $\frac{(-4.3)^9}{(-4.3)^5}$ **5.** $\frac{8^7 \times 8^4}{8^2} \times \frac{8^8}{8^3 \times 8^4}$ **6.** $\left(\frac{3}{5}\right)^3 \left(\frac{3}{5}\right)^7$

Find the sum. Write fractions in simplest form.

7. $6 + (-12)$ **8.** $-7.3 + 1.85$ **9.** $\frac{2}{9} + \left(-\frac{8}{9}\right)$ **10.** $-3\frac{3}{5} + 4\frac{1}{5}$

11. You have –10 points in a game. Your friend has 5 points. Who is closer to 0 points? Explain.

12. The side length of a square is 2.5^4 millimeters. Write the area as a power.

Evaluate the expression. Write fractions in simplest form.

13. $-41 + 29 + 16$ **14.** $18.75 + 12.25 + 19.5$ **15.** $-4\frac{1}{2} + 5\frac{1}{8} + \left(-3\frac{3}{8}\right)$

Write the product using exponents.

16. $\frac{7}{4} \cdot \frac{7}{4} \cdot \frac{7}{4} \cdot \frac{7}{4}$ **17.** $-(3.5 \cdot 3.5 \cdot 3.5 \cdot 3.5 \cdot 3.5)$

18. Your bank account balance is –\$10.45. You deposit \$26.80. Find the new account balance.

Name ______________________________ Date __________

Lesson 2.1 Review & Refresh (continued)

Find the sum. Write fractions in simplest form.

19. $(-16) + (-25)$ **20.** $-8.1 + (-9.7)$ **21.** $-\frac{1}{12} + \frac{11}{12}$ **22.** $5\frac{1}{10} + \left(-3\frac{2}{5}\right)$

23. The temperature was checked 5 different times of the day. The results are shown in the table.

a. List the temperatures from coldest to warmest.

b. Find the difference between the highest and lowest temperatures.

Time	Temperature
6:00 a.m.	–3°C
9:00 a.m.	–4°C
Noon	1°C
3:00 p.m.	5°C
6:00 p.m.	0°C

Evaluate the expression.

24. $\left(\frac{2}{3}\right)^4$ **25.** $\left(-\frac{1}{4}\right)^2$ **26.** 1.1^3 **27.** $\left(\frac{1}{10}\right)^3$

Complete the statement using <, >, or =.

28. $|-12|$ ____ 0 **29.** $-|3.1|$ _____ $-|-3.1|$

Lesson 2.1 Self-Assessment

Use the scale to rate your understanding of the learning target and the success criteria.

1 I don't understand yet. 2 I can do it with help. 3 I can do it on my own. 4 I can teach someone else.

	Rating	Date
2.1 Adding Rational Numbers		
Learning Target: Find sums of rational numbers.	1 2 3 4	
I can explain how to model addition of rational numbers on a number line.	1 2 3 4	
I can find sums of rational numbers by reasoning about absolute values.	1 2 3 4	
I can use properties of addition to efficiently add rational numbers.	1 2 3 4	

Name____ Date__________

Lesson 2.2 Review & Refresh

Find the sum or the difference. Write fractions in simplest form.

1. $-18 - 41$ **2.** $-20 + 8$ **3.** $\frac{4}{5} - \frac{9}{10}$ **4.** $-\frac{3}{4} + \frac{3}{16}$

5. $-6 - 3.5$ **6.** $-3.94 + 7.23$ **7.** $4 - 2\frac{2}{3}$ **8.** $-3\frac{1}{2} + \left(-4\frac{3}{4}\right)$

Order the numbers from least to greatest.

9. $-3.4, |-4.1|, |2.1|, -3.8, 2.7$ **10.** $|7.4|, |-3.8|, |-6.5|, -7.1, -5.4$

11. The length of a rectangle is 1.5^3 inches. The width of a rectangle is 1.5^4 inches. Find the area of the rectangle. Write as a power.

12. The table shows the change in height for a river over the course of 4 days. Find the total change in height of the river in feet.

Day	1	2	3	4
Change	$-\frac{1}{5}$	$1\frac{1}{4}$	$-\frac{1}{2}$	$-\frac{3}{5}$

Find the distance between the two numbers on a number line.

13. 3.6 and 8.1 **14.** –7.3 and 9.2 **15.** $-\frac{5}{12}$ and $\frac{11}{12}$

Evaluate the expression. Write fractions in simplest form.

16. $20 + 18 + (-16)$ **17.** $-9.3 + 3.7 + 8.8$ **18.** $\frac{3}{4} + \frac{1}{4} + \left(-\frac{7}{8}\right)$

19. You had 16 points in a game. You then lost 34 points. Find your current point total.

Name ______________________________ Date __________

Lesson 2.2 Review & Refresh (continued)

Simplify each expression. Write your answer as a power.

20. $\left(\left(-\frac{5}{6}\right)^3\right)^4$

21. $\left(-\frac{1}{10}\right)^8 \cdot \left(-\frac{1}{10}\right)^5$

22. $\frac{1.11^{12}}{1.11^7}$

Evaluate the expression.

23. $|-20|$

24. $\left|\frac{1}{3}\right|$

25. $-|3.7|$

26. $|-9.1|$

27. A container of milk contains $90\frac{1}{2}$ ounces. You drink $6\frac{3}{4}$ ounces of milk in every morning and $8\frac{1}{2}$ ounces every evening. How much is remaining after 3 days?

Write the distance between the points in the coordinate plane.

28. $(-8, -3.6), (-8, 8.1)$

29. $\left(-3\frac{3}{5}, 6\right), \left(-\frac{1}{10}, 6\right)$

Lesson 2.2 Self-Assessment

Use the scale to rate your understanding of the learning target and the success criteria.

1 I don't understand yet. 2 I can do it with help. 3 I can do it on my own. 4 I can teach someone else.

	Rating	Date
2.2 Subtracting Rational Numbers		
Learning Target: Find differences of rational numbers and find distances between numbers on a number line.	1 2 3 4	
I can explain how to model subtraction of rational numbers on a number line.	1 2 3 4	
I can find differences of rational numbers by reasoning about absolute values.	1 2 3 4	
I can find distances between numbers on a number line.	1 2 3 4	

Name____________________________________ Date__________

Lesson 2.3 Review & Refresh

Find the distance between the two numbers on a number line.

1. $-\frac{3}{10}$ and $\frac{5}{8}$ **2.** –10.86 and –4.52 **3.** $2\frac{1}{2}$ and $8\frac{3}{4}$

Write the product using exponents.

4. $(-1.3) \cdot (-1.3) \cdot (-1.3)$ **5.** $\frac{2}{5} \cdot \frac{2}{5} \cdot \frac{2}{5} \cdot \frac{2}{5} \cdot \frac{2}{5}$

Write the fraction or mixed numbers as a decimal.

6. $\frac{5}{16}$ **7.** $-\frac{1}{6}$ **8.** $2\frac{1}{10}$ **9.** $-9\frac{2}{3}$

10. In a town, the coldest temperature recorded is –15°F and the warmest temperature is 103°F. Find the difference of the temperatures.

11. The profit of a company each year is shown in the table in millions of dollars. Find the total amount of profit.

Year	2016	2017	2018	2019	2020
Profit	–3.1	–1.9	0.8	1.8	5.5

12. There are $10 \cdot 2^6$ apartments to be built. The number of apartments is equal between 5 buildings. Find the number of apartments.

Find the difference. Write fractions in simplest form.

13. 49 – (–32) **14.** –7.25 – (–1.5) **15.** $\frac{1}{12} - \frac{7}{12}$ **16.** $7\frac{1}{8} - 9\frac{1}{6}$

Evaluate the expression. Write fractions in simplest form.

17. $-\frac{4}{5} + \left(-\frac{3}{5}\right) + \frac{1}{5}$ **18.** 1.35 + (–1.58) + (–1.87) **19.** (–15) + (–31) + 24

Name ________________________________ Date __________

Lesson 2.3 Review & Refresh (continued)

Order the numbers from least to greatest.

20. $-\frac{1}{3}, \frac{4}{5}, -0.8, 0.4, -\frac{5}{6}$

21. $-1.8, 2\frac{1}{4}, -0.7, 1.3, 2\frac{2}{5}$

Write the decimal as a fraction or mixed number in simplest form.

22. 0.77 **23.** 0.806 **24.** 1.42 **25.** 3.1

Find the distance between the points in the coordinate plane.

26. $(-4.25, -9), (2.5, -9)$

27. $\left(8, -2\frac{2}{3}\right), \left(8, 7\frac{1}{3}\right)$

28. You have 5 quarters, 1 dime, 1 nickel, and 3 pennies. Write the dollar amount as decimal and as a fraction or mixed number.

Evaluate the expression.

29. -1.5^4

30. $\left(\frac{4}{5}\right)^3$

Lesson 2.3 Self-Assessment

Use the scale to rate your understanding of the learning target and the success criteria.

1 I don't understand yet. 2 I can do it with help. 3 I can do it on my own. 4 I can teach someone else.

	Rating	Date
2.3 Converting between Fractions and Decimals		
Learning Target: Convert between different forms of rational numbers.	1 2 3 4	
I can explain the difference between terminating and repeating decimals.	1 2 3 4	
I can write fractions and mixed numbers as decimals.	1 2 3 4	
I can write decimals as fractions and mixed numbers.	1 2 3 4	

Name____________________ Date__________

Lesson 2.4 Review & Refresh

1. The amount of water in a pool changes by –0.02 gallon per hour.

   a. Find the amount of change in one day.

   b. Find the amount of change in one week.

Write the decimal as a fraction or mixed number in simplest form.

2. 0.3
3. 0.291
4. 7.92
5. 9.563

Write the fraction or mixed number as a decimal.

6. $-\frac{2}{11}$
7. $\frac{11}{12}$
8. $-\frac{27}{22}$
9. $3\frac{1}{16}$

Find the sum or the difference. Write fractions in simplest form.

10. $-14 + (-9)$
11. $25 - 34$
12. $-5.9 + 4.6$
13. $8.2 - 9.7$
14. $-\frac{9}{10} + \left(-\frac{7}{10}\right)$
15. $-\frac{7}{8} - \left(-\frac{3}{8}\right)$
16. $-2\frac{2}{3} + 1\frac{1}{2}$
17. $-3\frac{5}{6} - 1\frac{1}{6}$

18. A 12.5-gallon gasoline tank is $\frac{1}{5}$ full. Find the number of gallons to fill the tank.

19. A submarine was at –210.8 feet and descended to –415.3 feet. Find the distance the submarine traveled.

Complete the statement using < or >.

20. $-8\frac{2}{3}$ ____ -8.4
21. $-7\frac{1}{11}$ ____ $-7.\overline{1}$
22. $-6\frac{9}{16}$ ____ $-6.\overline{5}$

Name ______________________________ Date __________

Lesson 2.4 Review & Refresh (continued)

Find the product. Write fractions in simplest form.

23. $-7 \cdot 12$

24. $(-8)^2$

25. $0\left(-\frac{20}{3}\right)$

26. $-\frac{1}{2}\left(-\frac{2}{3}\right)$

27. $4\left(-1\frac{2}{9}\right)$

28. $\left(5\frac{1}{2}\right)\left(-2\frac{2}{3}\right)$

29. $0.3 \times (-0.05)$

30. $(-0.2)(-0.7)$

31. A bank account has a balance of –$28.40. You deposit $58.70 and then make a payment of $36.90. Find the balance on the account.

Evaluate the expression. Write fractions in simplest form.

32. $17 + (-19) + (-8)$

33. $-12.1 + (-14.3) + 9$

34. $9\frac{1}{5} + \left(-6\frac{3}{5}\right) + 1\frac{1}{10}$

Lesson 2.4 Self-Assessment

Use the scale to rate your understanding of the learning target and the success criteria.

1 I don't understand yet. | 2 I can do it with help. | 3 I can do it on my own. | 4 I can teach someone else.

	Rating	Date
2.4 Multiplying Rational Numbers		
Learning Target: Find products of rational numbers.	1 2 3 4	
I can explain the rules for multiplying rational numbers.	1 2 3 4	
I can find products of rational numbers with the same sign.	1 2 3 4	
I can find products of rational numbers with different signs.	1 2 3 4	

Name____ Date__________

Lesson 2.5

Review & Refresh

Find the quotient. Write fractions in simplest form.

1. $\dfrac{\frac{7}{10}}{20}$ **2.** $\dfrac{\frac{3}{4}}{\frac{9}{16}}$ **3.** $\dfrac{\frac{3}{4}-\frac{7}{8}}{\frac{3}{8}}$

Find the product. Write fractions in simplest form.

4. $-3(0.08)(-0.2)^2$ **5.** $-\frac{3}{4}\times\frac{4}{9}\times\frac{1}{3}$ **6.** $1.4\times5\times(-1.8)$

7. Out of 40 questions on a quiz, you answer 6 incorrectly.

a. Write the correct number of questions as a decimal.

b. Write the correct number of questions as a fraction or mixed number.

8. A juice bottle is $\frac{9}{10}$ full. Your family drinks $\frac{2}{5}$ of what is remaining. Find the amount remaining.

9. You run 2.2 miles in 0.5 hour. Find the number of miles you run in 3.5 hours.

10. In a school, 504 students prefer open lunches. This is $\frac{3}{5}$ of the students in the school. Find the number of students in the school.

Write the decimal as a fraction or mixed numbers in simplest form.

11. 0.81 **12.** 0.64 **13.** 4.81 **14.** 2.225

Write the fraction or mixed numbers as a decimal.

15. $\frac{2}{3}$ **16.** $-\frac{3}{8}$ **17.** $-1\frac{4}{15}$ **18.** $5\frac{9}{20}$

Name ______________________________ Date __________

Lesson 2.5 Review & Refresh (continued)

Write the distance between the points in the coordinate plane.

19. $(4, -9.5), (4, -3.2)$

20. $(-3.6, 7), (-1.1, 7)$

21. You ride your bike $7\frac{3}{8}$ miles. Your friend rides $5\frac{2}{3}$ miles. Find how many more miles you ride.

22. For every tile drawn in a game, -1.5 points are scored. Find the number of points scored for drawing 9 tiles.

Find the product or the quotient. Write fractions in simplest form.

23. $-11 \div 1.1$

24. $3(-8)$

25. $-0.72 \div (-0.12)$

26. -7^2

27. $20 \div \left(-\frac{5}{8}\right)$

28. $-3\left(-3\frac{1}{10}\right)$

29. $-4\frac{1}{2} \div \left(-2\frac{2}{3}\right)$

30. $(-0.01)(0.8)$

Lesson 2.5 Self-Assessment

Use the scale to rate your understanding of the learning target and the success criteria.

1 I don't understand yet. | 2 I can do it with help. | 3 I can do it on my own. | 4 I can teach someone else.

	Rating	Date
2.5 Dividing Rational Numbers		
Learning Target: Find quotients of rational numbers.	1 2 3 4	
I can explain the rules for dividing rational numbers.	1 2 3 4	
I can find quotients of rational numbers with the same sign.	1 2 3 4	
I can find quotients of rational numbers with different signs.	1 2 3 4	

Name______________________________ Date__________

Lesson 2.6

Review & Refresh

Evaluate the expression. Write fractions in simplest form.

1. $8.25 - 7.5 \div 5^2$

2. $4.8 \div (-0.6) - 3.25$

3. $|-1.5 - 4| \cdot 1.1^2$

4. $-\left(\frac{3}{4}\right)^2 \div \left(-\frac{1}{2}\right)$

5. $-2\frac{1}{4} \times 1\frac{2}{3} - 3\frac{7}{12}$

6. $\frac{3}{5} - \frac{8}{9} - \frac{1}{3} + \frac{3}{10}$

Find the quotient. Write fractions in simplest form.

7. $\frac{\frac{17}{20}}{\frac{4}{5}}$

8. $\frac{\frac{7}{10}}{-\frac{3}{5} - \frac{4}{10}}$

9. $\frac{\frac{4}{9} + \frac{2}{3}}{\frac{5}{6} - \frac{7}{12}}$

10. The table shows the change in amount of snowpack in inches at a ski resort. Write the numbers from least to greatest.

Week	1	2	3	4
Change	-6.2	$-6\frac{3}{20}$	$-\frac{127}{20}$	-6.15

11. The water in an aquarium decreases by $\frac{7}{8}$ inch per day. Find the amount lost in one week.

12. A board 84 inches long is cut into strips that are $3\frac{1}{2}$ inches long. Find the number of strips that can be made.

13. The leading scorer of the basketball team averages 27.4 points per game. This is $\frac{1}{3}$ of the team's total number of points. Find the number of points the team scores.

Name ______________________________ Date __________

Lesson 2.6 Review & Refresh (continued)

Complete the statement using < or >.

14. -5.35 ____ $-5\frac{2}{5}$

15. $-4\frac{11}{15}$ ____ $-4\frac{13}{16}$

16. $-3\frac{13}{15}$ ____ $-3\frac{11}{13}$

Find the product or the quotient. Write fractions in simplest form.

17. $64 \div -4$

18. $\left(-1\frac{1}{4}\right)^2$

19. $-40.32 \div 7.2$

20. $3 \times -3 \times -8$

21. $-\frac{9}{10} \div \frac{3}{5}$

22. $\frac{2}{3} \cdot -\frac{4}{5} \cdot -15$

23. $-6\frac{6}{11} \div (-18)$

24. $-1.1 \times 1.2 \times -1.3$

25. You ride your bike for 3 days in a row. On Monday, you ride $3\frac{2}{3}$ miles. On Tuesday, you ride $1\frac{1}{2}$ times further. On Wednesday, you ride $1\frac{1}{4}$ miles less than Tuesday. Find the total number of miles.

Lesson 2.6 Self-Assessment

Use the scale to rate your understanding of the learning target and the success criteria.

1 I don't understand yet. | 2 I can do it with help. | 3 I can do it on my own. | 4 I can teach someone else.

	Rating	Date
2.6 Using Rational Number Operations		
Learning Target: Apply the order of operations to expressions involving rational numbers.	1 2 3 4	
I can use the order of operations to evaluate expressions.	1 2 3 4	
I can write and evaluate expressions to solve real-life problems.	1 2 3 4	

Name ______________________________ Date __________

Chapter 2

Chapter Self-Assessment

Use the scale to rate your understanding of the learning target and the success criteria.

1 I don't understand yet. 2 I can do it with help. 3 I can do it on my own. 4 I can teach someone else.

	Rating	Date
Chapter 2 Operations with Rational Numbers		
Learning Target: Understand operations with rational numbers.	1 2 3 4	
I can add and subtract rational numbers.	1 2 3 4	
I can multiply and divide rational numbers.	1 2 3 4	
I can convert between fractions and decimals.	1 2 3 4	
I can evaluate expressions involving rational numbers to solve real-life problems.	1 2 3 4	
2.1 Adding Rational Numbers		
Learning Target: Find sums of rational numbers.	1 2 3 4	
I can explain how to model addition of rational numbers on a number line.	1 2 3 4	
I can find sums of rational numbers by reasoning about absolute values.	1 2 3 4	
I can use properties of addition to efficiently add rational numbers.	1 2 3 4	
2.2 Subtracting Rational Numbers		
Learning Target: Find differences of rational numbers and find distances between numbers on a number line.	1 2 3 4	
I can explain how to model subtraction of rational numbers on a number line.	1 2 3 4	
I can find differences of rational numbers by reasoning about absolute values.	1 2 3 4	
I can find distances between numbers on a number line.	1 2 3 4	

Name ____ Date ___________

Chapter 2

Chapter Self-Assessment (continued)

	Rating	Date
2.3 Converting between Fractions and Decimals		
Learning Target: Convert between different forms of rational numbers.	1 2 3 4	
I can explain the difference between terminating and repeating decimals.	1 2 3 4	
I can write fractions and mixed numbers as decimals.	1 2 3 4	
I can write decimals as fractions and mixed numbers.	1 2 3 4	
2.4 Multiplying Rational Numbers		
Learning Target: Find products of rational numbers.	1 2 3 4	
I can explain the rules for multiplying rational numbers.	1 2 3 4	
I can find products of rational numbers with the same sign.	1 2 3 4	
I can find products of rational numbers with different signs.	1 2 3 4	
2.5 Dividing Rational Numbers		
Learning Target: Find quotients of rational numbers.	1 2 3 4	
I can explain the rules for dividing rational numbers.	1 2 3 4	
I can find quotients of rational numbers with the same sign.	1 2 3 4	
I can find quotients of rational numbers with different signs.	1 2 3 4	
2.6 Using Rational Number Operations		
Learning Target: Apply the order of operations to expressions involving rational numbers.	1 2 3 4	
I can use the order of operations to evaluate expressions.	1 2 3 4	
I can write and evaluate expressions to solve real-life problems.	1 2 3 4	

Name______________________________ Date__________

Chapter 2 B.E.S.T. Test Prep

1. Which expressions are positive?

Ⓐ $2(0.1)(-1.1)^2$

Ⓑ $14.3 - (-8.6)$

Ⓒ $(-5.5) + (-7.2)$

Ⓓ $-\frac{2}{3} - \left(-\frac{1}{6}\right)$

Ⓔ $-9.66 \div (-2.3)$

Ⓕ $-4\frac{2}{5} + 4\frac{1}{8}$

2. Which expressions are correct?

Ⓐ $\frac{15^8 \cdot 15^5}{15^3} = 15^{16}$

Ⓑ $\frac{12^{10} \cdot 12^4}{12^8} = 12^{32}$

Ⓒ $(6^4)^7 = 6^{28}$

Ⓓ $(9 \cdot 5)^4 = 9^4 \cdot 5$

Ⓔ $\left(\frac{1}{5}\right)^3 \left(\frac{1}{5}\right)^8 = \left(\frac{1}{5}\right)^{11}$

Ⓕ $\frac{(-5.4)^8}{(-5.4)^3} = (-5.4)^5$

3. A bank wants to share $8 \cdot 10^6$ dollars of dividends with its members. The bank has $2 \cdot 10^5$ members. How much does each member receive?

Ⓐ 20

Ⓑ 40

Ⓒ 60

Ⓓ 80

4. What is the value of $\frac{\frac{1}{6} - \frac{3}{8}}{\frac{1}{12}}$?

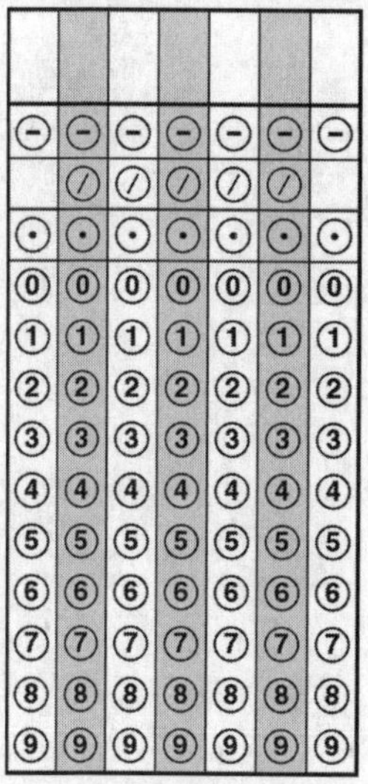

5. What is the value of $(-0.4)^3$?

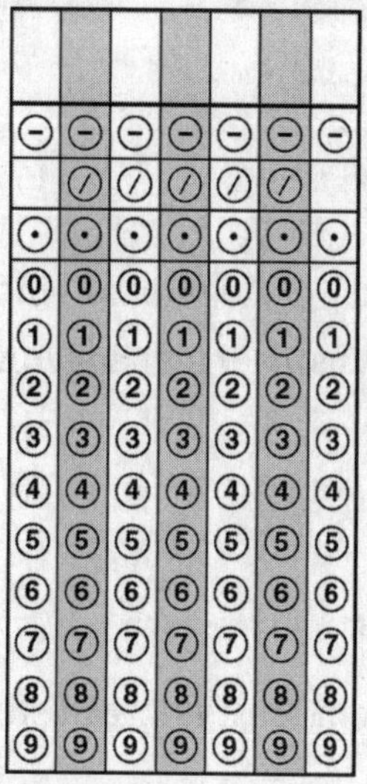

6. An airplane is 2^{14} feet in the air. Another plane is 2 times higher. What is the height of the other plane?

Ⓐ 4096 feet

Ⓑ 8192 feet

Ⓒ 16,384 feet

Ⓓ 32,768 feet

Name ______________________ Date __________

Chapter 2 B.E.S.T. Test Prep (continued)

7. Determine if the comparison is true or false.

	True	False
$-9\frac{1}{5} < -9.\overline{1}$	Ⓐ	Ⓑ
$16 > \lvert -16 \rvert$	Ⓒ	Ⓓ
$-7\frac{17}{19} < -7\frac{20}{21}$	Ⓔ	Ⓕ

8. The table shows the change in water temperature over the course of 5 hours. What is the total change, in °F, over 5 hours?

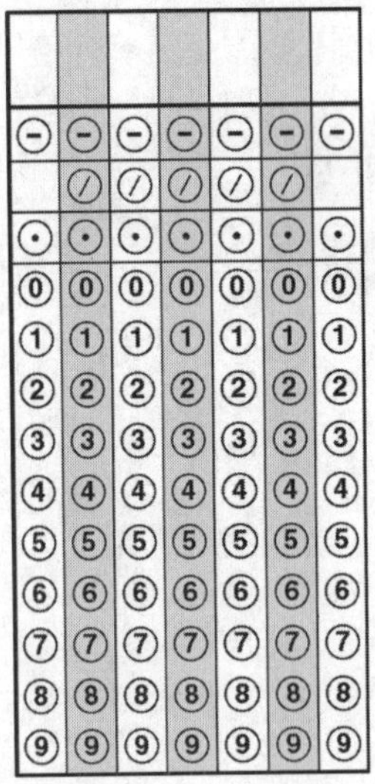

Hour	Temperature Change
1	–0.8°F
2	+1.4°F
3	+2.3°F
4	–0.9°F
5	–1.6°F

9. A person on a $3\frac{1}{2}$ meter diving board reaches a depth of $7\frac{3}{4}$ meters after diving in the water. What is the change in the person's distance?

Ⓐ $4\frac{1}{4}$ meters

Ⓑ $7\frac{1}{2}$ meters

Ⓒ $10\frac{3}{4}$ meters

Ⓓ $11\frac{1}{4}$ meters

10. Order the numbers from least to greatest: $-\frac{7}{9}, \frac{2}{3}, -\frac{4}{5}, \frac{9}{10}, -\frac{1}{8}$.

Ⓐ $-\frac{7}{9}, -\frac{4}{5}, -\frac{1}{8}, \frac{2}{3}, \frac{9}{10}$

Ⓑ $-\frac{4}{5}, -\frac{7}{9}, -\frac{1}{8}, \frac{2}{3}, \frac{9}{10}$

Ⓒ $-\frac{7}{9}, -\frac{1}{8}, -\frac{4}{5}, \frac{2}{3}, \frac{9}{10}$

Ⓓ $-\frac{4}{5}, -\frac{1}{8}, -\frac{7}{9}, \frac{2}{3}, \frac{9}{10}$

Name________________________________ Date__________

Chapter 2 B.E.S.T. Test Prep (continued)

11. The expression $-16t^2 + 40t$ represents the height of an object after t seconds. What is the height after 2 seconds?

Ⓐ 16 feet

Ⓑ 24 feet

Ⓒ 40 feet

Ⓓ 48 feet

12. This question has **two** parts.

The table shows the weight change, in pounds, of a dog over 6 months.

Month	1	2	3	4	5	6
Change (in lbs)	0.4	−1.2	1.1	0.8	−0.1	1.4

Part A

What is the average change, in pounds, each month?

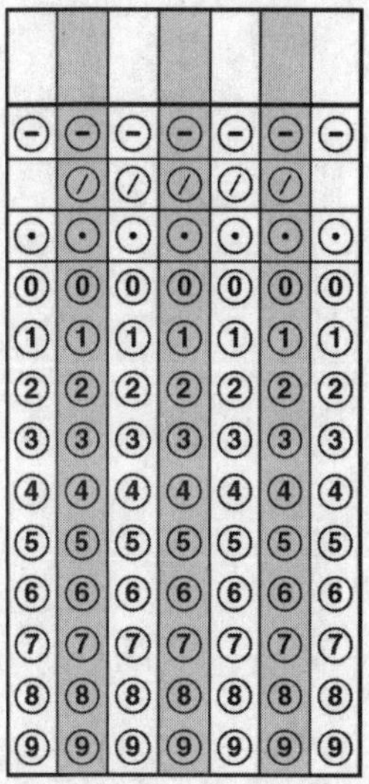

Part B

How much weight change, in pounds, must occur next month for the average weight change to be 0.5 pounds per month?

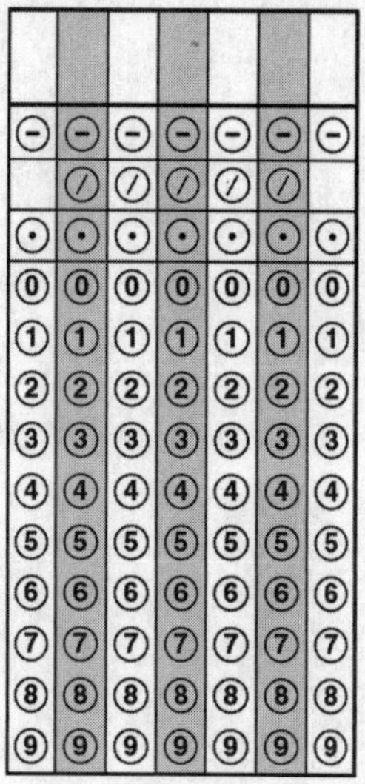

13. A cube has a side length of $1\frac{1}{2}$ inches. What is the expression that represents the surface area?

Ⓐ $\left(1\frac{1}{2}\right)^3$

Ⓑ $\left(1\frac{1}{2}\right)^2$

Ⓒ $6\left(1\frac{1}{2}\right)^3$

Ⓓ $6\left(1\frac{1}{2}\right)^2$

14. What is the distance between $-6\frac{1}{3}$ and $4\frac{5}{12}$?

Ⓐ $1\frac{3}{4}$

Ⓑ $1\frac{11}{12}$

Ⓒ $10\frac{3}{4}$

Ⓓ $10\frac{11}{12}$

Name ______________________________ Date __________

B.E.S.T. Test Prep (continued)

15. Your friend lives at an elevation of –16 feet. You live at an elevation of 12 feet.

Ⓐ You Ⓑ Your friend	live(s) closer to sea level. The difference in distance

between the two elevations is

Ⓐ 4 Ⓑ 16 Ⓒ 28	feet.

16. The table shows the change in production of items made at a factory. What is the average change?

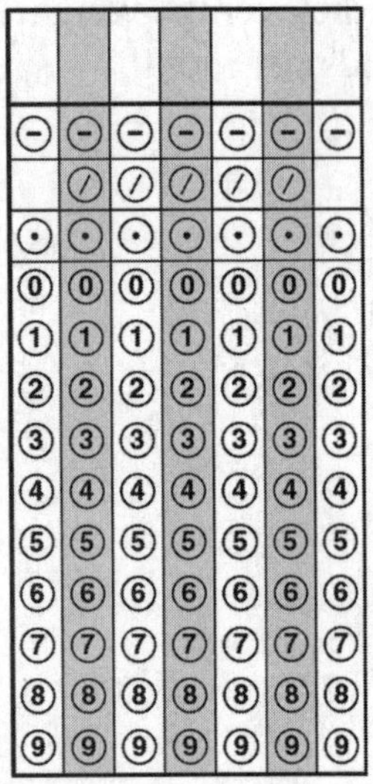

Week	Change in Production
1	300
2	–500
3	–400
4	–200
5	300

17. What is the value of $-|-7.2|$?

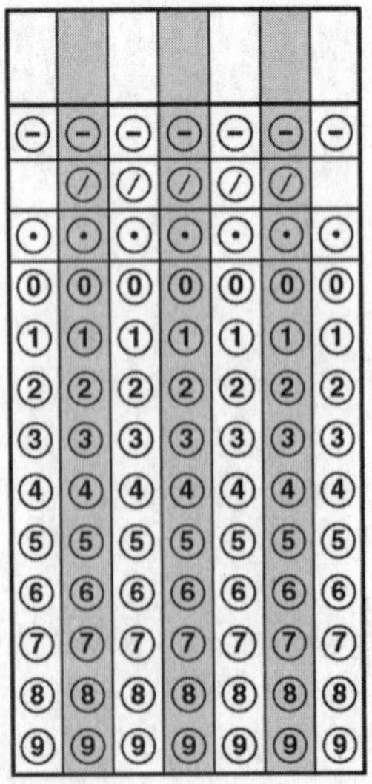

18. What is the value of $-45 + (-23) + 17$?

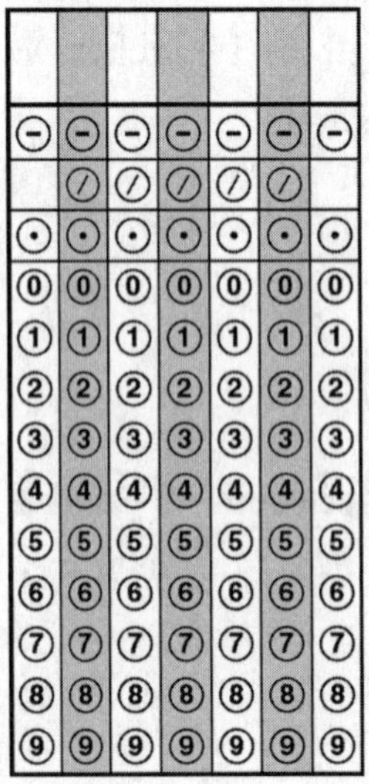

Name ____________________ Date __________

Lesson 3.1 Review & Refresh

Find the product or the quotient. Write fractions in simplest form.

1. $-\frac{3}{8}\left(\frac{8}{11}\right)$

2. $2\frac{2}{3} \div (-4)$

3. $\left(1\frac{1}{2}\right)^3$

4. $6\frac{1}{3} \div 4\frac{3}{4}$

Simplify the expression.

5. $8a + 10 - 6a$

6. $12b - 8 + 4$

7. $16a - 14 + 12a$

8. $4.4y - 3.3 + 2.2y - 1.1$

9. $\frac{2}{3}z + \frac{11}{12} - \frac{1}{3}z - \frac{5}{12}$

10. The volume of a rectangular prism pool is 8000 cubic feet. The pool is 5 feet long and 24 feet wide. Find the depth of the pool.

11. The table shows the daily change in water temperature of an aquarium. What is the average temperature change for the week?

Day	Sunday	Monday	Tuesday	Wednesday	Thursday	Friday	Saturday
Change	–0.1°F	–0.5°F	0.2°F	0.6°F	0.9°F	–0.1°F	–0.3°F

12. A power walker walks at a rate of 4.64 miles per hour. How many miles are walked in 1.5 hours?

13. A rectangle is 4.5 times long as it is wide.

a. Write an expression for the perimeter of the rectangle.

b. Write an expression for the area of the rectangle.

Name ______________________________ Date __________

Lesson 3.1 Review & Refresh (continued)

Evaluate the expression. Write fractions in simplest form.

14. $2.7 \times 3.1 - 1.8$

15. $0.4^2 \div |5.6 - 7.2|$

16. $\frac{3}{5} - \frac{8}{9} - \frac{2}{3} + \frac{1}{10}$

Identify the terms and the like terms in the expression.

17. $x + 4 + 2x$

18. $3y + 5 - 4 - 6y$

19. $5z + 6z - 8 + 2z^2$

Evaluate the expression. Write fractions in simplest form.

20. $\frac{\frac{11}{12}}{48}$

21. $\frac{\frac{4}{5}+\frac{7}{10}}{\frac{9}{20}}$

22. $\frac{\frac{5}{8}-\frac{9}{16}}{-\frac{7}{15}+\frac{3}{5}}$

23. You earn \$1.45 for every box of cookies sold. Find the amount earned when you sell 80 boxes.

Lesson 3.1 Self-Assessment

Use the scale to rate your understanding of the learning target and the success criteria.

1 I don't understand yet. | 2 I can do it with help. | 3 I can do it on my own. | 4 I can teach someone else.

	Rating	Date
3.1 Algebraic Expressions		
Learning Target: Simplify algebraic expressions.	1 2 3 4	
I can identify terms and like terms of algebraic expressions.	1 2 3 4	
I can combine like terms to simplify algebraic expressions.	1 2 3 4	
I can write and simplify algebraic expressions to solve real-life problems.	1 2 3 4	

Name____ Date__________

Lesson 3.2 Review & Refresh

Find the sum.

1. $(n + 16) + (n - 14)$

2. $(-7.2a + 8) + (-4.1a - 5)$

3. $(6 - m) + (4m - 8)$

4. $\left(\frac{2}{3}c + 4\right) + \left(\frac{1}{2}c - 6\right)$

5. The table shows your commute time to work in hours. Find the average commute time in minutes.

Day	Monday	Tuesday	Wednesday	Thursday	Friday
Time	$\frac{1}{2}$	$\frac{3}{4}$	$\frac{2}{5}$	$\frac{3}{5}$	$\frac{7}{10}$

Find the quotient. Write fractions in simplest form.

6. $\frac{2}{3} \div \left(-\frac{3}{4}\right)$

7. $-6.678 \div 3.18$

8. $-14 \div \frac{7}{8}$

9. $-0.24 \div (-0.06)$

Simplify the expression.

10. $7c + 8c - 3 - 4$

11. $6 + 8d - 9 + 12d$

12. $3x - \frac{9}{10} + 4x - \frac{7}{10}$

13. $-5.5y + 4.1 - 3.2 + 6.7y$

14. A triangle has sides of $0.3x + 0.5$, $0.4x + 0.6$ and $0.5x + 0.7$. Find the perimeter.

Name ______________________________ Date __________

Lesson 3.2 Review & Refresh (continued)

Find the difference.

15. $(4a - 6) - (8a + 10)$

16. $\left(-2 - \frac{8}{5}y\right) - \left(\frac{7}{10}y + 9\right)$

17. $(5b + 8) - (6b - 7)$

18. $(-6.4w - 3) - (2 - 5.5w)$

Evaluate the expression. Write fractions in simplest form.

19. $1.6^2 + 1.38 - 1.9$

20. $-\frac{2}{3} \div \left(\frac{1}{4}\right)^2$

21. $3\frac{1}{2} \cdot \left|1\frac{1}{4} - 1\frac{2}{3}\right|$

22. There are x customers who buy a 3.5-pound bag of red apples and a 4.25-pound bag of yellow apples. Write and simplify an expression to find the total number of pounds of apples bought.

Lesson 3.2 Self-Assessment

Use the scale to rate your understanding of the learning target and the success criteria.

1 I don't understand yet. 2 I can do it with help. 3 I can do it on my own. 4 I can teach someone else.

	Rating	Date
3.2 Adding and Subtracting Linear Expressions		
Learning Target: Find sums and differences of linear expressions.	1 2 3 4	
I can explain the difference between linear and nonlinear expressions.	1 2 3 4	
I can find opposites of terms that include variables.	1 2 3 4	
I can apply properties of operations to add and subtract linear expressions.	1 2 3 4	

Name ______________________________ Date __________

Lesson 3.3 Review & Refresh

Simplify the expression.

1. $4(a+3)$

2. $3.2(4-b)$

3. $-\frac{3}{4}(-8y+2z)$

4. $3a-4(2a+5)$

5. $2(3-x)+5(2x+7)$

6. The perimeter of a rectangle is $16x+24$. The length is $x+4$. Find the width.

Evaluate the expression. Write fractions in simplest form.

7. $\left(1\frac{1}{2}\cdot\frac{2}{3}\div 1\frac{1}{8}\right)^2$

8. $-2.2^2\cdot 1.5-3.87$

9. $-2\frac{1}{5}\cdot\left|5\frac{1}{8}-5\frac{3}{16}\right|$

Identify the terms and like terms in the expression.

10. $8y+6-4z+7-2y$

11. $7-9y+4x+6y-3x$

12. Your family buys 5.2 pounds of bananas at \$0.75 per pound and 6.4 pounds of apples at \$1.95 per pound. Find the amount of change if your family pays with a \$20 bill.

Determine whether the expressions are equivalent.

13. $4(-2x+3)+6x;\ 2x+12$

14. $-3(5-2x)+8;\ -2x-4$

Name ______________________________ Date __________

Lesson 3.3 Review & Refresh (continued)

Find the sum or the difference.

15. $(p - 12) + (2p + 10)$

16. $(7 - 3c) - (4c + 5)$

17. $\left(12 - \frac{4}{5}d\right) + \left(\frac{7}{10}d - 8\right)$

18. $\left(\frac{7}{4}y + 3\right) - \left(\frac{5}{4}y - 6\right)$

19. The change in stock price is shown in the table. Find the change in price for the week.

Day	Mon	Tues	Wed	Thurs	Fri
Change	$1\frac{1}{4}$	$-\frac{3}{5}$	$-2\frac{1}{2}$	$\frac{7}{10}$	$\frac{1}{5}$

Simplify the expression.

20. $3.5d - 4 + 4.8d - 2$

21. $8 - 7.2w + 4.4w - 3$

Lesson 3.3 Self-Assessment

Use the scale to rate your understanding of the learning target and the success criteria.

1 I don't understand yet. | 2 I can do it with help. | 3 I can do it on my own. | 4 I can teach someone else.

	Rating	Date
3.3 Writing Equivalent Expressions		
Learning Target: Apply properties of operations to generate equivalent expressions.	1 2 3 4	
I can explain how to apply the Distributive Property.	1 2 3 4	
I can use properties of operations to simplify algebraic expressions.	1 2 3 4	
I can determine whether two expressions are equivalent.	1 2 3 4	

Name ____ Date __________

Lesson 3.4

Review & Refresh

1. A square has a side length of x units.

   a. Write an expression for the perimeter.

   b. Write an expression for the area.

Solve the equation. Check your solution.

2. $-4 = a - 7$

3. $b + 10 = 25$

4. $1.6x = -6.4$

5. $\frac{z}{1.4} = 7$

6. $-1\frac{2}{3} = h - 2\frac{1}{2}$

7. $g + \frac{7}{8} = \frac{1}{2}$

8. You have $(8x + 60)$ dollars in a checking account. You have $(16x + 150)$ dollars in a savings account. Find the total amount in the accounts.

Simplify the expression.

9. $-2(4 - x)$

10. $6b + 8(7 - 2b)$

11. $5(2c + 3)$

Identify the terms and like terms in the expression.

12. $2x - 4 + 6x^2 + 8 - 10y$

13. $3x^2 - 2x + 4x^2 - x + 8$

Find the sum or the difference.

14. $(3x + 8) + (4x - 3) + (6x + 5)$

15. $(2 - 3y) - (y - 4) - (y + 5)$

16. At a restaurant, you and three friends share a bill evenly. Each person pays \$18. Write and solve an equation to find the total bill.

Name ______________________________ Date __________

Lesson 3.4 Review & Refresh (continued)

17. You have t toys. Your friend has 10 more than twice the number of toys you have. Write an expression to find the difference in toys.

18. Your family ate 28 muffins. This was $\frac{7}{10}$ of the muffins you made. Write and solve an equation to find the number of muffins you made.

Simplify the expression.

19. $\frac{4}{5}w + 6 + \frac{1}{10}w - 5$

20. $\frac{3}{4}z - \frac{1}{3}z - 4 + 12$

Find the sum or the difference.

21. $(4.4x + 7.2) + (8.5x + 3.9)$

22. $(4.6y + 3.2) - (2.8y + 5.1)$

Lesson 3.4 Self-Assessment

Use the scale to rate your understanding of the learning target and the success criteria.

1 I don't understand yet. | 2 I can do it with help. | 3 I can do it on my own. | 4 I can teach someone else.

	Rating	Date
3.4 Solving One-Step Equations		
Learning Target: Write and solve one-step equations.	1 2 3 4	
I can solve equations using addition or subtraction.	1 2 3 4	
I can solve equations using multiplication or division.	1 2 3 4	
I can apply one-step equations to solve real-life problems.	1 2 3 4	

Name________________________ Date__________

Lesson 3.5 Review & Refresh

1. A ride-share service charges \$2.20 per mile and a \$7.50 service fee. Write and solve an equation to find the number of miles for a \$24 ride.

Find the sum or the difference.

2. $(5 - 2x) + (4 - 6x) + (3x + 9)$

3. $(4y - 6) - (5 - 2y) - (3y + 1)$

Solve the equation. Check your solution.

4. $8h = -24$

5. $\frac{x}{-3} = -8$

6. $-8.3 + j = -9.5$

7. $9.2 + g = 4.8$

8. $-0.8x = 9.6$

9. $\frac{2}{3}a = 12$

10. A pool has a width twice of the length. The pool has a one-foot border around the pool.

    a. Write an expression for the perimeter.

    b. Write an expression for the area.

Simplify the expression.

11. $-5(4 + 2.1c + 3.3d)$

12. $\frac{4}{5}\left(\frac{2}{5}a + b - \frac{3}{5}c\right)$

13. A triangle has side lengths of 4.7 inches and 8.5 inches. The perimeter is 19.3 inches. Write and solve an equation to find the missing side length.

Name ______________________________ Date __________

Lesson 3.5 Review & Refresh (continued)

Solve the equation. Check your solution.

14. $-2(a + 4) = 2$

15. $10 - 4x = 18$

16. $\frac{1}{4}y - \frac{1}{3} = \frac{7}{12}$

17. $-2\left(p + \frac{3}{4}\right) = -4$

18. $1.4 = 6n - 10.6$

19. $1.1(x - 3) = 4.4$

20. In a game, you score $(2p + 5)$ points. Your friend scores $(4p + 7)$ points. Find the total points.

Find the sum or the difference.

21. $(3x + 4) + (6 - 5x)$

22. $(10c + 2) - (6c + 9)$

23. $(-3b + 1.1) + (4.8b - 2.6)$

24. $(3 - 2.2x) - (8.8x + 4)$

Lesson 3.5 Self-Assessment

Use the scale to rate your understanding of the learning target and the success criteria.

1 I don't understand yet. 2 I can do it with help. 3 I can do it on my own. 4 I can teach someone else.

	Rating	Date
3.5 Solving Two-Step Equations		
Learning Target: Write and solve two-step equations.	1 2 3 4	
I can apply properties of equality to produce equivalent expressions.	1 2 3 4	
I can solve two-step equations using the basic operations.	1 2 3 4	
I can apply two-step equations to solve real-life problems.	1 2 3 4	

Name ______________________________ Date __________

Lesson 3.6

Review & Refresh

Solve the equation. Check your solution.

1. $\frac{3}{4}b = -12$

2. $g - \frac{3}{5} = \frac{7}{10}$

3. $-3\frac{4}{5} = h + 4\frac{1}{10}$

Graph the inequality on a number line.

4. $a \geq 1.2$

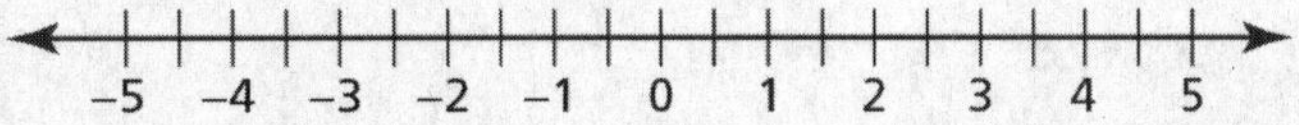

5. $b < 2\frac{1}{2}$

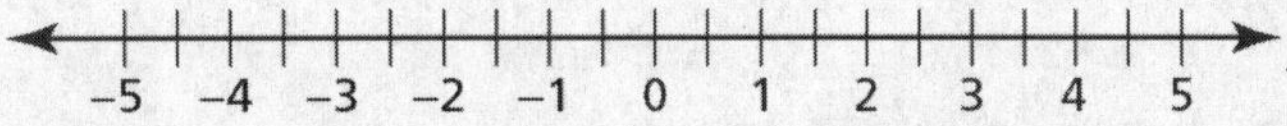

6. There were 40 cookies in a package. You eat 4 cookies each day. Write and solve an equation to find the number of days that pass until there are 8 cookies left.

7. The coldest temperature in a city was –9.4°F. The warmest temperature was 98.9°F. Write and solve an equation to find the difference in temperature.

Simplify the expression.

8. $4(2 - 3x) - 3(4x + 1)$

9. $3(-3a + 3b + c)$

10. $\frac{7}{10}\left(x - \frac{1}{10}y + \frac{1}{7}\right)$

11. $\frac{1}{2}(8a + 4c) - \frac{1}{3}(6c - 3a)$

12. At school, at least 75 students buy lunch each day. Write and graph an inequality that represents the situation.

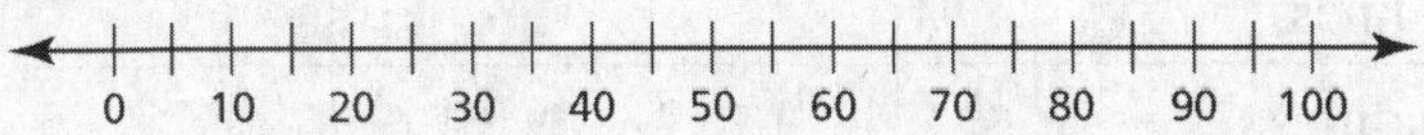

Name ______________________________ Date __________

Lesson 3.6 Review & Refresh (continued)

Solve the equation. Check your solution.

13. $-3x - 2 = -35$

14. $4x - 8x = 72$

15. $\frac{7}{6} = \frac{1}{2}x + \frac{2}{3}$

Tell whether the given value is a solution to the inequality.

16. $a + 10 \leq 12; a = -2$

17. $-16 > \frac{1}{2}g; g = -16$

18. $3x < \frac{2}{3}; x = 0$

19. $6.2 \geq b - 1.4; b = 8.6$

20. A garden is in the shape of a rectangle where the width is 16 feet. The perimeter is 84 feet. Write and solve an equation to find the length.

Write the inequality for the word sentence.

21. A number x is no more than 12.

22. 20 is less than the sum of a number a and 2.

Lesson 3.6 Self-Assessment

Use the scale to rate your understanding of the learning target and the success criteria.

1 I don't understand yet. 2 I can do it with help. 3 I can do it on my own. 4 I can teach someone else.

	Rating	Date
3.6 Writing and Graphing Inequalities		
Learning Target: Write inequalities and represent solutions of inequalities on number lines.	1 2 3 4	
I can write word sentences as inequalities.	1 2 3 4	
I can determine whether a value is a solution of an inequality.	1 2 3 4	
I can graph the solutions of inequalities.	1 2 3 4	

Name ______________________________ Date __________

Lesson 3.7 Review & Refresh

Solve the inequality. Graph the solution.

1. $a + 10 > 4$

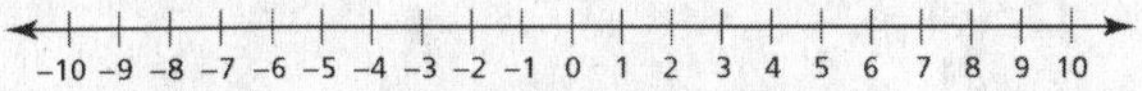

2. $6 < b - 3$

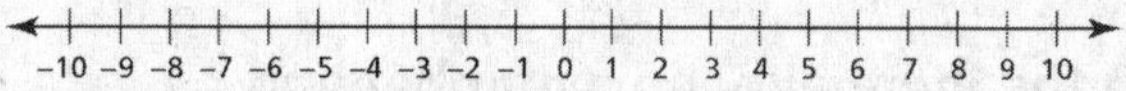

3. $-\frac{5}{8} \geq c + \frac{7}{8}$

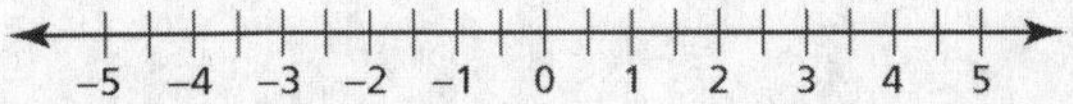

4. $-\frac{6}{5} + d \leq -\frac{4}{5}$

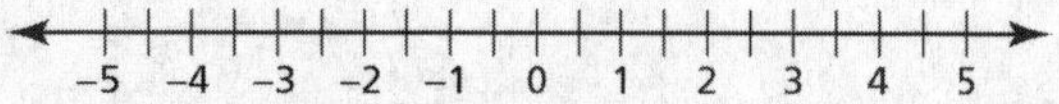

Solve the equation. Check your solution.

5. $3.5 = d - 4.1$

6. $24 + c = -8$

7. $-\frac{9}{2} = 8d$

8. $51 = 3(2c + 1)$

9. $-26 = 7t + 6t$

10. $-4m + 12.3 = 10.7$

11. Your grocery bill is \$74.36. Write and solve an equation to find the amount of change when paying with a \$100 bill.

12. The sum of three consecutive integers is –36. Write and solve an equation for the sum of the integers. Find all three integers.

13. Schools are open as long as the temperature is greater than –5°F. Write and graph an inequality to represent the situation.

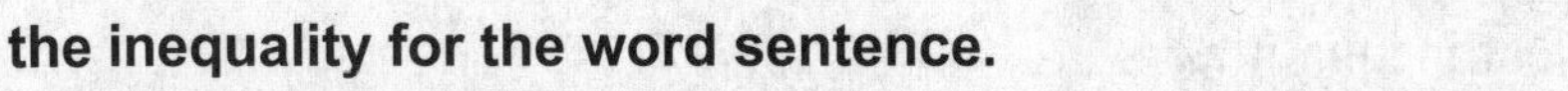

Write the inequality for the word sentence.

14. –14 is more than a number b minus 6.

15. A number y plus 5 is less than or equal to 15.

Name ______________________________ Date __________

Lesson 3.7 Review & Refresh (continued)

16. A bus can hold 65 people. Thirty-seven people board the bus. Write and solve an inequality to find how many more people can board the bus.

Graph the inequality on a number line.

17. $a > \frac{4}{5}$

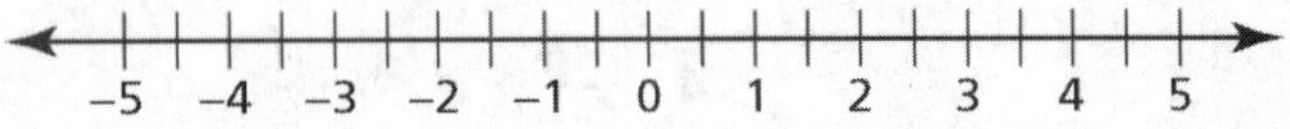

18. $d \leq -1\frac{1}{4}$

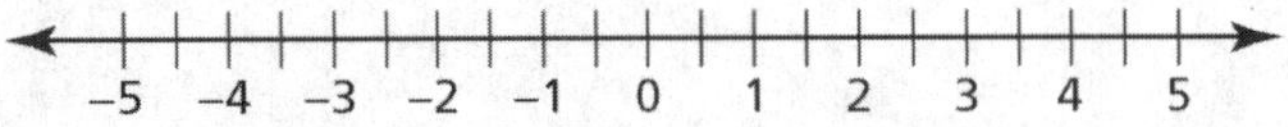

19. A triangle has two sides that measure 8 feet and 10 feet. The perimeter is no more than 24 feet. Write and solve an inequality to find the third side.

Solve the equation. Check your solution.

20. $-27.9 = 3p$

21. $\frac{y}{-4} = 6$

Lesson 3.7 Self-Assessment

Use the scale to rate your understanding of the learning target and the success criteria.

1 I don't understand yet. 2 I can do it with help. 3 I can do it on my own. 4 I can teach someone else.

	Rating	Date
3.7 Solving Inequalities Using Addition or Subtraction		
Learning Target: Write and solve inequalities using addition or subtraction.	1 2 3 4	
I can apply the Addition and Subtraction Properties of Inequality to produce equivalent inequalities.	1 2 3 4	
I can solve inequalities using addition or subtraction.	1 2 3 4	
I can apply inequalities involving addition or subtraction to solve real-life problems.	1 2 3 4	

Name______________________________ Date__________

Lesson 3.8 Review & Refresh

1. You sold half of your comic books and bought 12 more. You now have 48 comic books. Write and solve an equation to find the number of comic books you originally had.

2. You want to drive 150 miles in 2.5 hours. Write and solve an inequality to find the speed you must drive.

Solve the inequality. Graph the solution.

3. $d - 9 \leq -15$

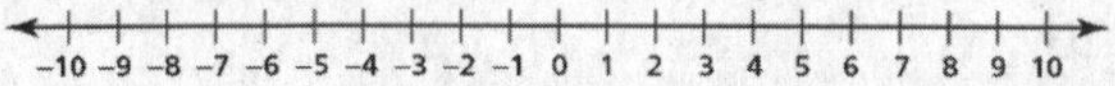

4. $4a > 16$

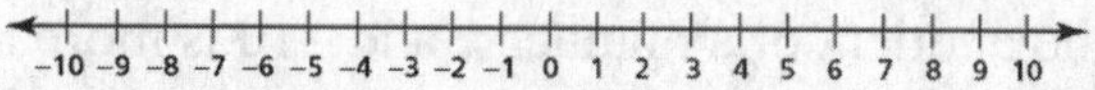

5. $b + 3.4 > 2.6$

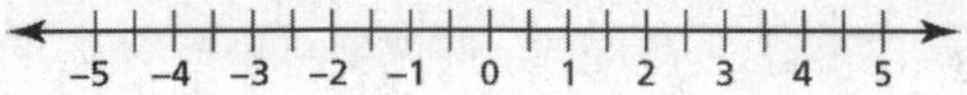

6. $-1.1y > 9.9$

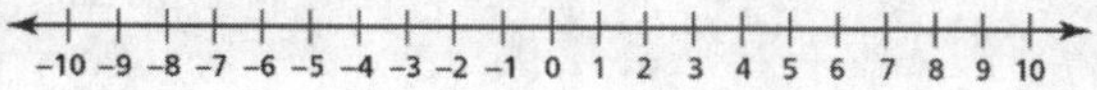

7. $a - \frac{4}{9} > \frac{5}{9}$

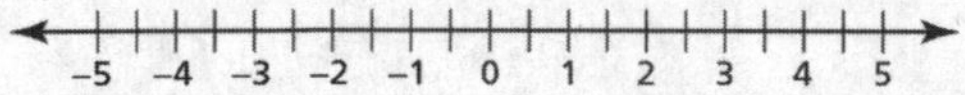

8. $\frac{x}{0.5} \geq 9$

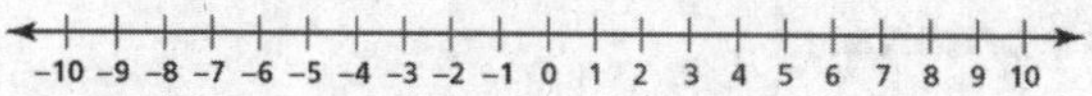

Solve the equation. Check your solution.

9. $3.1(2z - 2.8) = -9.3$

10. $-2.4w + 8 - 3.2w - 7 = 10.2$

11. $\frac{2}{3}z + \frac{3}{4} = \frac{5}{12}$

12. $-4(1.5y + 2) = -6.5$

Name ____________________ Date ________

Lesson 3.8 Review & Refresh (continued)

13. The maximum volume of a box is 200 cubic inches. Write and graph an inequality to represent the situation.

14. The width of the rectangle is 60 meters. The perimeter is 300 meters. Write and solve an equation to find the length.

Tell whether the given value is a solution to the inequality.

15. $d + 5 > 12; d = 7$

16. $3.5 + g > 5.5; g = 2.5$

Write the word sentence as an inequality. Then solve the inequality.

17. The quotient of a number x and -10 is more than 20.

18. The product of 3 and a number b is greater than or equal or 27.

Lesson 3.8 Self-Assessment

Use the scale to rate your understanding of the learning target and the success criteria.

1 I don't understand yet. 2 I can do it with help. 3 I can do it on my own. 4 I can teach someone else.

	Rating	Date
3.8 Solving Inequalities Using Multiplication or Division		
Learning Target: Write and solve inequalities using multiplication or division.	1 2 3 4	
I can apply the Multiplication and Division Properties of Inequality to produce equivalent inequalities.	1 2 3 4	
I can solve inequalities using multiplication or division.	1 2 3 4	
I can apply inequalities involving multiplication or division to solve real-life problems.	1 2 3 4	

Name ____________________ Date ________

Chapter 3

Chapter Self-Assessment

Use the scale to rate your understanding of the learning target and the success criteria.

1 I don't understand yet. | 2 I can do it with help. | 3 I can do it on my own. | 4 I can teach someone else.

	Rating	Date
Chapter 3 Expressions, Equations and Inequalities		
Learning Target: Understand expressions, equations and inequalities.	1 2 3 4	
I can identify an expression, equation and inequality.	1 2 3 4	
I can use algebraic properties to rewrite expressions.	1 2 3 4	
I can solve equations and inequalities.	1 2 3 4	
I can solve real-life problems.	1 2 3 4	
3.1 Algebraic Expressions		
Learning Target: Simplify algebraic expressions.	1 2 3 4	
I can identify terms and like terms of algebraic expressions.	1 2 3 4	
I can combine like terms to simplify algebraic expressions.	1 2 3 4	
I can write and simplify algebraic expressions to solve real-life problems.	1 2 3 4	
3.2 Adding and Subtracting Linear Expressions		
Learning Target: Find sums and differences of linear expressions.	1 2 3 4	
I can explain the difference between linear and nonlinear expressions.	1 2 3 4	
I can find opposites of terms that include variables.	1 2 3 4	
I can apply properties of operations to add and subtract linear expressions.	1 2 3 4	
3.3 Writing Equivalent Expressions		
Learning Target: Apply properties of operations to generate equivalent expressions.	1 2 3 4	
I can explain how to apply the Distributive Property.	1 2 3 4	
I can use properties of operations to simplify algebraic expressions.	1 2 3 4	
I can determine whether two expressions are equivalent.	1 2 3 4	

Name ______________________________ Date __________

Chapter 3

Chapter Self-Assessment (continued)

	Rating	Date
3.4 Solving One-Step Equations		
Learning Target: Write and solve one-step equations.	1 2 3 4	
I can solve equations using addition or subtraction.	1 2 3 4	
I can solve equations using multiplication or division.	1 2 3 4	
I can apply one-step equations to solve real-life problems.	1 2 3 4	
3.5 Solving Two-Step Equations		
Learning Target: Write and solve two-step equations.	1 2 3 4	
I can apply properties of equality to produce equivalent equations.	1 2 3 4	
I can solve two-step equations using the basic operations.	1 2 3 4	
I can apply two-step equations to solve real-life problems.	1 2 3 4	
3.6 Writing and Graphing Inequalities		
Learning Target: Write inequalities and represent solutions of inequalities on number lines.	1 2 3 4	
I can write word sentences as inequalities.	1 2 3 4	
I can determine whether a value is a solution of an inequality.	1 2 3 4	
I can graph the solutions of inequalities.	1 2 3 4	
3.7 Solving Inequalities Using Addition or Subtraction		
Learning Target: Write and solve inequalities using addition or subtraction.	1 2 3 4	
I can apply the Addition and Subtraction Properties of Inequality to produce equivalent inequalities.	1 2 3 4	
I can solve inequalities using addition or subtraction.	1 2 3 4	
I can apply inequalities involving addition or subtraction to solve real-life problems.	1 2 3 4	
3.8 Solving Inequalities Using Multiplication or Division		
Learning Target: Write and solve inequalities using multiplication or division.	1 2 3 4	
I can apply the Multiplication and Division Properties of Inequality to produce equivalent inequalities.	1 2 3 4	
I can solve inequalities using multiplication or division.	1 2 3 4	
I can apply inequalities involving multiplication or division to solve real-life problems.	1 2 3 4	

Name______________________________ Date__________

Chapter 3 B.E.S.T. Test Prep

1. What is the solution to $\frac{z}{-1.1} > 2$?

Ⓐ 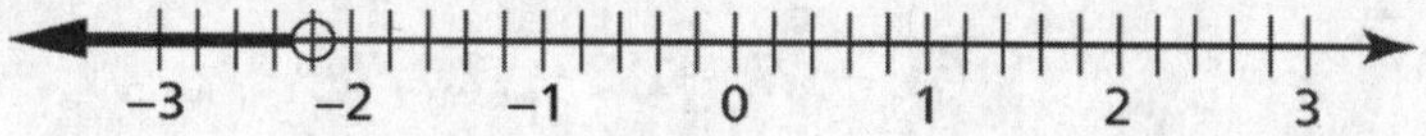

Ⓑ 

Ⓒ 

Ⓓ 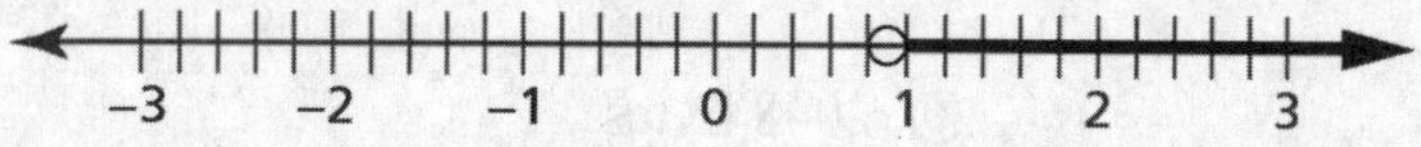

2. What is the value of $2(0.1)(1.1)^2$?

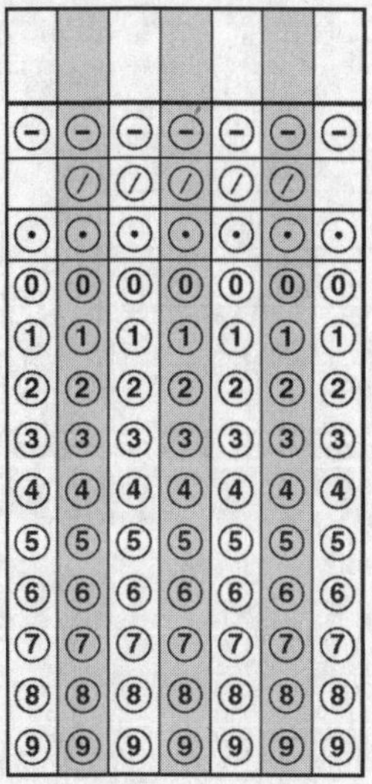

3. What is the solution to $4(1 - y) = 10$?

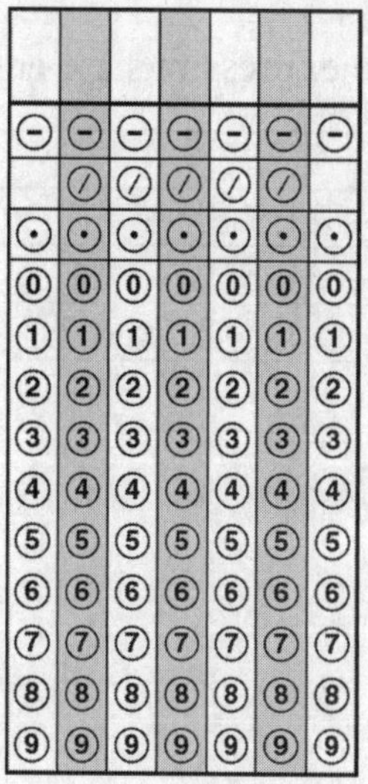

4. Which expressions are negative?

Ⓐ $|-12|$

Ⓑ $\left(-\frac{1}{10}\right)^4\left(-\frac{1}{10}\right)^5$

Ⓒ $\frac{(-2.5)^9}{(-2.5)^5}$

Ⓓ $-12.5 + (-14.4) + 18.6$

Ⓔ $-3\frac{1}{2} + 5\frac{3}{4} + \left(-2\frac{1}{4}\right)$

Ⓕ $28.9 - (-32.7)$

5. For which inequalities is $x = -2$ a solution?

Ⓐ $5x \geq -20$

Ⓑ $14 < x - 10$

Ⓒ $\frac{x}{5} > -3$

Ⓓ $2.2x \leq -4.4$

Ⓔ $-6.4 < x - 4.4$

Ⓕ $-8.5 \geq -7.5 + x$

Chapter 3 B.E.S.T. Test Prep (continued)

6. Order the numbers from least to greatest: $2.1, -1.7, 2\frac{1}{5}, -1, 2\frac{1}{11}$.

Ⓐ $-1, -1.7, 2\frac{1}{11}, 2.1, 2\frac{1}{5}$

Ⓑ $-1, -1.7, 2.1, 2\frac{1}{11}, 2\frac{1}{5}$

Ⓒ $-1.7, -1, 2\frac{1}{11}, 2.1, 2\frac{1}{5}$

Ⓓ $-1.7, -1, 2.1, 2\frac{1}{11}, 2\frac{1}{5}$

7. You download a file that is 8 kilobytes. One kilobyte is 2^{10} bytes. What is the file size in bytes?

Ⓐ 128 bytes

Ⓑ 512 bytes

Ⓒ 2048 bytes

Ⓓ 8192 bytes

8. Determine whether the expressions are equivalent.

	Yes	No
$4.5(2 - x) + 3.4(x + 2)$; $7.9x + 11$	Ⓐ	Ⓑ
$3.1(x + 1) - 2.1(2 - x)$; $5.2x - 1.1$	Ⓒ	Ⓓ
$2.5(x - 1) + 5.2(1 - x)$; $-2.7x + 2.7$	Ⓔ	Ⓕ

9. What is the value of $\left(-\frac{1}{10}\right)^2$?

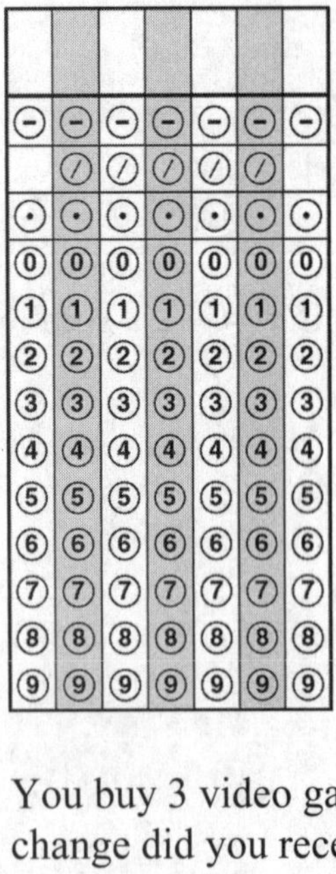

10. What is the value of $-2.2^2 + 1.5 \cdot (-0.8)$?

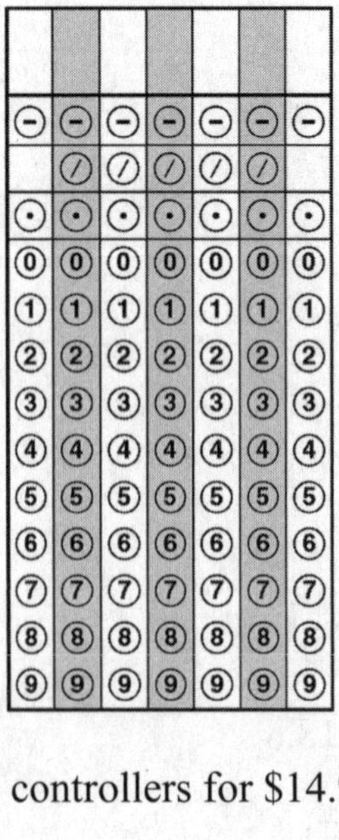

11. You buy 3 video games for $29.99 each and 2 controllers for $14.98 each. How much change did you receive if you paid $125?

Ⓐ $5.07

Ⓑ $5.17

Ⓒ $6.07

Ⓓ $6.17

Name____ Date__________

Chapter 3 B.E.S.T. Test Prep (continued)

12. An electrician charges $99 for a service call and $55 an hour. What is an equation that represents the number of h hours worked if the cost is $330? What are the number of hours?

Ⓐ $55h - 99 = 330$; 4.2 hours

Ⓑ $55h + 99 = 330$; 4.2 hours

Ⓒ $55h - 99 = 330$; 7.8 hours

Ⓓ $55h + 99 = 330$; 7.8 hours

13. A rating scale from –2 to 2 is used to rate a business. The responses are in the table. What is the average rating?

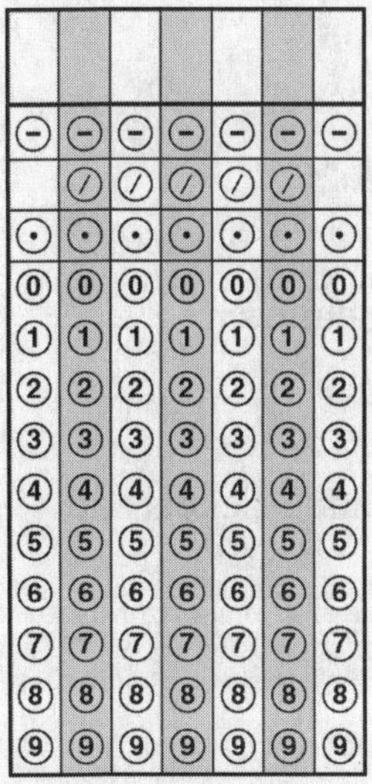

Rating	–2	–1.5	–1.0	–0.5	0	0.5	1.0	1.5	2.0
Responses	4	3	5	1	2	3	4	2	1

14. Which is $\left(\frac{2}{3}w - 4\right) + \left(\frac{1}{2}w + 8\right)$ simplified?

Ⓐ $\frac{7}{6}w - 4$

Ⓑ $\frac{7}{6}w + 4$

Ⓒ $\frac{3}{5}w - 4$

Ⓓ $\frac{3}{5}w + 4$

15. What is the value of $(9 - 12)^2 + 10 \cdot (-3)$?

Ⓐ –39

Ⓑ –21

Ⓒ 21

Ⓓ 39

16. You use a debit card to purchase several shirts. Your account balance after buying the shirts changes by –$84.84. You buy 4 shirts. What is the change in your account balance for each shirt you purchased?

Ⓐ –$21.21

Ⓑ –$4.00

Ⓒ $4.00

Ⓓ $21.21

Name ______________________________ Date __________

Chapter 3 B.E.S.T. Test Prep (continued)

17. One day at school, two-thirds of the students buy their lunch. There are 824 students who buy lunch on this day. There are s students in the school.

An equation for the number of students in school is [ ].

- Ⓐ $\frac{3}{2}s = 824$
- Ⓑ $\frac{2}{3}s = 824$
- Ⓒ $2s + 3 = 824$

The number of students in the school is [ ].

- Ⓐ 550
- Ⓑ 824
- Ⓒ 1236

18. This question has **two** parts.

The ticket prices for a movie theater are \$14 for adults and \$9.50 for children.

Part A

What is an expression for a adult tickets and c child tickets?

- Ⓐ $(14a)(9.50c)$
- Ⓑ $14c + 9.50a$
- Ⓒ $(14 + 9.50)(a + c)$
- Ⓓ $14a + 9.50c$

Part B

What is the cost for 2 adult tickets and 3 child tickets?

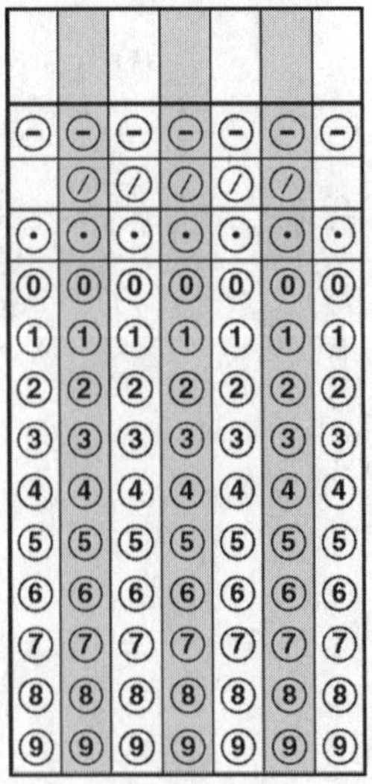

19. What is the distance between $-1\frac{1}{3}$ and -5?

- Ⓐ $3\frac{1}{3}$
- Ⓑ $3\frac{2}{3}$
- Ⓒ $4\frac{1}{3}$
- Ⓓ $4\frac{2}{3}$

Name____ Date__________

Lesson 4.1

Review & Refresh

Find the missing values in the ratio table. Then write the equivalent ratios.

1.

Miles	25		$62\frac{1}{2}$	
Hour	$\frac{1}{2}$	$\frac{3}{4}$		$1\frac{7}{8}$

2.

Feet	8	14		25
Yards	$2\frac{2}{3}$		$5\frac{1}{3}$	

Tell whether the given value is a solution to the inequality.

3. $4f \geq 8,; f = -2$

4. $-7 \geq \frac{a}{6}; a = -42$

5. $z + 12 < 20; z = 7$

Solve the inequality. Graph the solution.

6. $2.7 \geq -0.3d$

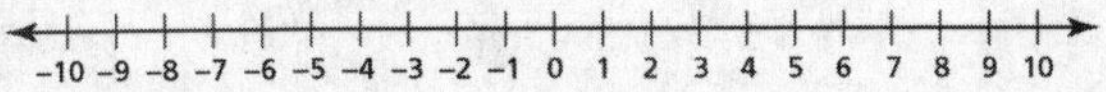

7. $-10 < \frac{c}{4}$

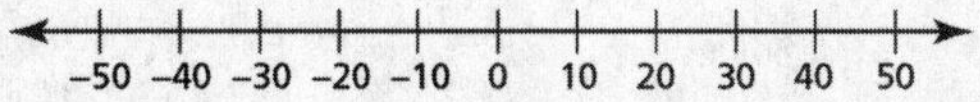

8. $\frac{2}{3} > b + \frac{1}{3}$

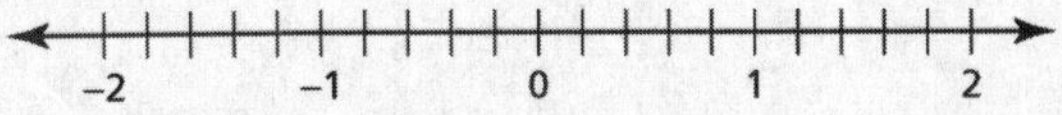

9. $12 \geq 7 + a$

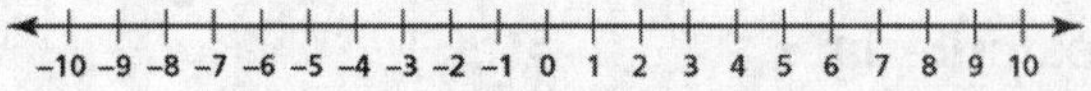

10. You walk 800 feet every $\frac{1}{3}$ hour. How many feet do you walk in $1\frac{1}{2}$ hours?

11. You have \$45 to spend at a store. You spend \$18. Write and solve an inequality that shows how much more you can spend.

Write the word sentence as an inequality. Then solve the inequality.

12. Eight times a number b is less than 60.

Name ____________________ Date ________

Lesson 4.1 Review & Refresh (continued)

13. You mix 0.5 cup of lemonade mix for every 6 cups of water to make lemonade. Find the number of cups of lemonade mix needed for 15 cups of water.

14. To win a game, you need to score at least 20 points on your next turn. Write and graph an inequality that represents the situation.

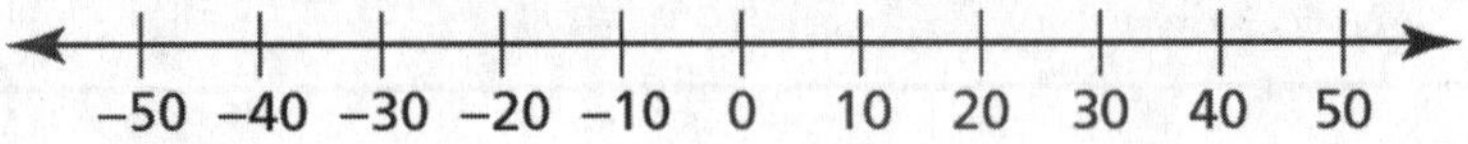

15. A rectangle has a width of 20 centimeters. Write and solve an inequality that represents the length if the area is no more than 120 centimeters.

16. A tennis team purchases 5000 tennis balls for $1000. During the season, the team buys 2000 more tennis balls. Find the cost of the 2000 additional tennis balls.

Lesson 4.1 Self-Assessment

Use the scale to rate your understanding of the learning target and the success criteria.

1 I don't understand yet. | 2 I can do it with help. | 3 I can do it on my own. | 4 I can teach someone else.

	Rating	Date
4.1 Ratios and Ratio Tables		
Learning Target: Understand ratios of rational numbers and use ratio tables to represent equivalent ratios.	1 2 3 4	
I can write and interpret ratios involving rational numbers.	1 2 3 4	
I can use various operations to create tables of equivalent ratios.	1 2 3 4	
I can use ratio tables to solve ratio problems.	1 2 3 4	

Name ______________________________ Date __________

Lesson 4.2 Review & Refresh

Solve the inequality. Graph the solution.

1. $1.7 < a + 2.8$

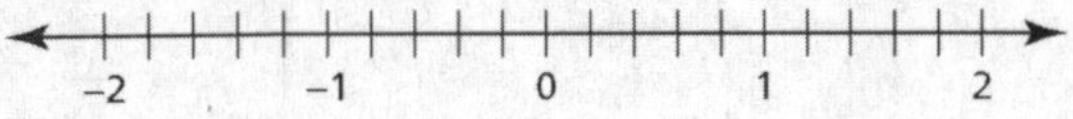

2. $c - 8.3 \geq -7.1$

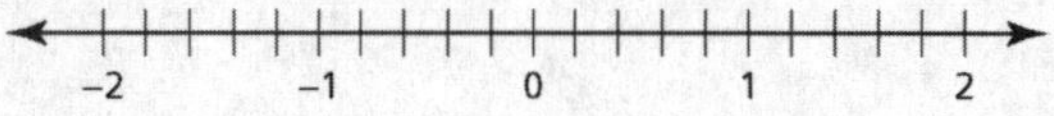

3. $-48 \leq -6b$

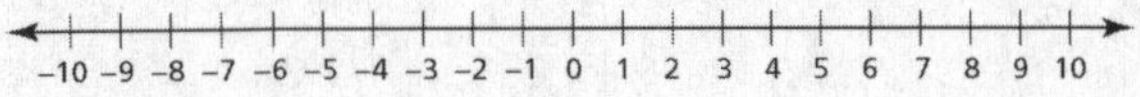

4. $\frac{d}{2} > 3$

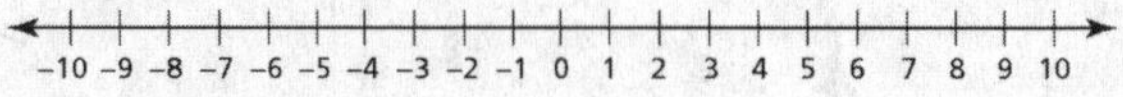

Represent the ratio relationship using a graph.

5.

Girls	10	20	30
Boys	15	30	45

6.

Pieces of Fish	2	3	4
Ounces of Fries	12	18	24

7. A cookie recipe has the ingredients listed in the table. Write the ratio. Then find and interpret the value of the ratio.

$2\frac{1}{4}$ cups flour
$\frac{3}{4}$ cup brown sugar
2 cups chocolate chips
$\frac{1}{48}$ cup vanilla

a. Flour to brown sugar

b. Brown sugar to chocolate chips

c. Flour to chocolate chips

d. Chocolate chips to vanilla

Name ____ Date __________

Lesson 4.2 Review & Refresh (continued)

8. You lose 30 points at the start of a game. You need at least 125 points to win. Write and solve an inequality that represents the number of points you need to win.

9. You ride your bike $1\frac{1}{4}$ miles in 30 minutes. Your friend rides his bike $\frac{3}{4}$ mile in 15 minutes. Graph each ratio relationship in the same coordinate plane. Determine who rides faster.

10. You earn \$12.50 per hour. You want to save at least \$200. Write and solve an inequality that represents the number of hours you must work.

11. A basketball team averages 72 points over 36 minutes. Find the number of points the team averages for 48 minutes.

Lesson 4.2 Self-Assessment

Use the scale to rate your understanding of the learning target and the success criteria.

1 I don't understand yet. | 2 I can do it with help. | 3 I can do it on my own. | 4 I can teach someone else.

	Rating	Date
4.2 Graphing Ratio Relationships		
Learning Target: Represent ratio relationships in a coordinate plane.	1 2 3 4	
I can create and plot ordered pairs from a ratio relationship.	1 2 3 4	
I can create graphs to solve ratio problems.	1 2 3 4	
I can create graphs to compare ratios.	1 2 3 4	

Name____ Date__________

Lesson 4.3

Review & Refresh

1. You buy apples for \$2 per pound.

a. Represent the ratio relationship using a graph.

b. Find the cost of 7.5 pounds of apples.

Find the missing values in the ratio table. Then write the equivalent ratios.

2.

Flour (cups)	1.25	2		3.25
Sugar (cups)	0.75		1.5	

3.

Calories	45		180	
Minutes	10	20		60

Solve the inequality. Graph the solution.

4. $\frac{a}{2} < 2.5$

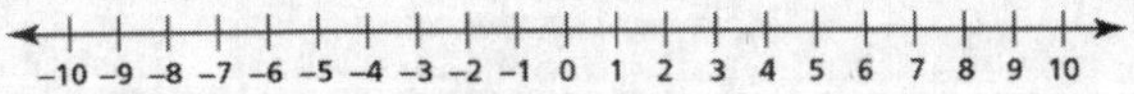

5. $-3b \leq 21$

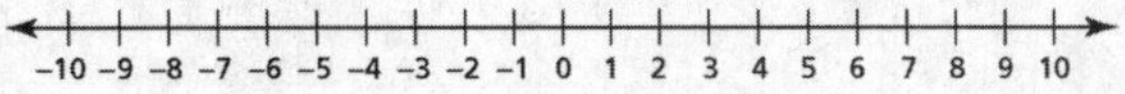

Represent the ratio relationship using a graph.

6.

Lemons	5	15	25
Limes	15	45	75

7.

Minutes	10	20	30
Meters Walked	750	1500	2250

Find the unit rate.

8. 216 words in 4.5 minutes

9. $\frac{1}{4}$ pound : 6 days

Name ______________________________ Date __________

Lesson 4.3 Review & Refresh (continued)

10. In 2015, the population of a town was about 5200 people. In 2020, the population of the town was about 5900 people. Find the average rate of population change per year.

11. You can paint 200 square feet in $\frac{3}{4}$ of an hour. Find the number of square feet you can paint in $1\frac{3}{4}$ hours.

Write the word sentence as an inequality. Then solve the inequality.

12. A number y divided by 12 is greater than 4.

Tell whether the rates are equivalent. Justify your answer.

13. 8 ounces in 1.5 years
2 pounds in 6 years

14. 10 miles in 1 hour
$\frac{1}{4}$ mile every 2 minutes

15. You ride your bike $1\frac{1}{2}$ miles in $\frac{3}{5}$ hour. Find the distance you ride in $1\frac{1}{2}$ hours.

Lesson 4.3 Self-Assessment

Use the scale to rate your understanding of the learning target and the success criteria.

1 I don't understand yet. | 2 I can do it with help. | 3 I can do it on my own. | 4 I can teach someone else.

	Rating	Date
4.3 Rates and Unit Rates		
Learning Target: Understand rates involving fractions and use unit rates to solve problems.	1 2 3 4	
I can find unit rates for rates involving fractions.	1 2 3 4	
I can use unit rates to solve rate problems.	1 2 3 4	

Name ______________________________ Date __________

Lesson 4.4

Review & Refresh

Find the unit rate.

1. 160 miles in 2.5 hours
2. $7.56 for 4 pounds
3. $1\frac{1}{2}$ grams of fat : $\frac{1}{4}$ ounce
4. 28 points in 16 minutes

Complete the statement. Round to the nearest hundredth if necessary.

5. 45 kg ≈ ____ lb
6. 8 qt ≈ ____ L
7. 24 ft ≈ ____ m
8. 36 cm ≈ ____ in.
9. 4 mi ≈ ____ km
10. 3 cu ft ≈ ____ gal

Find the missing values in the ratio table. Then write the equivalent ratios.

11.

Minutes	2	5		15
Words Typed	80		440	

12.

Dogs	4		20	
Cats	32	96		200

13. You buy 2.8 pounds of peanuts for $8.40. Your friend buys 1.6 pounds of peanuts for $6.40. Graph each ratio relationship in the same coordinate plane. Determine who pays less per pound.

14. The distance between two towns is 400 kilometers. Find the distance between the towns to the nearest hundredth mile.

Name ____ Date __________

Lesson 4.4 Review & Refresh (continued)

15. You score 5 points for every correct answer in a game.

a. Represent the ratio relationship using a graph.

b. Find the number of points you score for 17 correct answers.

Complete the statement using < or >.

16. 40 oz ____ 4 kg **17.** 5 ft ____ 50 cm **18.** 7 L ____ 7 qt

19. Your drive 12 miles in $\frac{1}{4}$ hour. Find the number of miles driven in $1\frac{3}{4}$ hours.

20. You can mow $\frac{1}{3}$ of an acre in $\frac{5}{6}$ of an hour. Find the number of acres you can mow in 2 hours.

Lesson 4.4 Self-Assessment

Use the scale to rate your understanding of the learning target and the success criteria.

1 I don't understand yet. 2 I can do it with help. 3 I can do it on my own. 4 I can teach someone else.

	Rating	Date
4.4 Converting Measures between Systems		
Learning Target: Use ratio reasoning to convert units of measure between systems.	1 2 3 4	
I can convert units of measure between systems using ratio tables.	1 2 3 4	
I can convert units of measure between systems using conversion factors.	1 2 3 4	
I can convert rates using conversion factors.	1 2 3 4	
I can convert currencies using exchange rates.	1 2 3 4	

Name____ Date__________

Lesson 4.5 Review & Refresh

Tell whether the ratios form a proportion.

1. 1 to 4 and 8 to 32

2. 0.9 to 0.3 and 3.9 to 3.3

3. $\frac{3}{10}$ to $\frac{5}{8}$ and $\frac{3}{5}$ to $\frac{5}{4}$

Complete the statement. Round to the nearest hundredth if necessary.

4. 19 in. ≈____ cm

5. 9 km ≈____ mi

6. 5 gal ≈____ cu ft

Find the unit rate.

7. $9.75 for 12 cans

8. $4\frac{1}{2}$ miles in $1\frac{1}{2}$ hours

Tell whether *x* and *y* are proportional.

9.

x	3	6	9
y	3	6	9

10.

x	2	3	4
y	7	8	9

11. You make 3 ribbons and use 4.5 inches of string. Your friend makes 4 ribbons and uses 5 inches of string. Graph each ratio relationship in the same coordinate plane. Determine who uses more string.

12. You and your friend are walking a 4-mile race. You walk $\frac{1}{5}$ mile in 10 minutes. Your friend walks $\frac{2}{3}$ mile in 30 minutes.

a. Determine who finishes first.

b. Find the difference in finishing times.

Name ______________________________ Date ________

Lesson 4.5

Review & Refresh (continued)

Complete the statement. Round to the nearest hundredth if necessary.

13. $\frac{10 \text{ km}}{\text{h}} \approx \frac{\_\_\_\_ \text{ mi}}{\text{min}}$ **14.** $\frac{7 \text{ m}}{\text{min}} \approx \frac{\_\_\_\_ \text{ ft}}{\text{sec}}$ **15.** $\frac{3 \text{ gal}}{\text{min}} \approx \frac{\_\_\_\_ \text{ L}}{\text{hr}}$

16. An office had 800 employees in 2012 and 660 employees in 2019. Find the average rate of change in the number of employees per year.

17. You earn $256.50 for 18 hours of work. You friend earns $327.75 for 23 hours of work. Do these rates form a proportion? Justify your answer.

Use the exchange rate 1 U.S. Dollar (USD) ≈ 6.54 Chinese Yuan (RMB) to convert between currencies. Round to the nearest hundredth if necessary.

18. 45 USD ≈ ____ RMB **19.** 75 RMB ≈ ____ USD **20.** 250 RMB ≈ ____ USD

Lesson 4.5

Self-Assessment

Use the scale to rate your understanding of the learning target and the success criteria.

1 I don't understand yet. | 2 I can do it with help. | 3 I can do it on my own. | 4 I can teach someone else.

	Rating	Date
4.5 Identifying Proportional Relationships		
Learning Target: Determine whether two quantities are in a proportional relationship.	1 2 3 4	
I can determine whether ratios form a proportion.	1 2 3 4	
I can explain how to determine whether quantities are proportional.	1 2 3 4	
I can distinguish between proportional and nonproportional situations.	1 2 3 4	

Name______________________________ Date__________

Lesson 4.6 Review & Refresh

1. You and your friend drive 12 miles to work. You drive $2\frac{1}{2}$ miles in 4 minutes. Your friend drives 2 miles in 3 minutes.

a. Who gets to work first?

b. Find the difference in the time it takes each of you to get to work.

Solve the proportion.

2. $\frac{2}{3} = \frac{94}{a}$ **3.** $\frac{15}{2} = \frac{g}{6}$ **4.** $\frac{3.1}{5} = \frac{m}{4}$ **5.** $\frac{n}{1.1} = \frac{9}{9.9}$

Tell whether x and y are proportional.

6.

x	$\frac{3}{4}$	1	$\frac{5}{4}$
y	$\frac{10}{3}$	$\frac{13}{3}$	$\frac{16}{3}$

7.

x	$\frac{1}{3}$	$\frac{2}{3}$	1
y	$\frac{5}{18}$	$\frac{5}{9}$	$\frac{5}{6}$

8. A square garden has a side length of 20 meters.

a. Find the perimeter of the garden to the nearest hundredth of a foot.

b. Find the area of the garden to the nearest hundredth of a square foot.

Tell whether the rates are equivalent. Justify your answer.

9. 4 inches in 2.5 years

1 foot in 7.5 years

10. $2\frac{1}{2}$ miles in $\frac{1}{2}$ hour

$\frac{1}{4}$ mile in $\frac{1}{10}$ hour

Find the value of x so that the ratios are equivalent.

11. 1 : 16 and 8 : x **12.** x : 0.5 and 8 : 4 **13.** x : $\frac{1}{4}$ and 16 : 1

Name ____ Date __________

Lesson 4.6 Review & Refresh (continued)

Complete the statement using < or >.

14. 20 in. ____ 45 cm **15.** 20 lb ____ 16 kg **6.** 55 ft ____ 18 m

17. There are 400 people at a play. The ratio of males to females is 1 : 4. Find the number of females.

18. During a basketball season, you score 240 points in 30 games. Your friend scores 225 points in 25 games. Do these rates form a proportion? Justify your answer.

19. You can type 25 words in $\frac{1}{2}$ minute. Find the number of words typed in 6 minutes.

Lesson 4.6 Self-Assessment

Use the scale to rate your understanding of the learning target and the success criteria.

1 I don't understand yet. 2 I can do it with help. 3 I can do it on my own. 4 I can teach someone else.

	Rating	Date
4.6 Writing and Solving Proportions		
Learning Target: Use proportions to solve ratio problems.	1 2 3 4	
I can solve proportions using various methods.	1 2 3 4	
I can find a missing value that makes two ratios equivalent.	1 2 3 4	
I can use proportions to represent and solve real-life problems.	1 2 3 4	

Name________________________________ Date__________

Lesson 4.7

Review & Refresh

Tell whether x and y are proportional. If so, find the constant of proportionality. Explain your reasoning.

1.

x	−3	−2	2	3
y	−4	−1	1	4

2.

x	−4	−2	2	4
y	−12	−6	6	12

Complete the statement. Round to the nearest hundredth if necessary.

3. 25 lb ≈____ kg

4. 6 L ≈____ qt

5. 15 m ≈____ ft

Tell whether the rates form a proportion.

6. 16 players for 24 teams
20 players for 32 teams

7. 10 inches in 6 hours
80 inches in 2 days

8. Four large deluxe pizzas costs $67.80. Find the cost of 9 large deluxe pizzas.

Graph the equation.

9. $y = 3x$

10. $y = x + 2$

Name ____________________ Date ________

Lesson 4.7 Review & Refresh (continued)

Solve the proportion.

11. $\frac{3.6}{7.2} = \frac{r}{2}$

12. $\frac{p}{12} = \frac{3}{1.5}$

13. $\frac{18}{h} = \frac{2}{7}$

14. $\frac{40}{c} = \frac{8}{27}$

Tell whether the ratios form a proportion.

15. 7 to 9 and 17.5 to 22.5

16. 1 to 5 and 15 to 20

17. $\frac{3}{4}$ to $\frac{5}{7}$ and $\frac{2}{3}$ to $\frac{1}{2}$

Identify the constant of proportionality in the situation.

18. A car travels 120 miles in 1.5 hours.

19. There are 200 people who live within 5 square miles.

20. You earn 112 points for correctly answering 14 questions. Find the number of points you earn for correctly answering 25 questions.

Lesson 4.7 Self-Assessment

Use the scale to rate your understanding of the learning target and the success criteria.

1 I don't understand yet. 2 I can do it with help. 3 I can do it on my own. 4 I can teach someone else.

	Rating	Date
4.7 Using Graphs of Proportional Relationships		
Learning Target: Represent proportional relationships using graphs and equations.	1 2 3 4	
I can graph an equation in two variables.	1 2 3 4	
I can determine whether quantities are proportional using a graph.	1 2 3 4	
I can find the unit rate of a proportional relationship using a graph.	1 2 3 4	
I can create equations to represent proportional relationships.	1 2 3 4	

Name____ Date__________

Lesson 4.8 Review & Refresh

1. A model of a building has a scale of 1 cm : 6 m. The dimensions of the scale model are 8 centimeters, 4 centimeters, and 15 centimeters. Find the actual dimensions of the building.

Find the value of x so that the ratios are equivalent.

2. 3 : 5 and x : 20

3. 1.5 : 3.25 and 9 : x

4. $\frac{3}{5}$: 2 and x : 7

5. You walk $1\frac{3}{4}$ miles in 50 minutes. Your friend walks $1\frac{2}{3}$ miles in 40 minutes. Do these rates form a proportion? Justify your answer.

Graph the equation.

6. $y = \frac{1}{2}x$

7. $y = 2x + 1$

Find the missing dimension. Use the scale 1 : 6.

	Item	Model	Actual
8.	Car	Length: 7.25 in.	Length: ____ ft
9.	Building	Height: ____ cm	Height: 108 m
10.	Picture	Width: 4.4 in.	Width: ____ in.
11.	Dog	Length: ____ cm	Length: 36 cm

Name ______________________________ Date __________

Lesson 4.8 Review & Refresh (continued)

12. You make \$12 per hour.

a. Write an equation that represents the amount you earned.

b. Graph the equation.

c. Use your equation to find the amount you earned for working 24 hours.

Tell whether the rates form a proportion.

13. $\frac{2}{3}$ cups for every 2 gallons
3 cups for every $4\frac{1}{3}$ gallons

14. 2.4 meters every 5 minutes
6.72 meters every 14 minutes

15. The ratio of boys to girls in a summer camp class is 1 : 2. There are 24 students in the class. Find the number of boys and girls.

Identify the constant of proportionality in the situation.

16. A doctor sees 60 patients in 10 hours.

Lesson 4.8 Self-Assessment

Use the scale to rate your understanding of the learning target and the success criteria.

1 I don't understand yet. | 2 I can do it with help. | 3 I can do it on my own. | 4 I can teach someone else.

	Rating	Date
4.8 Scale Drawings		
Learning Target: Solve problems involving scale drawings.	1 2 3 4	
I can find an actual distance in a scale drawing.	1 2 3 4	
I can explain the meaning of scale and scale factor.	1 2 3 4	
I can use a scale drawing to find the actual lengths and areas of real-life objects.	1 2 3 4	

Name ______________________________ Date __________

Chapter 4

Chapter Self-Assessment

Use the scale to rate your understanding of the learning target and the success criteria.

1 I don't understand yet. | 2 I can do it with help. | 3 I can do it on my own. | 4 I can teach someone else.

	Rating	Date
Chapter 4 Ratios and Proportions		
Learning Target: Understand ratios and proportions.	1 2 3 4	
I can write and interpret ratios.	1 2 3 4	
I can describe ratio relationships and proportional relationships.	1 2 3 4	
I can represent equivalent ratios.	1 2 3 4	
I can model ratio relationships and proportional relationships to solve real-life problems.	1 2 3 4	
4.1 Ratios and Ratio Tables		
Learning Target: Understand ratios of rational numbers and use ratio tables to represent equivalent ratios.	1 2 3 4	
I can write and interpret ratios involving rational numbers.	1 2 3 4	
I can use various operations to create tables of equivalent ratios.	1 2 3 4	
I can use ratio tables to solve ratio problems.	1 2 3 4	
4.2 Graphing Ratio Relationships		
Learning Target: Represent ratio relationships in a coordinate plane.	1 2 3 4	
I can create and plot ordered pairs from a ratio relationship.	1 2 3 4	
I can create graphs to solve ratio problems.	1 2 3 4	
I can create graphs to compare ratios.	1 2 3 4	
4.3 Rates and Units Rates		
Learning Target: Understand rates involving fractions and use unit rates to solve problems.	1 2 3 4	
I can find unit rates for rates involving fractions.	1 2 3 4	
I can use unit rates to solve rate problems.	1 2 3 4	

Name ______________________________ Date __________

Chapter 4

Chapter Self-Assessment (continued)

	Rating	Date
4.4 Converting Measures between Systems		
Learning Target: Use ratio reasoning to convert units of measure between systems.	1 2 3 4	
I can convert units of measure between systems using ratio tables.	1 2 3 4	
I can convert units of measure between systems using conversion factors.	1 2 3 4	
I can convert rates using conversion factors.	1 2 3 4	
I can convert currencies using exchange rates.	1 2 3 4	
4.5 Identifying Proportional Relationships		
Learning Target: Determine whether two quantities are in a proportional relationship.	1 2 3 4	
I can determine whether ratios form a proportion.	1 2 3 4	
I can explain how to determine whether quantities are proportional.	1 2 3 4	
I can distinguish between proportional and nonproportional situations.	1 2 3 4	
4.6 Writing and Solving Proportions		
Learning Target: Use proportions to solve ratio problems.	1 2 3 4	
I can solve proportions using various methods.	1 2 3 4	
I can find a missing value that makes two ratios equivalent.	1 2 3 4	
I can use proportions to represent and solve real-life problems.	1 2 3 4	
4.7 Using Graphs of Proportional Relationships		
Learning Target: Represent proportional relationships using graphs and equations.	1 2 3 4	
I can graph an equation in two variables.	1 2 3 4	
I can determine whether quantities are proportional using a graph.	1 2 3 4	
I can find the unit rate of a proportional relationship using a graph.	1 2 3 4	
I can create equations to represent proportional relationships.	1 2 3 4	
4.8 Scale Drawings		
Learning Target: Solve problems involving scale drawings.	1 2 3 4	
I can find an actual distance in a scale drawing.	1 2 3 4	
I can explain the meaning of scale and scale factor.	1 2 3 4	
I can use a scale drawing to find the actual lengths and areas of real-life objects.	1 2 3 4	

Name____ Date__________

Chapter 4 B.E.S.T. Test Prep

1. Determine whether x and y are proportional.

<table>
<tr><th></th><th>Yes</th><th>No</th></tr>
<tr><td><table><tr><td>x</td><td>4</td><td>7</td><td>10</td></tr><tr><td>y</td><td>12</td><td>21</td><td>30</td></tr></table></td><td>Ⓐ</td><td>Ⓑ</td></tr>
<tr><td><table><tr><td>x</td><td>0.5</td><td>1.5</td><td>2.5</td></tr><tr><td>y</td><td>2.5</td><td>7.5</td><td>12.5</td></tr></table></td><td>Ⓒ</td><td>Ⓓ</td></tr>
<tr><td><table><tr><td>x</td><td>0.25</td><td>0.5</td><td>0.75</td></tr><tr><td>y</td><td>4</td><td>10</td><td>16</td></tr></table></td><td>Ⓔ</td><td>Ⓕ</td></tr>
</table>

2. You spent $\frac{2}{3}$ of your money. The next day, you get \$18. You now have \$36. Which equation can you use to find how much money you started with? What is that amount?

Ⓐ $\frac{2}{3}m + 18 = 36$; \$81

Ⓑ $\frac{2}{3}m + 18 = 36$; \$27

Ⓒ $\frac{2}{3}m - 18 = 36$; \$81

Ⓓ $\frac{2}{3}m - 18 = 36$; \$27

3. What is the value of $-0.01(-400)(0.5)$?

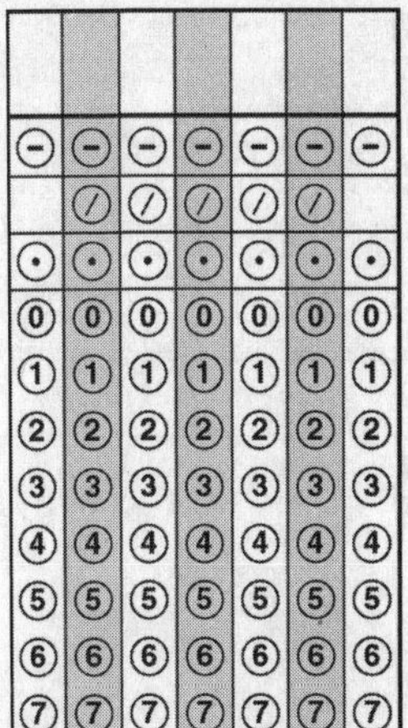

4. What is the decimal value of $4\frac{11}{16}$?

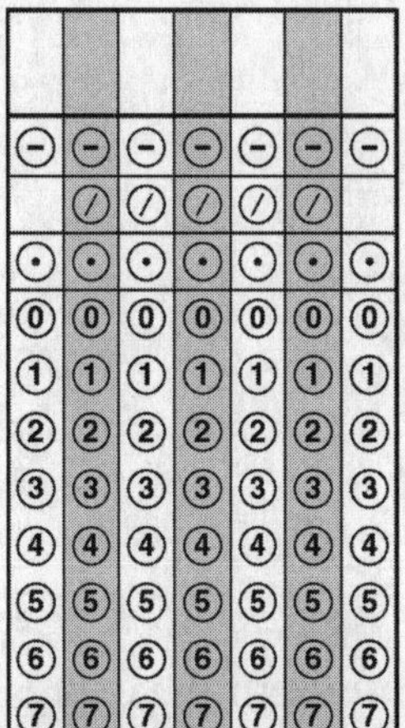

Name ______________________________ Date __________

Chapter 4 B.E.S.T. Test Prep (continued)

5. Which statements are true?

Ⓐ $40 \text{ mm} \overset{?}{>} 4 \text{ in.}$

Ⓑ $8 \text{ in.} \overset{?}{<} 27 \text{ cm}$

Ⓒ $10 \text{ lb} \overset{?}{>} 200 \text{ g}$

Ⓓ $25 \text{ lb} \overset{?}{<} 12 \text{ kg}$

Ⓔ $12 \text{ gal} \overset{?}{>} 40 \text{ L}$

Ⓕ $2 \text{ gal} \overset{?}{>} 6500 \text{ mL}$

6. Which equations have a negative solution?

Ⓐ $-6 = -12 + b$

Ⓑ $7.4 + f = 2.1$

Ⓒ $4\frac{2}{3} + j = 8\frac{1}{6}$

Ⓓ $-12y = 120$

Ⓔ $\frac{w}{-5} = -2.3$

Ⓕ $\frac{7}{10}c = 6$

7. You pick $8n + 28$ strawberries. Your friend picks $4n + 10$ strawberries. How many more strawberries did you pick than your friend?

Ⓐ $12n + 38$

Ⓑ $12n + 18$

Ⓒ $4n + 38$

Ⓓ $4n + 18$

8. What is the value of -6^4?

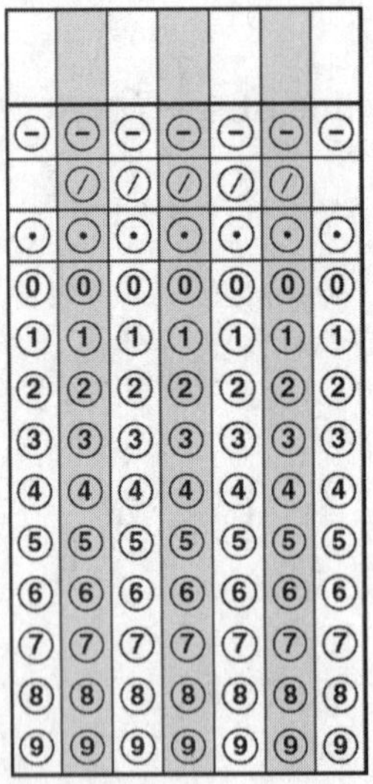

9. What is the unit rate, in miles per gallon, for 80.85 miles on 3.3 gallons?

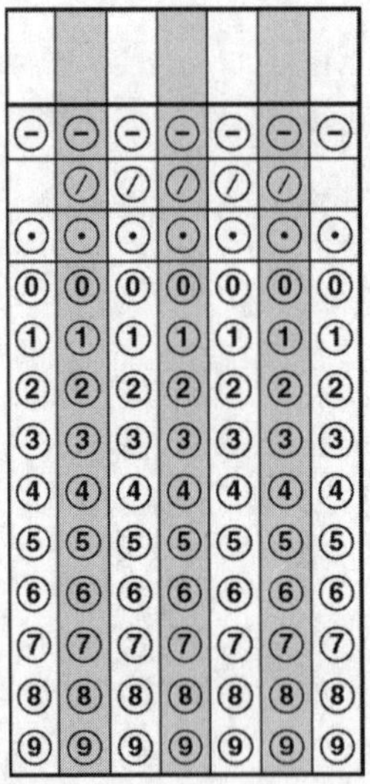

10. What is the simplified form of the expression $5(2 - x) - 3(x + 2)$?

Ⓐ $12 - 2x$

Ⓑ $12 - 4x$

Ⓒ $4 - 8x$

Ⓓ $4 - 2x$

Name______________________________ Date__________

Chapter 4 B.E.S.T. Test Prep (continued)

11. There are 5 blue marbles for every 3 yellow marbles in a bag. There are 24 yellow marbles in the bag. How many total marbles are in the bag?

Ⓐ 40 marbles
Ⓑ 60 marbles
Ⓒ 64 marbles
Ⓓ 84 marbles

12. What is the expression $(-0.3)(-0.3)(-0.3)(-0.3)$ as an exponent?

Ⓐ $(-0.4)^3$
Ⓑ $-(0.4)^3$
Ⓒ $(-0.3)^4$
Ⓓ $-(0.3)^4$

13. There are 500 people allowed to attend a show at a movie theater. There are 60 people already at the movie theater. An inequality that represents the number of p people that can attend is

Ⓐ $p - 60 \leq 500$
Ⓑ $p + 60 \leq 500$
Ⓒ $p - 60 \geq 500$
Ⓓ $p + 60 \geq 500$

.

The solution to the inequality is

Ⓐ $p \geq 540$
Ⓑ $p \leq 540$

.

14. What is the value of j in $\frac{7}{10} = \frac{j}{3.1}$?

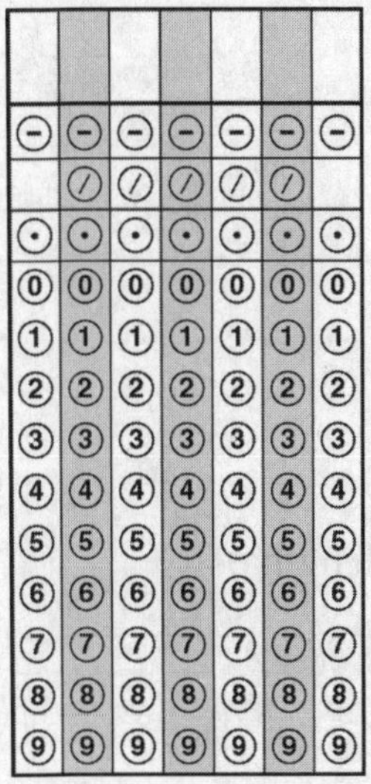

15. What is the distance between $-4\frac{3}{5}$ and $7\frac{2}{5}$ on a number line?

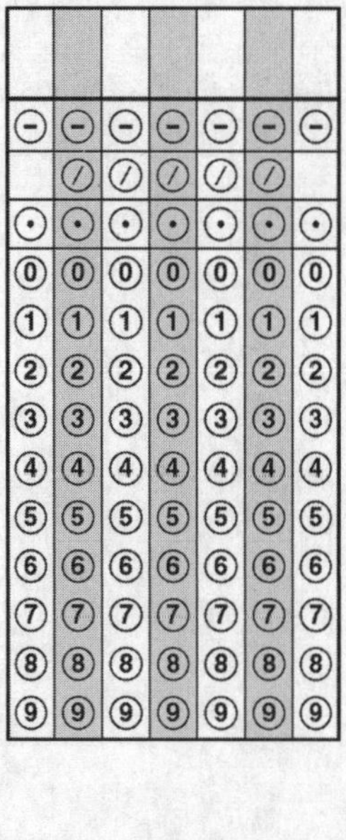

Name ______________________ Date __________

Chapter 4 B.E.S.T. Test Prep (continued)

16. This question has **two** parts.

A roller coaster has 640 riders per hour.

Part A

What is an equation that represents r riders for h hours?

Ⓐ $h = 640 + r$

Ⓑ $r = 640 + h$

Ⓒ $h = 640r$

Ⓓ $r = 640h$

Part B

How many riders are there in 6 hours?

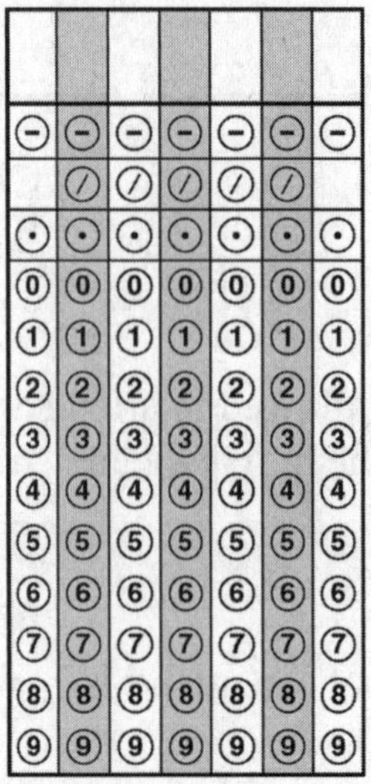

17. The table shows the change in weight for a wrestler in pounds. What are the weights in order from least to greatest?

Week	1	2	3	4	5
Weight Change	$\frac{2}{11}$	-0.1	$\frac{7}{9}$	0.4	$-\frac{2}{3}$

Ⓐ $-0.1, -\frac{2}{3}, 0.4, \frac{2}{11}, \frac{7}{9}$

Ⓑ $-0.1, -\frac{2}{3}, \frac{2}{11}, 0.4, \frac{7}{9}$

Ⓒ $-\frac{2}{3}, -0.1, 0.4, \frac{2}{11}, \frac{7}{9}$

Ⓓ $-\frac{2}{3}, -0.1, \frac{2}{11}, 0.4, \frac{7}{9}$

18. What is the expression $\frac{4}{5}y - \frac{3}{5}y + 6 - 7$ simplified?

Ⓐ $\frac{1}{5}y - 1$

Ⓑ $\frac{1}{5}y + 1$

Ⓒ $-\frac{1}{5}y - 1$

Ⓓ $-\frac{1}{5}y + 1$

19. The scale drawing has a scale of 1 in. : 250 ft. What is the actual length of a segment that is 5 inches?

Ⓐ 50 feet

Ⓑ 250 feet

Ⓒ 1000 feet

Ⓓ 1250 feet

Name____ Date____________

Lesson 5.1

Review & Refresh

Solve the proportion.

1. $\frac{14}{3} = \frac{56}{b}$ **2.** $\frac{12}{d} = \frac{8}{3}$ **3.** $\frac{4}{f} = \frac{2.5}{3.5}$ **4.** $\frac{1.8}{1.2} = \frac{l}{3.6}$

Tell whether x and y are proportional. If so, find the constant of proportionality. Explain your reasoning.

5.

x	3	5	7	9
y	6	10	14	18

6.

x	−8	−6	−4	−2
y	−10	−8	−6	−4

Write the decimal as a percent.

7. 0.36 **8.** 0.008 **9.** 2.15 **10.** 3.456

11. The table shows the number of students in school on a weekly basis. Order the grades from least to greatest.

Grade	6	7	8
Percent	$93.\bar{3}\%$	$\frac{47}{50}$	0.925

Interpret each point on the graph. Then identify the unit rate.

12.

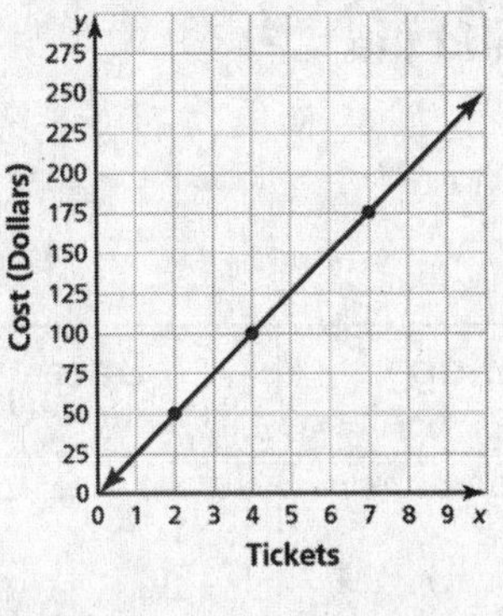

Interpret the constant of proportionality in the situation.

13. A company mows 28 lawns in 8 hours.

Name ______________________________ Date __________

Lesson 5.1 Review & Refresh (continued)

14. A football team has 90 players. The ratio of seventh graders to all other players is 4 : 5. Find the number of seventh graders on the team.

15. A drawing of a rectangular park has a scale of 1 in. : 400 ft. The park on the scale drawing is 10 inches by 15 inches.

a. Find the perimeter and area of the scale drawing.

b. Find the perimeter and area of the actual park.

Write the fraction as a decimal and a percent.

16. $\frac{73}{100}$ **17.** $\frac{1}{3}$ **18.** $\frac{17}{5}$ **19.** $\frac{23}{9}$

Find the value of x so that the ratios are equivalent.

20. $4 : x$ and $10 : 40$ **21.** $2.2 : 1.1$ and $x : 8.8$

Lesson 5.1 Self-Assessment

Use the scale to rate your understanding of the learning target and the success criteria.

1 I don't understand yet. 2 I can do it with help. 3 I can do it on my own. 4 I can teach someone else.

	Rating	Date
5.1 Fractions, Decimals, and Percents		
Learning Target: Rewrite fractions, decimals, and percents using different representations.	1 2 3 4	
I can write percents as decimals and decimals as percents.	1 2 3 4	
I can write fractions as decimals and percents.	1 2 3 4	
I can compare and order fractions, decimals, and percents.	1 2 3 4	

Name______________________________ Date__________

Lesson 5.2

Review & Refresh

1. The model of the bottom of a storage unit is shown. The scale is 1 cm : 5 m.
   a. Find the perimeter and area of the scale drawing.

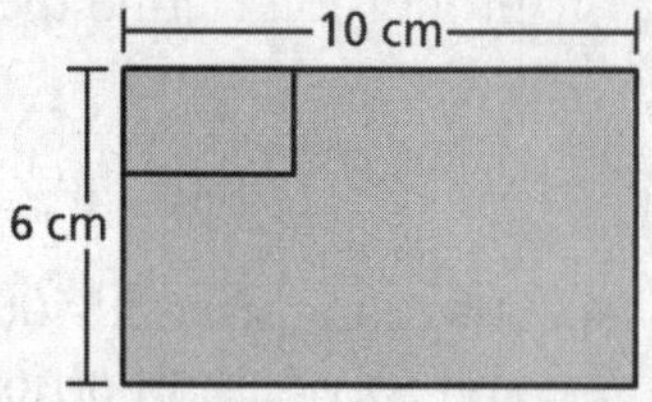

   b. Find the perimeter and area of the actual storage unit.

Write the percent as a decimal.

2. 28%
3. 45%
4. 125%
5. $9.\overline{6}\%$

Write and solve a proportion to answer the question.

6. What percent of 36 is 12?
7. 80% of what number is 16?
8. What number is 0.6% of 40?
9. 108 is what percent of 64?

Interpret each point on the graph. Then identify the unit rate.

10.

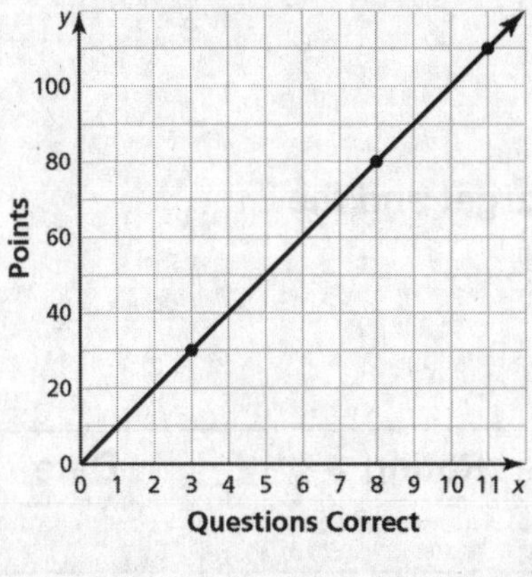

Order the numbers from least to greatest.

11. $\frac{1}{3}, 0.333, 33\%, 0.3$
12. $0.\overline{8}, 0.8, 88.8\%, \frac{22}{25}$

Name ______________________________ Date ________

Lesson 5.2 Review & Refresh (continued)

13. You earned \$12 per hour. You received an 8% raise. Write and solve a proportion to find the amount of the raise.

14. A group raised \$5500 this year, which is 110% more than last year. Write and solve a proportion to find last year's total.

Write the fraction as a decimal and a percent.

15. $\frac{5}{8}$ **16.** $\frac{1}{500}$ **17.** $\frac{7}{11}$ **18.** $\frac{13}{4}$

19. On Friday, $\frac{1}{6}$ of the work force was not at work. On Monday, $8.\overline{3}\%$ was not at work. Find the number of times more absences on Friday than on Monday.

Identify the constant of proportionality in the situation.

20. You run 2.5 miles in 30 minutes.

21. You talk with 12 customers in 1.5 hours.

Lesson 5.2 Self-Assessment

Use the scale to rate your understanding of the learning target and the success criteria.

1 I don't understand yet. 2 I can do it with help. 3 I can do it on my own. 4 I can teach someone else.

	Rating	Date
5.2 The Percent Proportion		
Learning Target: Use the percent proportion to find missing quantities.	1 2 3 4	
I can write proportions to represent percent problems.	1 2 3 4	
I can solve a proportion to find a percent, a part, or a whole.	1 2 3 4	

Name____ Date__________

Lesson 5.3 Review & Refresh

Write and solve a percent equation to answer the question.

1. 5 is what percent of 200?

2. 45% of what number is 90?

3. What number is $\frac{1}{5}$% of 40?

4. What percent of 90 is 15?

5. A drawing of a rectangular desktop has a scale of 1 in. = 2.5 in. The desktop on the scale drawing is 8 inches by 18 inches. Find the dimensions of the actual desktop.

Write the decimal as a percent.

6. 0.45

7. 0.2

8. 1.75

9. 0.0001

Write the fraction as a decimal and a percent.

10. $\frac{3}{5}$

11. $\frac{1}{2500}$

12. $\frac{15}{2}$

13. $\frac{17}{6}$

Write and solve a proportion to answer the question.

14. 36 is 10% of what number?

15. 20% of 0.5 is what number?

16. What percent of 80 is 70?

17. 150% of what number is 6.5?

18. The table shows the percentages of three-point shots made by four different players. Order the players from least to greatest.

Player	A	B	C	D
Made	0.37	$\frac{3}{8}$	36.5%	$\frac{9}{25}$

Name ________________________________ Date __________

Lesson 5.3 Review & Refresh (continued)

19. You answered 25 out of 30 questions correct on a test. Write and solve a proportion to find the percent of correct questions.

20. A gym has seats for 1500 people. A game has 12% empty seats. Write and solve a proportion to find the number of empty seats.

21. A basketball team scored 78 points. This is 120% more than the last game. Write and solve a percent equation to find the points scored in the last game.

22. A part of jeans cost $36 and the sales tax rate is 7.5%. Write and solve a percent equation to find the amount of tax.

Write the percent as a decimal.

23. 37.6% **24.** 300% **25.** 10.25% **26.** $4.\overline{4}\%$

Lesson 5.3 Self-Assessment

Use the scale to rate your understanding of the learning target and the success criteria.

1 I don't understand yet. 2 I can do it with help. 3 I can do it on my own. 4 I can teach someone else.

	Rating	Date
5.3 The Percent Equation		
Learning Target: Use the percent equation to find missing quantities.	1 2 3 4	
I can write equations to represent percent problems.	1 2 3 4	
I can use the percent equation to find a percent, a part, or a whole.	1 2 3 4	

Name____ Date__________

Lesson 5.4

Review & Refresh

Identify the percent of change as increase or decrease. Then find the percent of change. Round to the nearest tenth of a percent if necessary.

1. 40 feet to 80 feet

2. 400 minutes to 100 minutes

3. \$75 to \$40

4. 75 hours to 85 hours

Write and solve a percent equation to answer the question.

5. 16 is 40% of what number?

6. 32% of 80 is what number?

7. What percent of 48 is 72?

8. 0.1% of what number is 4?

Write and solve a proportion to answer the question.

9. 8% of 90 is what number?

10. 50 is what percent of 60?

Write the fraction as a decimal and a percent.

11. $\frac{33}{50}$

12. $\frac{1}{75}$

13. $\frac{8}{9}$

14. $\frac{13}{8}$

15. The expenses of a company were $\frac{16}{25}$ of the revenue in 2019. In 2020, the expenses were 60% of the revenue. Find the number of times greater the expenses were in 2019.

16. You estimate that the length of a piece of wood is $7\frac{7}{8}$ feet. The actual length is 8 feet. Find the percent error.

Name ________________________________ Date __________

Lesson 5.4

Review & Refresh (continued)

17. There were 9 employees out of 120 on vacation. Write and solve a percent equation to find the percent of employees on vacation.

18. A player makes 12 free throws in a game. This is 60% of the free throws attempted. Write and solve a proportion to find the number of free throws attempted.

19. The population of a town was 8000 in 2010 and 8800 in 2020. Find the percent of change.

20. You have placed 375 out of 500 pieces in a puzzle. Write and solve a proportion to find the percent of pieces *not* in the puzzle.

Order the numbers from least to greatest.

21. $\frac{7}{9}, 77.7\%, \frac{39}{50}, 0.77$

Lesson 5.4

Self-Assessment

Use the scale to rate your understanding of the learning target and the success criteria.

1 I don't understand yet. | 2 I can do it with help. | 3 I can do it on my own. | 4 I can teach someone else.

	Rating	Date
5.4 Percents of Increase and Decrease		
Learning Target: Find percents of change in quantities.	1 2 3 4	
I can explain the meaning of percent of change.	1 2 3 4	
I can find the percent of increase or decrease in a quantity.	1 2 3 4	
I can find the percent error of a quantity.	1 2 3 4	

Name ______________________________ Date ________

Lesson 5.5

Review & Refresh

1. The bill at a department store is $145. There is a 15% discount when you check out. Find the final price.

Identify the percent of change as increase or decrease. Then find the percent of change. Round to the nearest tenth of a percent if necessary.

2. 36 inches to 40 inches

3. 150 pounds to 120 pounds

4. The sun was out 21 out of 30 days in April. Write and solve a proportion to find the percent of sunny days.

Write and solve a percent equation to answer the question.

5. 0.3% of 10 is what number?

6. What percent of 90 is 50?

7. A store pays $25 for a book. Find the selling price with a 40% markup.

Write and solve a proportion to answer the question.

8. 75 is 125% of what number?

9. 2.5% of 0.25 is what number?

10. You run a 100-yard dash is 16.5 seconds in the spring and 14.8 seconds in the fall. Find the percent of change.

11. A 3-gallon container of juice is 70% full. Write and solve a percent equation to find the number of gallons left.

Name ______________________ Date ________

Lesson 5.5 Review & Refresh (continued)

Find the sale price.

12. Original price: $75, discount: 10%

13. Original price: $200, discount: 45%

14. The estimated weight of a suitcase was 45 kilograms. The actual weight is 48 kilograms. Find the percent error.

Find the selling price.

15. Cost to store: $20, markup: 125%

16. Cost to store: $210, markup: 30%

17. You answered 35 out of 40 questions correctly in a game. Write and solve a percent equation to find the number percent questions correct.

Find the original price.

18. Sale price: $18, discount: 10%

19. Sale price: $56, discount: 30%

Lesson 5.5 Self-Assessment

Use the scale to rate your understanding of the learning target and the success criteria.

1 I don't understand yet. 2 I can do it with help. 3 I can do it on my own. 4 I can teach someone else.

	Rating	Date
5.5 Discounts and Markups		
Learning Target: Solve percent problems involving discounts and markups.	1 2 3 4	
I can use percent models to solve problems involving discounts and markups.	1 2 3 4	
I can write and solve equations to solve problems involving discounts and markups.	1 2 3 4	

Name____ Date__________

Lesson 5.6

Review & Refresh

1. A dog weighed 12 pounds last year. This year the dog weighs 15 pounds. Find the percent of change.

2. There are 44 students out of group of 80 who say dogs are their favorite pet. Write and solve a percent equation to find the percent.

An account earns simple annual interest. Find the interest earned. Find the balance of the account.

3. \$500 at 3% for 2 years

4. \$1600 at 5.5% for 18 months

5. A bag of snacks is 24 ounces. The acceptable percent error when filling the bag is 3%. Bag A is 24.5 ounces and Bag B is 23 ounces. Explain whether each bag has an acceptable weight.

Find the percent discount.

6. Original price: \$150, sale price: \$52.50

7. Original price: \$300, sale price: \$270

Write and solve a percent equation to answer the question.

8. 52 is 125% of what number?

9. What number is 27% of 32?

10. Store A has a phone for \$250 with a 60% markup. Store B has the same phone for \$295 with a 40% markup. Find the phone that costs less. Find the difference in the prices.

Name ______________________ Date ________

Lesson 5.6 Review & Refresh (continued)

Find the annual interest rate.

11. $I = \$125, P = \$2500, t = 2$ years

12. $I = \$33.75, P = \$300, t = 30$ months

13. Find the number of years for \$1000 to double at a simple annual interest rate of 4%.

14. The height of a tower to be built was changed from 500 feet to 450 feet. Find the percent of change for the height.

Find the sale price.

15. Original price: \$425, discount: 60%

16. Original price: \$78, discount: 5%

17. Find the amount paid for a loan with \$5000 borrowed at 7% simple annual interest for 3 years.

Lesson 5.6 Self-Assessment

Use the scale to rate your understanding of the learning target and the success criteria.

1 I don't understand yet. | 2 I can do it with help. | 3 I can do it on my own. | 4 I can teach someone else.

	Rating	Date
5.6 Simple Interest		
Learning Target: Understand and apply the simple interest formula.	1 2 3 4	
I can explain the meaning of simple interest.	1 2 3 4	
I can use the simple interest formula to solve problems.	1 2 3 4	

Name____ Date__________

Chapter 5

Chapter Self-Assessment

Use the scale to rate your understanding of the learning target and the success criteria.

1 I don't understand yet. | 2 I can do it with help. | 3 I can do it on my own. | 4 I can teach someone else.

	Rating	Date
Chapter 5 Percents		
Learning Target: Understand fractions, decimals, and percents.	1 2 3 4	
I can rewrite fractions, decimals, and percents.	1 2 3 4	
I can compare and order fractions, decimals, and percents.	1 2 3 4	
I can use the percent proportion or percent equation to find a percent, a part, or a whole.	1 2 3 4	
I can apply percents to solve real-life problems.	1 2 3 4	
5.1 Fractions, Decimals and Percents		
Learning Target: Rewrite fractions, decimals and percents using different representations.	1 2 3 4	
I can write percents as decimals and decimals as percents.	1 2 3 4	
I can write fractions as decimals and percents.	1 2 3 4	
I can compare and order fractions, decimals and percents.	1 2 3 4	
5.2 The Percent Proportion		
Learning Target: Use the percent proportion to find missing quantities.	1 2 3 4	
I can write proportions to represent percent problems.	1 2 3 4	
I can solve a proportion to find a percent, a part, or a whole.	1 2 3 4	

Name ______________________ Date __________

Chapter 5

Chapter Self-Assessment (continued)

	Rating	Date
5.3 The Percent Equation		
Learning Target: Use the percent equation to find missing quantities.	1 2 3 4	
I can write equations to represent percent problems.	1 2 3 4	
I can use the percent equation to find a percent, a part, or a whole.	1 2 3 4	
5.4 Percents of Increase and Decrease		
Learning Target: Find percents of change in quantities.	1 2 3 4	
I can explain the meaning of percent of change.	1 2 3 4	
I can find the percent of increase or decrease in a quantity.	1 2 3 4	
I can find the percent error of a quantity.	1 2 3 4	
5.5 Discounts and Markups		
Learning Target: Solve percent problems involving discounts and markups.	1 2 3 4	
I can use percent models to solve problems involving discounts and markups.	1 2 3 4	
I can write and solve equations to solve problems involving discounts and markups.	1 2 3 4	
5.6 Simple Interest		
Learning Target: Understand and apply the simple interest formula.	1 2 3 4	
I can explain the meaning of simple interest.	1 2 3 4	
I can use the simple interest formula to solve problems.	1 2 3 4	

Name____ Date __________

Chapter 5 B.E.S.T. Test Prep

1. Solve $-2 + 7d = 68$ for d.

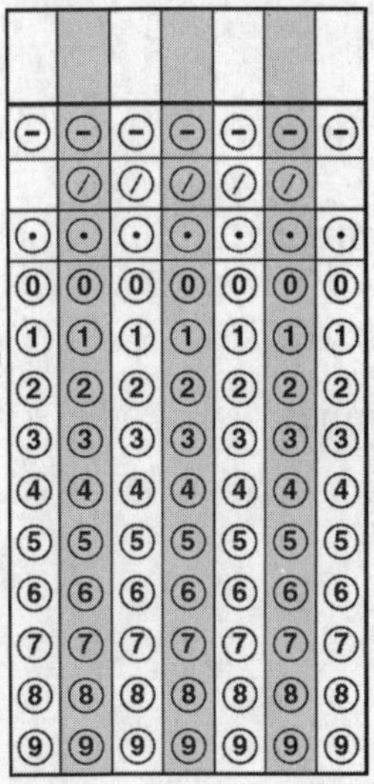

2. What is the value of $\left|7\frac{1}{8} - 7\frac{3}{16}\right| \cdot -3\frac{1}{5}$?

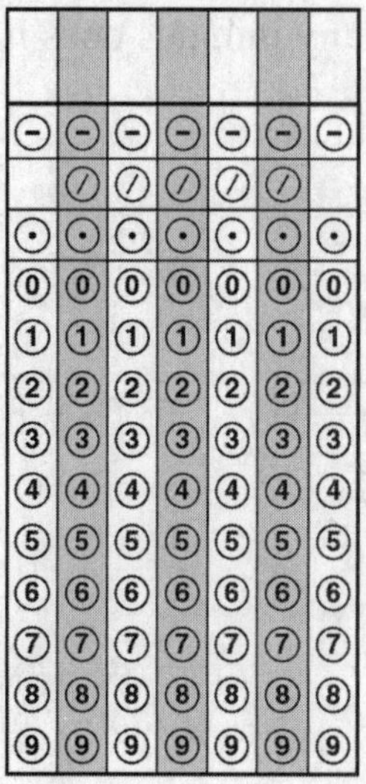

3. What is the expression $\frac{9^7 \cdot 9^3}{9^4} \cdot \frac{9^9 \cdot 9^4}{9^2}$ simplified?

Ⓐ 9^{17}

Ⓑ 9^{27}

Ⓒ 9^{59}

Ⓓ 9^{69}

4. Two bags of lawn fertilizer cover 7500 square feet. How many square feet are covered with 7 bags?

Ⓐ 22,500 ft^2

Ⓑ 26,250 ft^2

Ⓒ 42,250 ft^2

Ⓓ 52,500 ft^2

5. A salesperson earns $2500 with a 5% commission rate. How much did the salesperson sell?

Ⓐ $12,500

Ⓑ $15,000

Ⓒ $50,000

Ⓓ $52,500

6. Tell whether the ratios form a proportion.

	Yes	No
8 to 3 and 16.5 to 6.5	Ⓐ	Ⓑ
0.8 to 0.3 and 7.2 to 2.7	Ⓒ	Ⓓ
0.08 to 0.03 and 4.5 to 1.5	Ⓔ	Ⓕ

Name ______________________________ Date __________

Chapter 5 B.E.S.T. Test Prep (continued)

7. You drove 18 minutes to school yesterday. Today you drive 27 minutes to school. What is an equation to find how many more minutes it takes you to get to school? How many minutes does it take?

Ⓐ $18m = 27$; 1.5 minutes

Ⓑ $\frac{m}{18} = 27$; 1.5 minutes

Ⓒ $m - 18 = 27$; 9 minutes

Ⓓ $m + 18 = 27$; 9 minutes

8. What is the value of $\dfrac{\frac{7}{12} - \frac{1}{4}}{\frac{2}{3}}$?

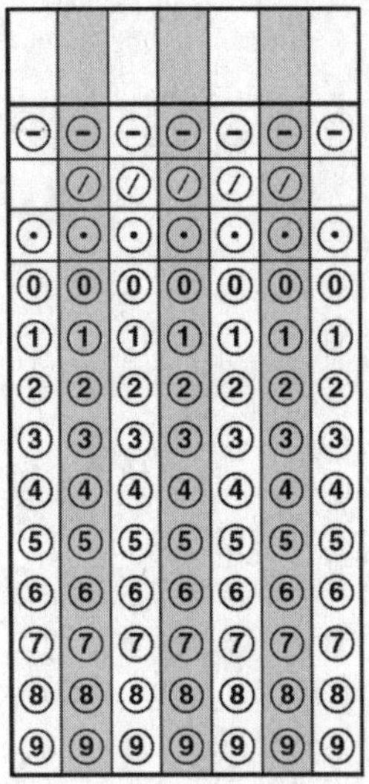

9. 27 is 15% of what number?

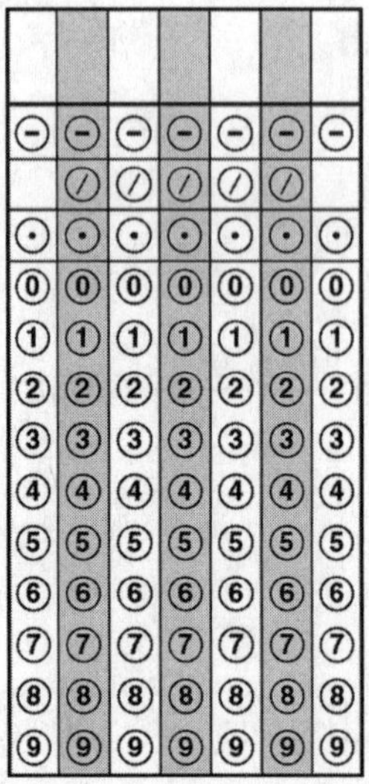

10. Last season, a player averaged 4.8 points per basketball game. This year, the player averaged 8.4 points per game. What is the percent of change?

Ⓐ 25% decrease

Ⓑ 75% decrease

Ⓒ 75% increase

Ⓓ 175% increase

11. A hole was to be dug to 60 feet below the surface. The depth of the hole is reduced by $\frac{3}{5}$. How many feet below the surface is the hole to be dug?

Ⓐ –40 feet

Ⓑ –24 feet

Ⓒ –20 feet

Ⓓ –4 feet

Name______________________________ Date__________

B.E.S.T. Test Prep (continued)

12. What is equivalent to $\frac{14}{5}$?

Ⓐ 2.8

Ⓑ 2.4

Ⓒ $2\frac{4}{5}$

Ⓓ $4\frac{2}{5}$

Ⓔ 250%

Ⓕ 280%

13. Which statements are true?

Ⓐ 8 m < 30 ft

Ⓑ 15 in < 30 cm

Ⓒ 7 qt < 7 L

Ⓓ 30 gal > 100 L

Ⓔ 6 kg > 10 lb

Ⓕ 32 oz > 800 g

14. You deposit $1000 in an account that earns 2% annual simple interest.

The amount in the account after 1 year is [Ⓐ $1002 / Ⓑ $1020 / Ⓒ $1022]. The amount in the account after 3 years is [Ⓐ $1040.00 / Ⓑ $1040.40 / Ⓒ $1060.00 / Ⓓ $1061.21].

15. The coldest temperature in a town was −19.4°F. The warmest temperature was 87.9°F. What is the difference in temperatures?

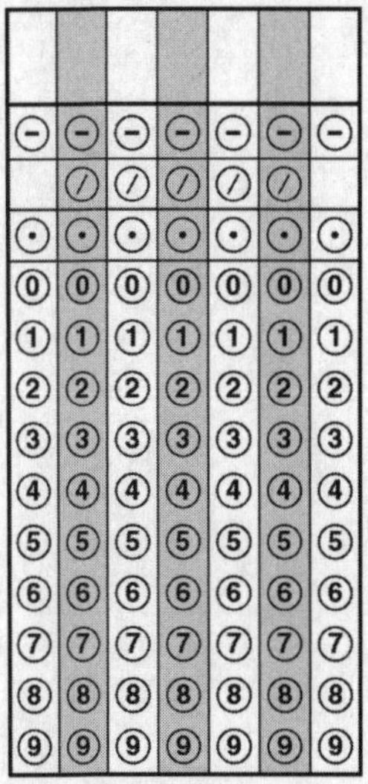

16. What is the constant of proportionality for the table?

x	−5	−4	−3	−2
y	−10	−8	−6	−4

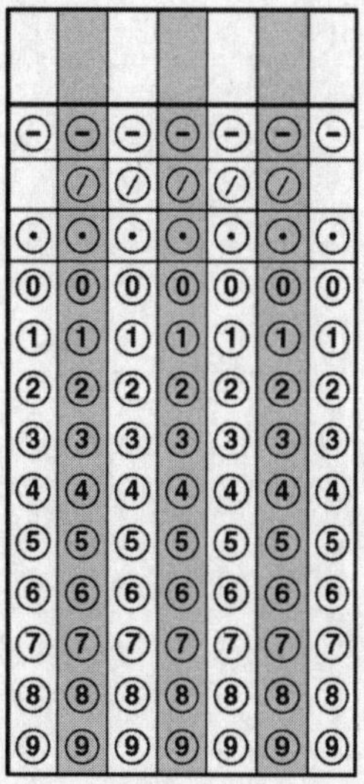

Name ______________________________ Date __________

B.E.S.T. Test Prep (continued)

17. What is the expression $(5 - 2z) - (z + 4) - (3 - 5z)$ simplified?

Ⓐ $-8z - 5$

Ⓑ $-8z - 2$

Ⓒ $2z - 5$

Ⓓ $2z - 2$

18. A sweatshirt that was originally \$49 is on sale for 75% off. What is the final price of the sweatshirt?

Ⓐ \$12.25

Ⓑ \$24.00

Ⓒ \$26.00

Ⓓ \$36.75

19. There are 250 seventh graders in a school, and 42% buy their lunch one day. What is the percent equation that represents the students who buy their lunch?

Ⓐ $250 = 42\% \cdot p$

Ⓑ $42 = 250\% \cdot p$

Ⓒ $a = 42\% \cdot 250$

Ⓓ $a = 250\% \cdot 42$

20. This question has **two** parts.

A drawing of a floor plan for a rectangular living room has a scale of 2 inches : 5 feet. The room on the scale drawing is 8 inches by 9 inches.

Part A

What is the actual perimeter of the room in feet?

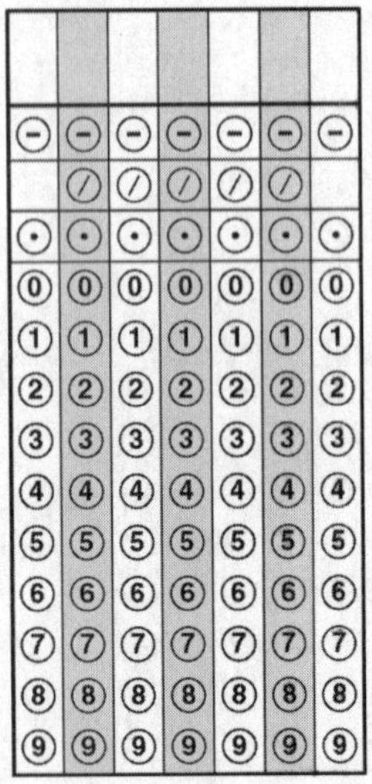

Part B

What is the actual area of the room in square feet?

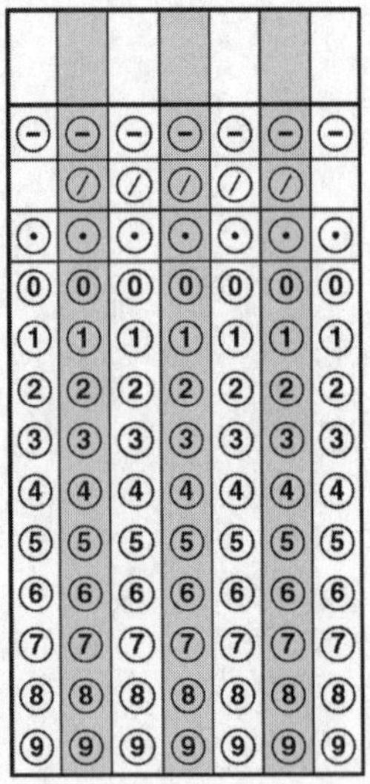

Name_______________________________________ Date__________

Lesson 6.1

Review & Refresh

1. A six-sided number cube is used in a game.

   a. Find the sample space. How many possible outcomes are there?

   b. In how many ways can rolling an odd number occur?

   c. In how many ways can rolling a number greater than 7 occur?

Identify the percent of change as an increase or decrease. Then find the percent of change. Round to the nearest tenth of a percent if necessary.

2. 100 pounds to 110 pounds

3. 60 inches to 50 inches

4. 72 miles to 88 miles

5. 80 hours to 60 hours

An account earns simple annual interest. Find (a) the interest earned and (b) the balance of the account.

6. \$1250 at 4% for 7 years

7. \$5000 at 1.5% for 66 months

Describe the likelihood of the event given its probability.

8. The probability you make a shot is $\frac{7}{10}$.

9. There is a 0% chance of snow tomorrow.

Find the selling price.

10. Cost to seller: \$80; % markup: 25%

11. Cost to seller: \$35; % markup: 75%

12. A football team scores 42 points in their first game. In the second game, the team scores 7 points. Find the percent of change in the point totals.

Name ______________________________ Date __________

Lesson 6.1 Review & Refresh (continued)

13. An \$18,000 car is sold at 10% off. Find the final price.

14. The table shows the numbers of shots attempted during the first quarter of a basketball game. Out of 90 shots taken, how many can you expect to be missed? Justify your reasoning.

Two-Point Shots	||||
Three-Point Shots		
Misses	𝍸 𝍸

An account earns simple interest. Find the amount of time.

15. $I = \$80, P = \$800, r = 2\%$

16. $I = \$243.75, P = \$2500, r = 1.5\%$

Find the original price.

17. Sale price: \$42; % discount: 40%

18. Sale price: \$18; % discount: 85%

Lesson 6.1 Self-Assessment

Use the scale to rate your understanding of the learning target and the success criteria.

1 I don't understand yet. 2 I can do it with help. 3 I can do it on my own. 4 I can teach someone else.

	Rating	Date
6.1 Probability		
Learning Target: Understand how the probability of an event indicates its likelihood.	1 2 3 4	
I can find the sample space of an experiment.	1 2 3 4	
I can use probability and relative frequency to describe the likelihood of an event.	1 2 3 4	
I can use relative frequency to make predictions.	1 2 3 4	

Name____ Date__________

Lesson 6.2

Review & Refresh

1. Cards numbered 1 to 20 are used for a game. Find the theoretical probability of the event.

   a. selecting an even-numbered card

   b. selecting a card that is a multiple of 3

   c. selecting a card with the number 25

   d. selecting a card with the number 11

Describe the likelihood of the event given its probability.

2. Your basketball team has a 1 in 3 chance of winning its next game.

3. A coin has a 50% chance of landing on heads.

Find the sale price.

4. Original price: \$104; % discount: 60%

5. Original price: \$29.50; % discount: 36%

Find the annual interest rate.

6. $I = \$360, P = \$4000, t = 3$ years

7. $I = \$6.25,\ P = \$1250, t = 6$ months

8. You want to determine whether a six-sided number cube is *fair*. You roll the number cube and record the number of times you roll each number.

Number	1	2	3	4	5	6
Results	||||	|||	||||	||	||	||||

   a. Describe the likelihood that you roll a 1 on your next roll.

   b. Describe the likelihood that you roll an even number on your next roll.

   c. Do you think the cube is *fair*? Explain.

Find the percent discount.

9. Original price: \$80; Sale price: \$50

10. Original price: \$200; Sale price: \$30

Name ______________________________ Date ________

Lesson 6.2 Review & Refresh (continued)

11. The table shows the results of flipping two coins 200 times each.

HH	HT	TH	TT
54	43	61	42

a. Compare the theoretical probability and the experimental probability of one coin landing on heads and the other coin landing on tails.

b. Find the number of times one coin landing on heads and the other coin landing on tails would occur when each coin is flipped 1000 times using the theoretical probability and the experimental probability.

Find the amount paid for a loan.

12. \$4000 at 5.5% for 5 years

13. \$7500 at 10% for 6.5 years

14. There are 5 defective pencils out of 1000 pencils randomly selected. Find the experimental probability that the screw is defective.

15. There are 12 boys and 13 girls in a class. Find the theoretical probability of selecting a girl as a partner for a project.

Lesson 6.2 Self-Assessment

Use the scale to rate your understanding of the learning target and the success criteria.

1 I don't understand yet. 2 I can do it with help. 3 I can do it on my own. 4 I can teach someone else.

	Rating	Date
6.2 Experimental and Theoretical Probability		
Learning Target: Develop probability models using experimental and theoretical probability.	1 2 3 4	
I can explain the meanings of experimental and theoretical probabilities.	1 2 3 4	
I can find experimental and theoretical probabilities.	1 2 3 4	
I can compare experimental and theoretical probabilities.	1 2 3 4	
I can use simulations to find experimental probabilities.	1 2 3 4	

Name____ Date__________

Lesson 6.3

Review & Refresh

Display the data in a circle graph.

1.

Favorite Season			
Spring	**Summer**	**Fall**	**Winter**
25%	50%	10%	15%

2. A six-sided number cube is rolled 80 times in a game. Compare the theoretical probability and the experimental probability for the events.

Number	1	2	3	4	5	6
Results	12	15	13	10	18	12

a. rolling an even number

b. rolling a 5

c. rolling a 3 or a 6

An account earns simple interest. Find the amount of time.

3. $I = \$41.25, P = \$250, r = 5.5\%$

4. $I = \$64,\ P = \$640, r = 4\%$

5. The circle graph shows the favorite games of a group of students. Four students say other games.

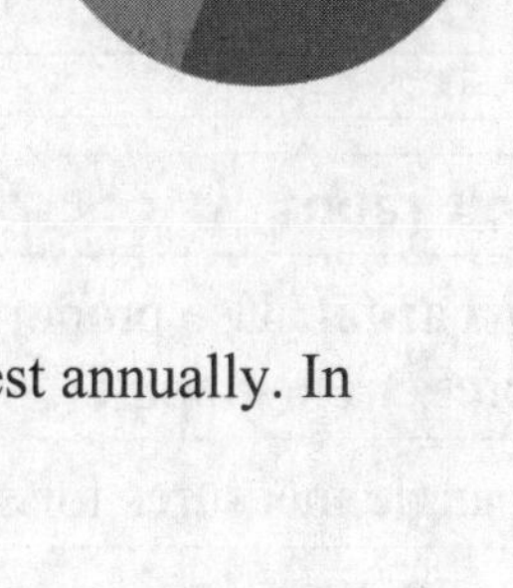

a. How many students were surveyed?

b. Find the probability of a student *not* selecting board games.

6. You deposit $2500 in an account earning 3.25% simple interest annually. In how many years will the account have $3500?

Name ____________________ Date __________

Lesson 6.3 Review & Refresh (continued)

7. A spinner with 10 equal sections numbered 1–10 is used in a game.

a. Find the sample space. How many possible outcomes are there?

b. In how many ways can choosing an even number occur?

c. In how many ways can choosing a number less than 4 occur?

An account earns simple annual interest. Find (a) the interest earned and (b) the balance of the account.

8. $775 at 1.25% for 3 years

9. $8000 at 2% for 1.25 years

10. The data shows the percentages of children and their favorite fruit.

Favorite Fruit			
Apple	**Bananas**	**Oranges**	**Other**
24	48	10	18

a. Display the data in a circle graph.

b. You survey 150 more students. Find the number of students that you would expect to say banana.

c. You survey 150 more students. Find the number of students that you would expect to say apple or orange.

Lesson 6.3 Self-Assessment

Use the scale to rate your understanding of the learning target and the success criteria.

1 I don't understand yet. 2 I can do it with help. 3 I can do it on my own. 4 I can teach someone else.

	Rating	Date
6.3 Circle Graphs		
Learning Target: Use proportional reasoning to make and interpret circle graphs.	1 2 3 4	
I can find angle measures for sections of a circle graph.	1 2 3 4	
I can make circle graphs.	1 2 3 4	
I can interpret circle graphs.	1 2 3 4	

Name____ Date___________

Lesson 6.4 Review & Refresh

Create an appropriate data display to represent the data.

1.

Daily Minutes Read by Students			
20	35	38	40
45	42	50	37
39	44	46	24
27	36	33	29

2. A bag contains red, blue, and green marbles. The marbles are drawn and then put back in the bag. The results are shown.

Red	5
Yellow	8
Blue	2

a. What is the likelihood the next marble is yellow?

b. What is the likelihood the next marble is blue?

c. What is the likelihood the next marble is green?

3. The results of 30 spins are shown. Find the experimental probability of the event.

Red	10
Orange	8
Yellow	5
Green	7

a. spinning blue

b. spinning yellow

c. spinning red or orange

4. A coin flip is simulated 100 times. Compare the theoretical and experimental probabilities of the event.

Heads	47
Tails	53

Display the data in a circle graph.

5.

Monthly Expenses				
Car	**Rent**	**Groceries**	**Utilities**	**Misc.**
$500	$700	$300	$300	$200

Name ______________________________ Date __________

Lesson 6.4 Review & Refresh (continued)

6. Create an appropriate data display to represent the data.

Days Absent from School			
4	7	3	5
12	15	18	20
25	31	9	16
5	2	7	11

7. The number of song downloads for six months is shown. Explain what type of data display you would use to display the data.

Song Downloads					
Jan	**Feb**	**Mar**	**Apr**	**May**	**Jun**
450	600	550	750	800	950

8. You spin the spinner. Find the theoretical probability of the event.

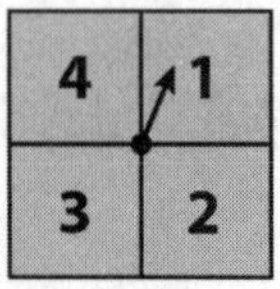

   a. spinning a 1

   b. spinning an even number

9. There is a 1 in 10 chance of school closing tomorrow. Describe the likelihood of school closing.

Lesson 6.4 Self-Assessment

Use the scale to rate your understanding of the learning target and the success criteria.

1 I don't understand yet. | 2 I can do it with help. | 3 I can do it on my own. | 4 I can teach someone else.

	Rating	Date
6.4 Choosing a Data Display		
Learning Target: Use appropriate data displays to represent situations.	1 2 3 4	
I can choose and create appropriate data displays for situations.	1 2 3 4	
I can identify misleading data displays.	1 2 3 4	
I can analyze a variety of data displays.	1 2 3 4	

Name____ Date__________

Chapter 6 Chapter Self-Assessment

Use the scale to rate your understanding of the learning target and the success criteria.

1 I don't understand yet. 2 I can do it with help. 3 I can do it on my own. 4 I can teach someone else.

	Rating	Date
Chapter 6 Probability and Data Displays		
Learning Target: Understand probability and representing data.	1 2 3 4	
I can find the sample space of an experiment.	1 2 3 4	
I can find experimental and theoretical probabilities.	1 2 3 4	
I can make and interpret a circle graph.	1 2 3 4	
I can use appropriate data displays to represent a situation.	1 2 3 4	
6.1 Probability		
Learning Target: Understand how the probability of an event indicates its likelihood.	1 2 3 4	
I can find the sample space of an experiment.	1 2 3 4	
I can use probability and relative frequency to describe the likelihood of an event.	1 2 3 4	
I can use relative frequency to make predictions.	1 2 3 4	
6.2 Experimental and Theoretical Probability		
Learning Target: Develop probability models using experimental and theoretical probability.	1 2 3 4	
I can explain the meanings of experimental and theoretical probabilities.	1 2 3 4	
I can find experimental and theoretical probabilities.	1 2 3 4	
I can compare experimental and theoretical probabilities.	1 2 3 4	
I can use simulations to find experimental probabilities.	1 2 3 4	

Name ____________________ Date ________

Chapter 6

Chapter Self-Assessment (continued)

	Rating	Date
6.3 Circle Graphs		
Learning Target: Use proportional reasoning to make and interpret circle graphs.	1 2 3 4	
I can find angle measures for sections of a circle graph.	1 2 3 4	
I can make circle graphs.	1 2 3 4	
I can interpret circle graphs.	1 2 3 4	
6.4 Choosing a Data Display		
Learning Target: Use appropriate data displays to represent situations.	1 2 3 4	
I can choose and create appropriate data displays for situations.	1 2 3 4	
I can identify misleading data displays.	1 2 3 4	
I can analyze a variety of data displays.	1 2 3 4	

Name________________________________ Date__________

Chapter 6 B.E.S.T. Test Prep

1. You borrow $750 to buy gifts. The simple annual interest rate is 10.2% and there are equal payments for 18 months. What is your monthly payment?

Ⓐ $41.67

Ⓑ $45.92

Ⓒ $48.04

Ⓓ $50.17

2. Which graph represents the ratio relationship?

Iced Tea (cups)	4	8	12
Lemonade (cups)	8	16	24

Ⓐ
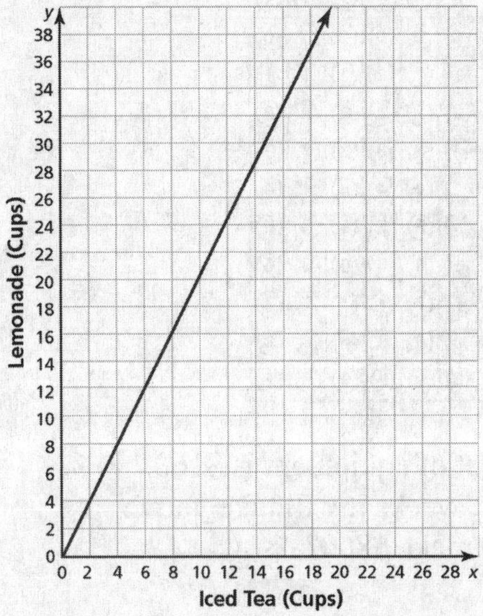

Ⓑ
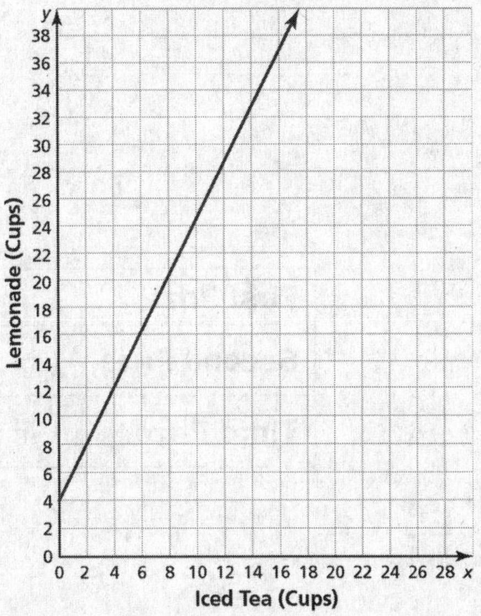

Ⓒ
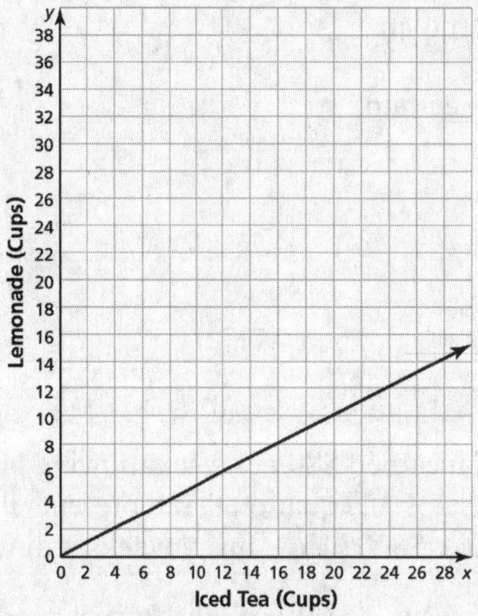

Ⓓ
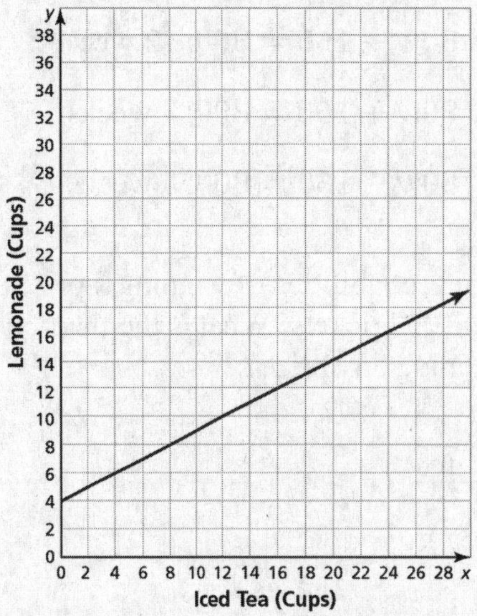

Name ______________________________ Date __________

Chapter 6 B.E.S.T. Test Prep (continued)

3. This question has **two** parts.

You roll a number cube and record the number of times you roll an even number and the number of times you roll an odd number.

Even	𝍸 |||
Odd	𝍸 𝍸 ||

Part A

Describe the likelihood that you roll an odd number on your next roll.

Ⓐ unlikely

Ⓑ equally likely to happen or not happen

Ⓒ likely

Ⓓ certain

Part B

Out of 200 rolls, how many times can you expect to roll an even number?

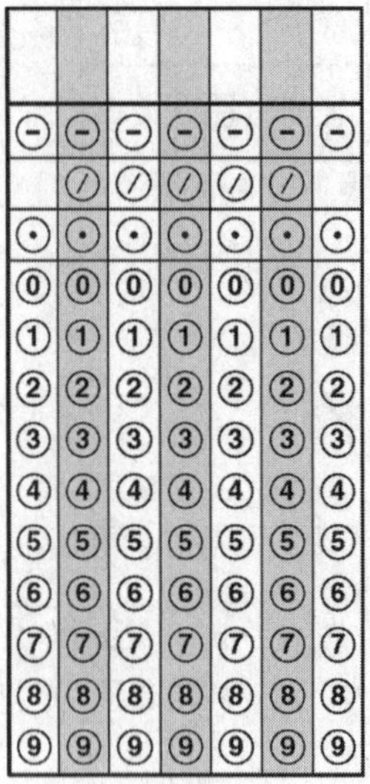

4. You earned \$80 per week mowing lawns. The cost of equipment is \$160. What is an equation that represents the number of weeks it will take you to make \$800? How many weeks will it take you to make \$800?

Ⓐ $80w + 160 = 800$; 12 weeks

Ⓑ $80w - 160 = 800$; 12 weeks

Ⓒ $80w + 160 = 800$; 8 weeks

Ⓓ $80w - 160 = 800$; 8 weeks

5. The probabilities of winning a prize are shown. There are 1000 tickets. What is the theoretical probability of winning any prize?

First Prize	1 in 1000
Second Prize	1 in 100
Third Prize	1 in 10

Ⓐ $\frac{3}{100}$

Ⓑ $\frac{11}{100}$

Ⓒ $\frac{3}{1000}$

Ⓓ $\frac{111}{1000}$

Name____ Date__________

B.E.S.T. Test Prep (continued)

6. Which equations have a positive solution?

Ⓐ $c - 14 = 20$

Ⓑ $f + 6.3 = -14.9$

Ⓒ $-4\frac{3}{8} + k = -5\frac{3}{4}$

Ⓓ $-16 = d - 32$

Ⓔ $\frac{x}{-2.4} = -4.5$

Ⓕ $-32 = 16z$

7. There are 2 defective screws out of 100 screws randomly selected. What is the experimental probability that the screw is defective?

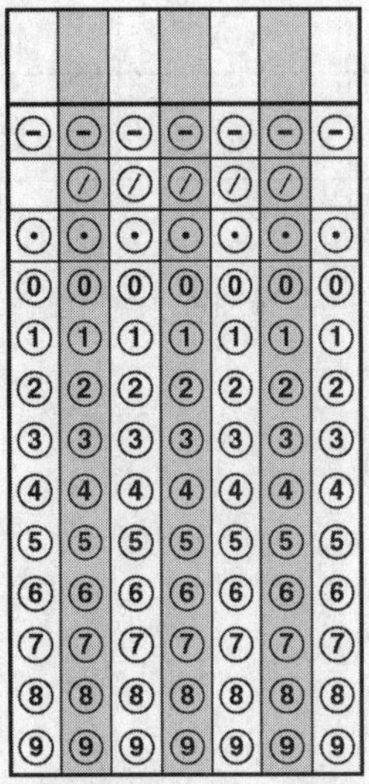

8. A billboard has dimensions of 90 feet long by 60 feet wide.

The perimeter of the billboard is approximately [Ⓐ 45.72 / Ⓑ 91.44 / Ⓒ 137.16] meters.

and the area in is approximately [Ⓐ 501.69 / Ⓑ 822.90 / Ⓒ 1645.20] square meters.

9. The circle graph shows the students' favorite sports. You survey 200 more students. How many students will say that soccer or tennis is their favorite sport?

Ⓐ 15

Ⓑ 20

Ⓒ 30

Ⓓ 45

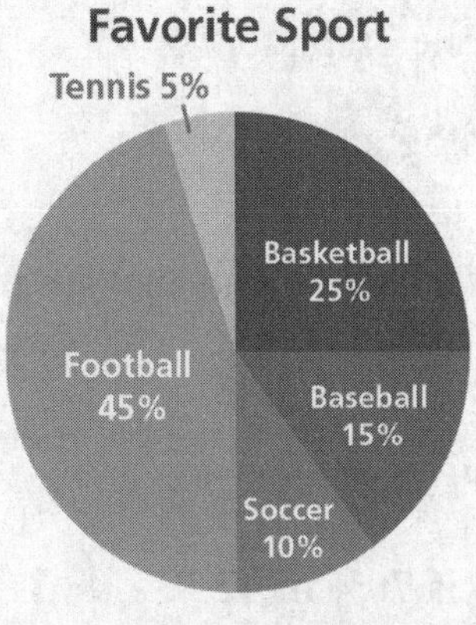

Name ______________________________ Date __________

Chapter 6 B.E.S.T. Test Prep (continued)

10. Determine whether the given value makes the inequality *true* or *false*.

	True	False
$x = 8; x + 3 < 15$	Ⓐ	Ⓑ
$h = 7; 2h \geq 14$	Ⓒ	Ⓓ
$b = 12; \frac{b}{4} > 4$	Ⓔ	Ⓕ

11. What is $27.43 - 19.76 + (-36.41)$?

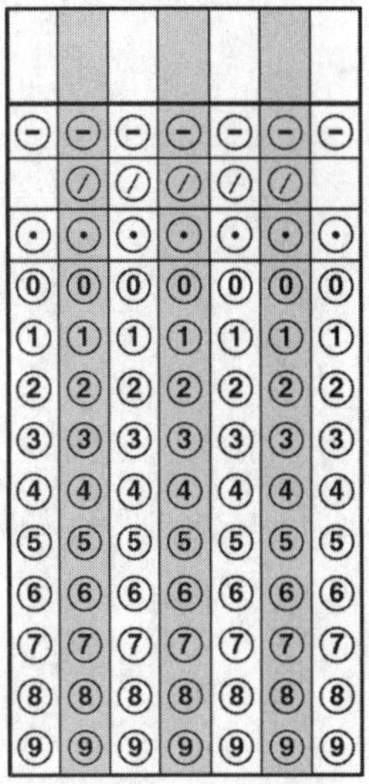

12. What is the unit rate for 6 grams of protein in every $\frac{2}{3}$ of an ounce?

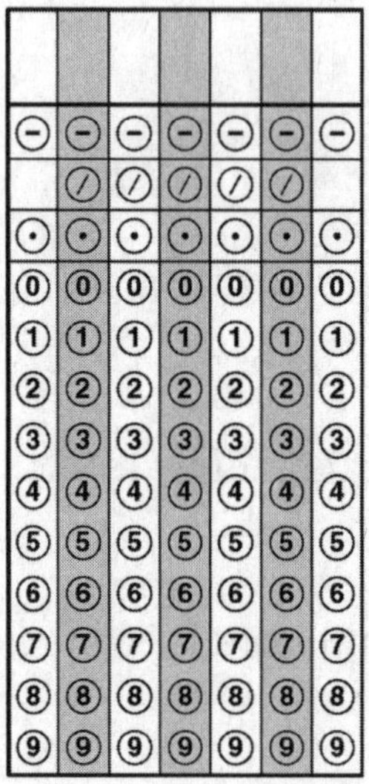

13. Which data display is best for the data?

Ⓐ bar graph

Ⓑ dot plot

Ⓒ circle graph

Ⓓ histogram

Hourly Wages of Employees			
\$11.50	\$12.50	\$11.00	\$14.50
\$15.00	\$13.50	\$13.00	\$16.50
\$13.00	\$16.50	\$14.50	\$17.50
\$11.50	\$14.00	\$17.50	\$17.00

14. Select all statements that are true.

Ⓐ 32 is 60% of 48.

Ⓑ 2.5% of 800 is 20.

Ⓒ 28 is 70% of 42.

Ⓓ 17.5 is 10% of 175.

Ⓔ 10 is 0.4% of 250.

Ⓕ 77.5 is 125% of 62.

Name ______________________________ Date __________

Lesson 7.1 Review & Refresh

1. The table shows the results of flipping a coin 50 times. Find the experimental probability for heads and tails.

Heads	Tails
28	22

Which data display is misleading? Explain your reasoning.

2.

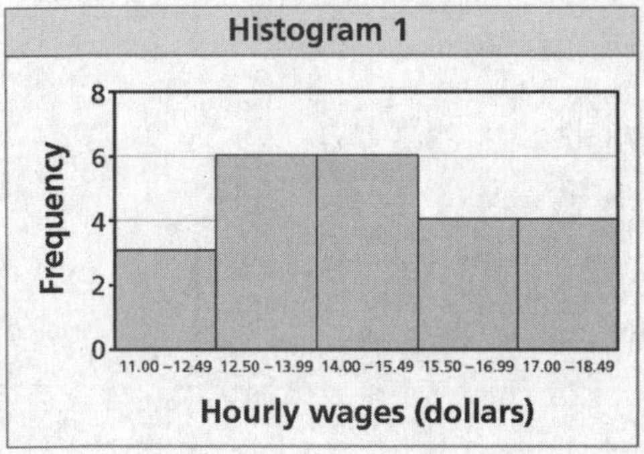

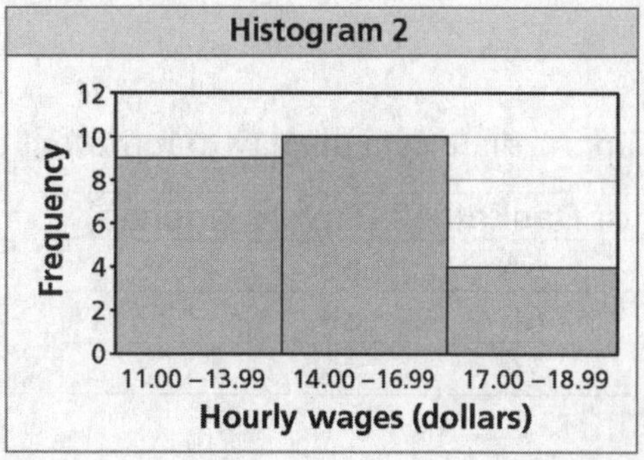

Find the mean, median, and mode of the data.

3. 12, 17, 19, 13, 14, 15, 8, 2, 8

4. 47, 58, 62, 18, 23, 25, 29, 37, 41, 65

5. A card game has red, orange, yellow, and green cards numbered 1–5 for each color. Find the theoretical probability of the event.

a. an odd card

b. an orange card

c. a red 3 or a green 5 card

6. The table shows the number of vacation days available to employees. Find the range and interquartile range of the number of vacation days available.

Vacation Days				
15	13	12	18	14
7	5	20	25	24
16	12	8	10	19

Find the outliers of the data.

7. 23, 28, 19, 4, 15, 26, 50, 27, 11

8. 45, 48, 32, 36, 39, 55, 57, 12, 33, 36, 40

Name ______________________________ Date __________

Lesson 7.1 Review & Refresh (continued)

9. Display the data in a circle graph.

Favorite Summer Activity				
Riding Bikes	**Play with Friends**	**Go to a Park**	**Camping**	**Swimming**
15%	30%	15%	5%	35%

10. Create an appropriate data display to represent the data.

Heights of Basketball Players (inches)			
64	64	66	68
70	66	68	72
74	76	70	78

11. The table shows the quiz scores for a class. Find the mean, median, and mode of the quiz scores.

Quiz Scores				
18	16	14	20	20
20	17	15	19	13
16	15	20	18	17

Lesson 7.1 Self-Assessment

Use the scale to rate your understanding of the learning target and the success criteria.

1 I don't understand yet. 2 I can do it with help. 3 I can do it on my own. 4 I can teach someone else.

	Rating	Date
7.1 Measures of Center and Variation		
Learning Target: Understand measures of center and variation.	1 2 3 4	
I can find the mean, median, and mode of a data set.	1 2 3 4	
I can find the range and interquartile range of a data set.	1 2 3 4	
I can identify outliers in a data set.	1 2 3 4	
I can describe how outliers affect the measures of center and variation of a data set.	1 2 3 4	

Name____ Date__________

Lesson 7.2

Review & Refresh

Choose the most appropriate measures to describe the center and the variation. Explain your reasoning.

1. Number of Shopping Trips in a Month

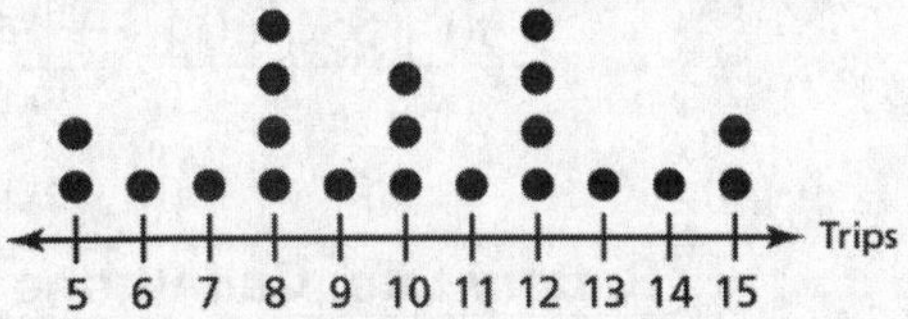

2. Runs Scored by a Baseball Team

Stem	Leaf
0	0 1 2 2 2 3 3 3 4 4 5 5 6 7 8 8 9
1	0 1 2 4 4 5 6
2	0 1 3

Key: 2|1 = 21

Find the range and interquartile range of the data.

3. 12.5, 14.5, 13, 11, 10.5, 7, 9, 8.5

4. 45, 35, 75, 15, 85, 85, 25, 65, 55

5. The circle graph shows the favorite color of a group of first graders. Fifty students said yellow was their favorite color.

a. Find the number of students surveyed.

b. Find the probability of a student *not* choosing red.

Favorite Color

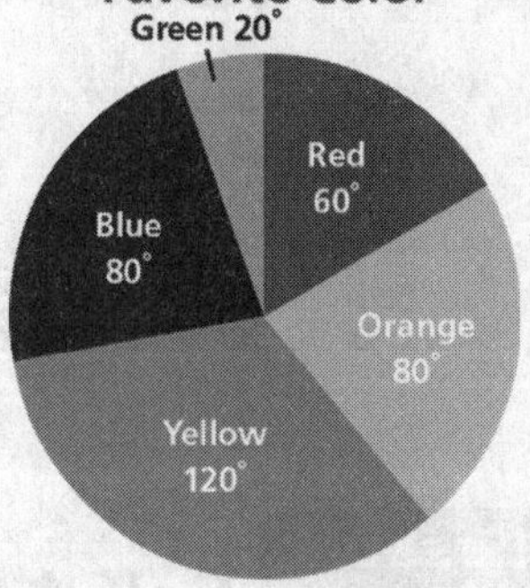

6. Create an appropriate data display to represent the data.

Books Sold Each Month					
Jan	Feb	Mar	Apr	May	Jun
450	700	750	600	650	800
Jul	Aug	Sept	Oct	Nov	Dec
550	750	900	1000	800	650

7. Describe the centers and the variation of the data set.

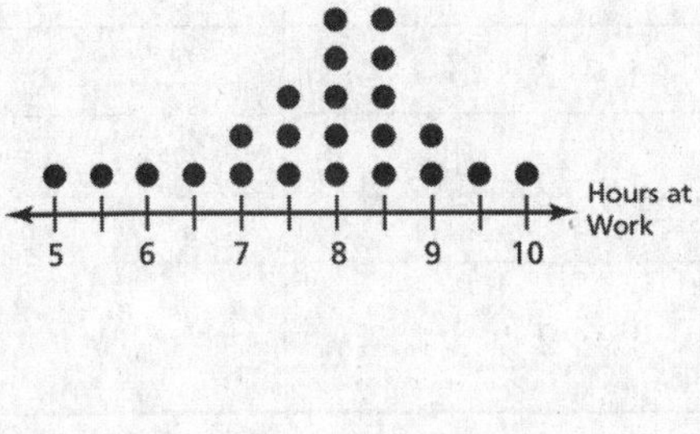

Name ______________________________ Date ________

Lesson 7.2 Review & Refresh (continued)

8. The table shows the number of books read by a group of students during the school year. Find the mean, median, and mode number of books read.

Books Read				
40	45	35	50	40
40	40	45	45	45
30	55	60	50	65

9. The tables show the battery life, in hours, of two different cell phones. Which cell phone would you choose? Explain your reasoning.

Battery Life: Cell Phone A					
10	9	10	11	10	10.5
9.5	8.5	8	12	14	11.5

Battery Life: Cell Phone B					
13	12	11.5	11	10.5	10.5
11	12.5	11	13	12	11.5

10. Which data display is misleading? Explain your reasoning.

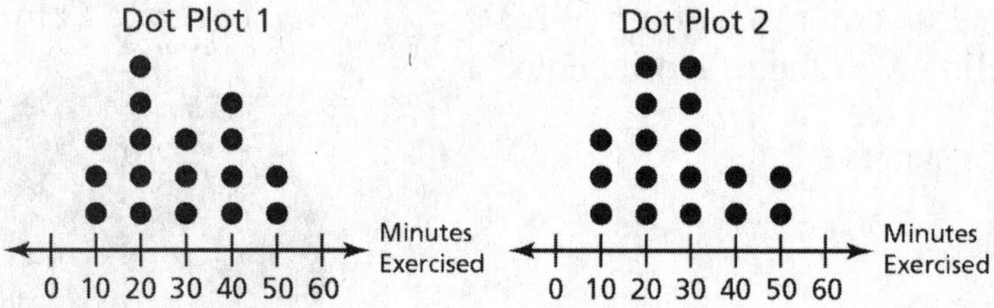

Lesson 7.2 Self-Assessment

Use the scale to rate your understanding of the learning target and the success criteria.

1 I don't understand yet. 2 I can do it with help. 3 I can do it on my own. 4 I can teach someone else.

	Rating	Date
7.2 Choosing Appropriate Measures		
Learning Target: Determine which measures of center and variation are appropriate to describe a data set.	1 2 3 4	
I can determine whether a data set contains outliers.	1 2 3 4	
I can explain whether a measure of center is appropriate to describe a data set.	1 2 3 4	
I can explain whether a measure of variation is appropriate to describe a data set.	1 2 3 4	

Name____ Date__________

Lesson 7.3

Review & Refresh

1. The table shows the number of text messages sent between 20 friends on one day.

Text Messages Sent				
50	40	60	80	75
5	30	25	50	55
60	60	75	80	90
95	90	70	75	80

a. Find and interpret the measures of center and variation.

b. Identify outliers. Explain the affect of the outliers on the measures of center and variation.

Determine whether the sample is *biased* or *unbiased.* Explain your reasoning.

2. You want to estimate the number of students who buy a school lunch. You surveyed every fifth person who entered the cafeteria.

3. You want to estimate the number of people who want to build a new basketball arena. You survey every 15th person at a basketball game.

4. Create an appropriate data display to represent the data.

Monthly Expenses (dollars)			
Cable	Phone	Internet	Gas
100	40	75	40
Water	Electric	Insurance	Security
40	80	100	25

Find the mean, median, and mode of the data.

5.

Stem	Leaf
4	5 6 6 8
5	0 1 2 3 4 5
6	1 3

Key: 4|5 = 45

6.

Stem	Leaf
0	5 7 8 8 9 9
1	2 3 5 6
2	0 1 2 5 6
3	0 5

Key: 0|5 = 5

Name ______________________________ Date ________

Lesson 7.3 Review & Refresh (continued)

Describe the center and the variation of the data set.

7. The number of packages delivered to houses in a neighborhood in one month are represented by the data set: {16, 18, 22, 24, 25, 27, 28, 30, 32, 35, 38}.

8. The minutes of exercise from a group of friends in one day are represented by the data set: {20, 25, 30, 30, 35, 35, 40, 45, 50, 60, 65, 70, 90}.

Determine whether you should survey a sample or the population. Explain your reasoning.

9. You want to know the average age of residents in a city.

10. You want to know the favorite subject of students in your homeroom.

11. The table shows the amount spent at a grocery store by a family every 12 weeks. Find the range and the interquartile range of the amount spent.

Grocery Bill (Dollars)					
150	125	175	100	150	200
100	75	75	150	250	175

Lesson 7.3 Self-Assessment

Use the scale to rate your understanding of the learning target and the success criteria.

1 I don't understand yet. | 2 I can do it with help. | 3 I can do it on my own. | 4 I can teach someone else.

	Rating	Date
7.3 Samples and Populations		
Learning Target: Understand how to use random samples to make conclusions about a population.	1 2 3 4	
I can explain why a sample is biased or unbiased.	1 2 3 4	
I can explain why conclusions made from a biased sample may not be valid.	1 2 3 4	
I can explain use an unbiased sample to make a conclusion about a population.	1 2 3 4	

Name____ Date__________

Lesson 7.4 Review & Refresh

1. Two data sets contain an equal number of values. The double box-and-whisker plot represents the values in the data sets.

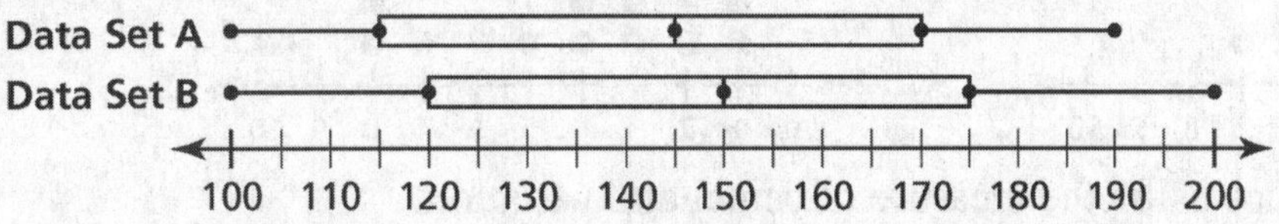

   a. Compare the data sets using the measures of center and variation.

   b. Explain which data set is more likely to contain a value of 110.

   c. Explain which data set is more likely to contain a value of 190.

2. You ask 100 randomly selected houses in a neighborhood about trash pick-up options. The results are in the table on the right. There are 500 houses in the neighborhood. Estimate the number of households that would choose company A.

Trash Company		
A	B	C
58	27	15

In Exercises 3 and 4, determine whether the conclusion is *valid* or *invalid*. Explain your reasoning.

3. You survey 200 students at a football game about their favorite sport. 150 students say football. You conclude that 75% of the students like football.

4. You randomly select and ask 100 students about their favorite type of book. 15 students respond with biographies. You conclude that 15% of students like biographies.

5. The table shows the time, in minutes, it takes 15 employees to get to work. Find the mean, median, and mode number of minutes. Find the range and interquartile range of minutes.

Minutes to Work				
15	24	20	18	33
36	30	27	14	19
36	44	12	31	46

Name ______________________________ Date __________

Lesson 7.4 Review & Refresh (continued)

6. The dot plots show the number of fish caught in a competition.

Group A

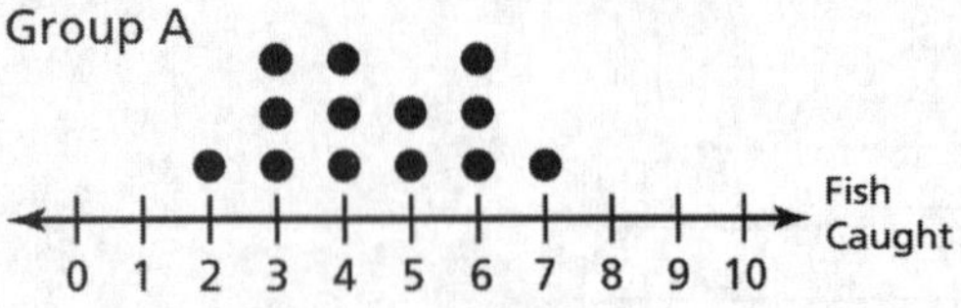

Group B

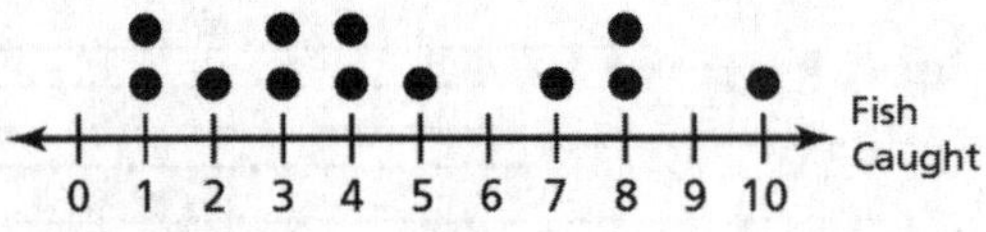

a. Compare the groups using the measure of center and variation.

b. Explain which group was more consistent in catching fish.

Choose the most appropriate measures to describe the center and the variation. Explain your reasoning.

7. Number of Wins Each Week

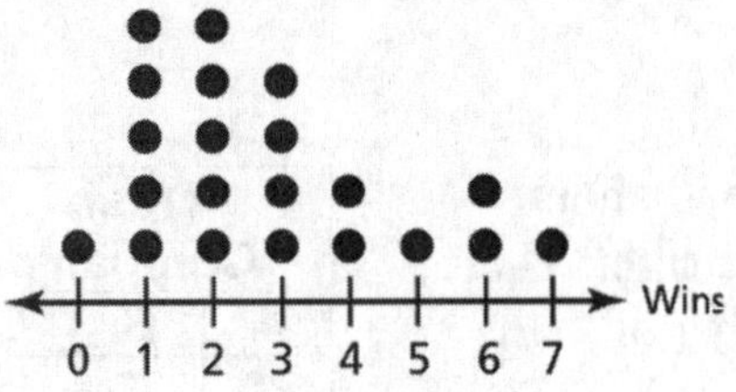

8. Number of Times Volunteered

Stem	Leaf
1	5 7 8
2	0 2 3 4 5 5 6 7 8 9
3	1 2 5

Key: 2|0 = 20

Lesson 7.4 Self-Assessment

Use the scale to rate your understanding of the learning target and the success criteria.

1 I don't understand yet. | 2 I can do it with help. | 3 I can do it on my own. | 4 I can teach someone else.

	Rating	Date
7.4 Comparing Populations		
Learning Target: Compare populations using measures of center, measures of variation, and random samples.	1 2 3 4	
I can compare populations using measures of center and variation.	1 2 3 4	
I can compare random samples using measures of center and variation.	1 2 3 4	
I can compare populations using multiple random samples.	1 2 3 4	

Name ____ Date ________

Chapter 7

Chapter Self-Assessment

Use the scale to rate your understanding of the learning target and the success criteria.

1 I don't understand yet. | 2 I can do it with help. | 3 I can do it on my own. | 4 I can teach someone else.

	Rating	Date
Chapter 7 Statistics		
Learning Target: Understand statistics.	1 2 3 4	
I can find measures of center and variation of a data set.	1 2 3 4	
I can explain which measure(s) is/are appropriate in describing a data set.	1 2 3 4	
I can use an unbiased sample to make a conclusion about a population.	1 2 3 4	
I can compare populations.	1 2 3 4	
7.1 Measures of Center and Variation		
Learning Target: Understand measures of center and variation.	1 2 3 4	
I can find the mean, median, and mode of a data set.	1 2 3 4	
I can find the range and interquartile range of a data set.	1 2 3 4	
I can identify outliers in a data set.	1 2 3 4	
I can describe how outliers affect the measures of center and variation of a data set.	1 2 3 4	
7.2 Choosing Appropriate Measures		
Learning Target: Determine which measures of center and variation are appropriate to describe a data set.	1 2 3 4	
I can determine whether a data set contains outliers.	1 2 3 4	
I can explain whether a measure of center is appropriate to describe a data set.	1 2 3 4	
I can explain whether a measure of variation is appropriate to describe a data set.	1 2 3 4	

Name ______________________________ Date __________

Chapter 7

Chapter Self-Assessment (continued)

	Rating	Date
7.3 Samples and Populations		
Learning Target: Understand how to use random samples to make conclusions about a population.	1 2 3 4	
I can explain why a sample is biased or unbiased.	1 2 3 4	
I can explain why conclusions made from a biased sample may not be valid.	1 2 3 4	
I can use an unbiased sample to make a conclusion about a population.	1 2 3 4	
7.4 Comparing Populations		
Learning Target: Compare populations using measures of center, measures of variation, and random samples.	1 2 3 4	
I can compare populations using measures of center and variation.	1 2 3 4	
I can compare random samples using measures of center and variation.	1 2 3 4	
I can compare populations using multiple random samples.	1 2 3 4	

Name_______________________________________ Date__________

Chapter 7 B.E.S.T. Test Prep

1. Which event is likely to happen?

Ⓐ There is a 10% chance that you will make the shot.

Ⓑ There is a $\frac{2}{5}$ chance that you select a 5 next turn.

Ⓒ It will be sunny $\frac{2}{3}$ of the days in August.

Ⓓ The probability of the sun setting is 100%.

2. What is the total amount paid, in dollars, for an $8500 loan at 10% annual interest for 3.5 years?

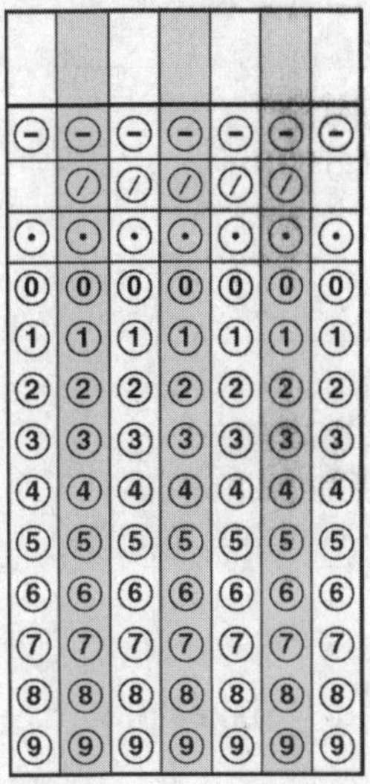

3. Dog food costs $35 and is marked up 42%. What is the final cost, in dollars, of the dog food?

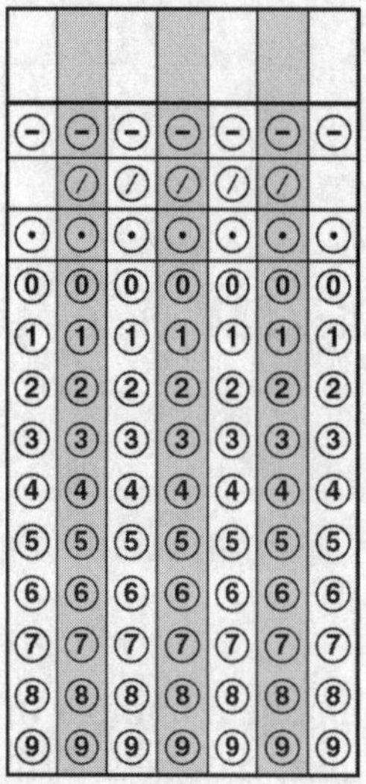

4. The data set shows the points scored by a player in 10 rounds of a game.
{100, 250, 250, 300, 450, 500, 500, 500, 650, 800}

Determine whether the statement is *true* or *false*.

	True	False
The mean score is 430 points.	Ⓐ	Ⓑ
The median score is 450 points.	Ⓒ	Ⓓ
The mode score is 500 points.	Ⓔ	Ⓕ

5. The exchange rate is 1 U.S. Dollar (USD) to approximately 0.82 Euro (EUR). What is the conversion of 80 EUR to USD?

Ⓐ 65.6 USD

Ⓑ 79.2 USD

Ⓒ 80.8 USD

Ⓓ 97.6 USD

Name ______________________________ Date __________

Chapter 7 B.E.S.T. Test Prep (continued)

6. You ask 50 randomly selected employees about their commute time to work. There are 800 employees in the company. Approximately how many employees have a commute greater than 30 minutes?

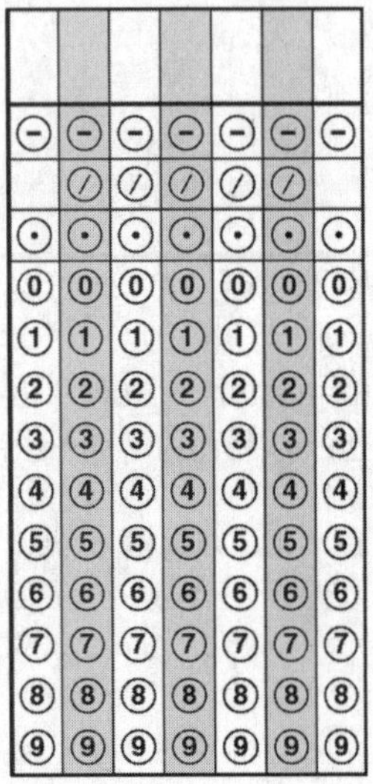

Commute Time			
10-19	20-29	30-39	40+
7	13	19	11

7. What is the correct order of $44.\overline{4}\%, 0.444, \frac{9}{20}, \frac{11}{25}$ from least to greatest?

Ⓐ $0.444, \frac{11}{25}, 44.\overline{4}\%, \frac{9}{20}$

Ⓑ $\frac{11}{25}, 0.444, 44.\overline{4}\%, \frac{9}{20}$

Ⓒ $44.\overline{4}\% \frac{11}{25}, 0.444, \frac{9}{20}$

Ⓓ $44.\overline{4}\%, 0.444, \frac{11}{25}, \frac{9}{20}$

8. Two data sets contain an equal number of values. The double box-and-whisker plot represents the values in the data sets. Which statements are true?

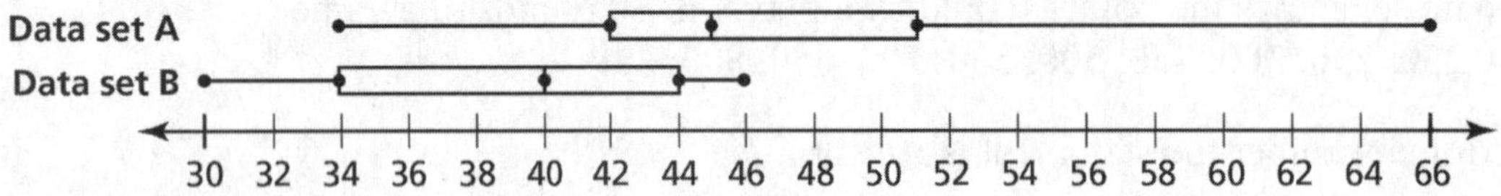

Ⓐ Data Set B has the greatest measure of variation.

Ⓑ Data Set A is more likely to have a value of 46.

Ⓒ Data set B is more likely to have a value of 32.

Ⓓ Data set A is more likely to have a value that differs by 10 from the center.

Ⓔ Data set B is more likely to have a value that differs by 15 from the center.

Ⓕ Data Set A has the greatest measure of center.

Name______________________________ Date__________

Chapter 7 B.E.S.T. Test Prep (continued)

9. This question has **two** parts.

The table shows the number of customers a store had when it is was open.

Customers					
15	18	24	16	10	17
19	13	11	8	5	7

Part A

What is the range?

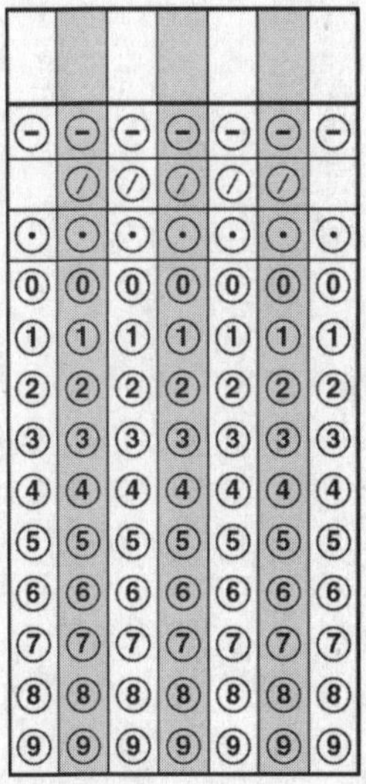

Part B

What is the interquartile range?

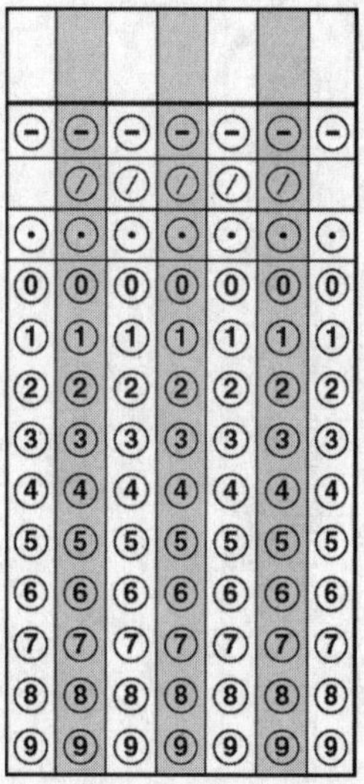

10. You want to estimate the number of students and their favorite subject. You survey every other student in every mathematics class. Your sample is

Ⓐ biased Ⓑ unbiased	because the sample	Ⓐ is Ⓑ is not	random.

11. Which decimal is equivalent to $\frac{9}{8}$?

Ⓐ 0.8

Ⓑ $0.\overline{8}$

Ⓒ 1.125

Ⓓ $1.\overline{125}$

12. A school's math club includes 15% of all students in the seventh grade. There are 180 seventh graders in the school. What is the number of seventh graders in the math club?

Ⓐ 12 students

Ⓑ 23 students

Ⓒ 27 students

Ⓓ 40 students

Name ______________________ Date __________

Chapter 7 B.E.S.T. Test Prep (continued)

13. Which graph shows a proportional relationship?

Ⓐ
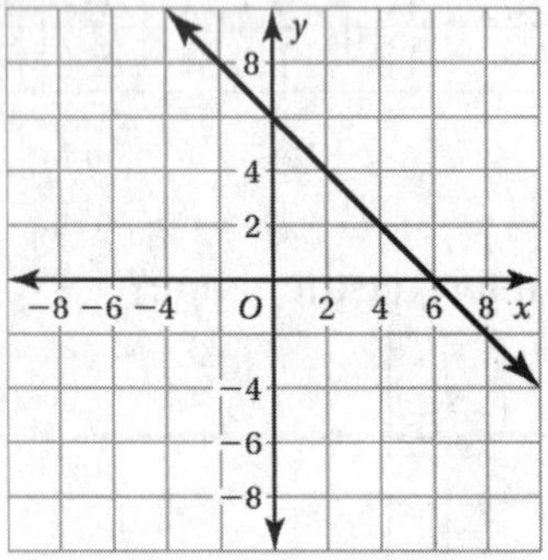

Ⓒ
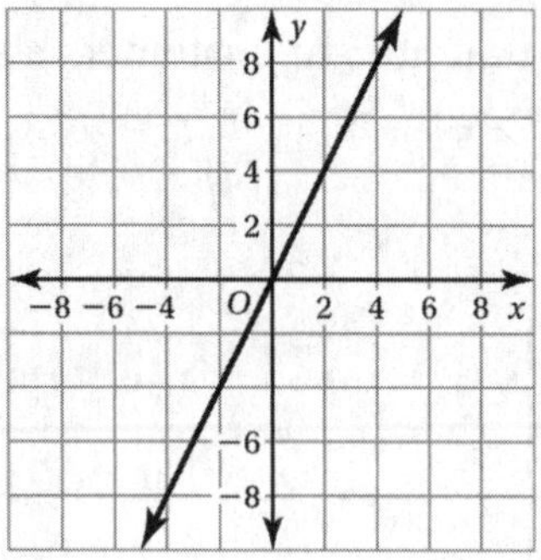

Ⓑ
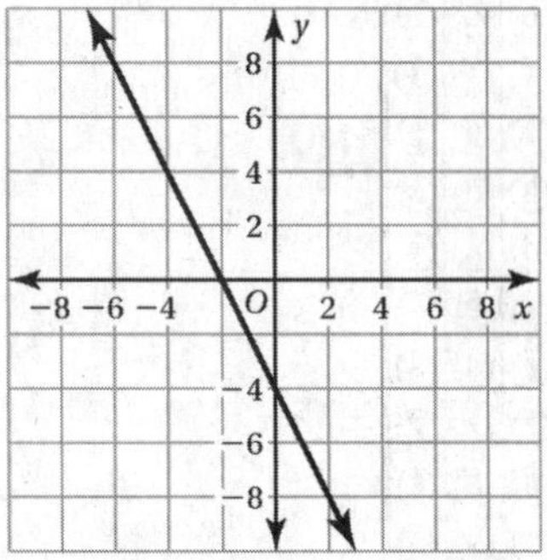

Ⓓ
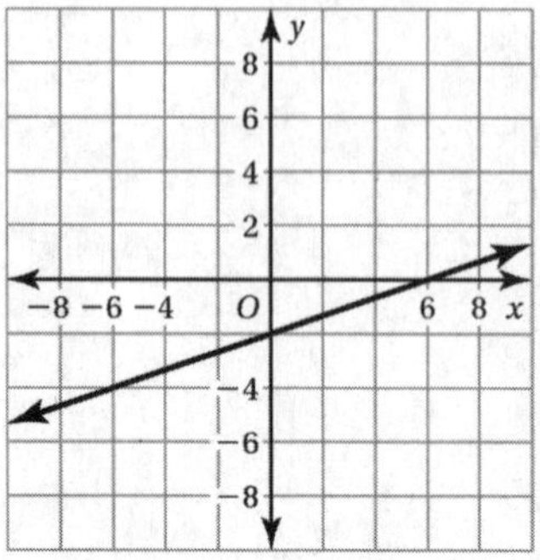

14. The depth of the pool decreases every hour by $\frac{2}{5}$ of an inch. What is the change, in inches, to the depth after 10 hours?

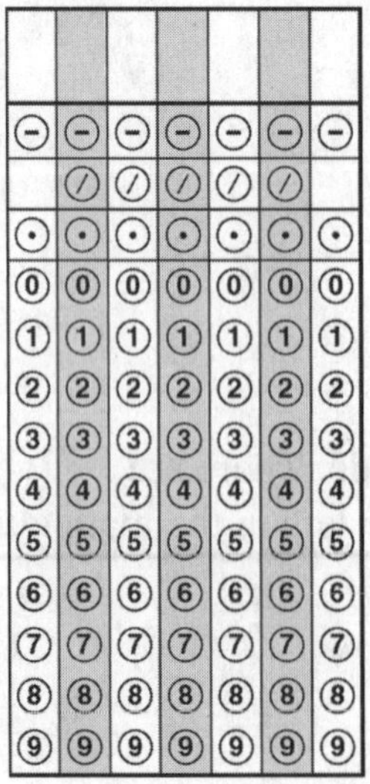

15. Which expressions are simplified correctly? Select all that apply.

Ⓐ $\left(2\frac{1}{2}\right)^2 = 2^2\left(\frac{1}{2}\right)^2$

Ⓑ $(0.3)^7(0.3)^2 = (0.3)^9$

Ⓒ $\left(1\frac{1}{3}\right)^3 = 3\left(\frac{1}{3}\right)^3$

Ⓓ $(0.4)^2(0.4)^4 = (0.4)^8$

Ⓔ $\left(4\frac{1}{4}\right)^2 = \left(\frac{17}{4}\right)^2$

Ⓕ $(0.5)^5(0.5)^5 = (0.5)^{10}$

Name_______________________________ Date__________

Lesson 8.1 Review & Refresh

1. The tables show the number of rainy days in two different cities. Which city should someone who prefers less rainy days choose to live in? Explain.

City A Rainy Days					
12	14	13	18	16	12
9	11	7	8	10	14

City B Rainy Days					
15	16	17	19	20	15
14	18	20	16	17	19

Find the area of the parallelogram.

2.

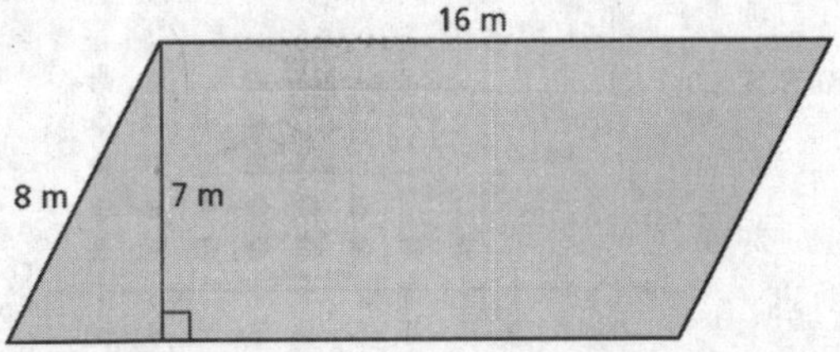

3.

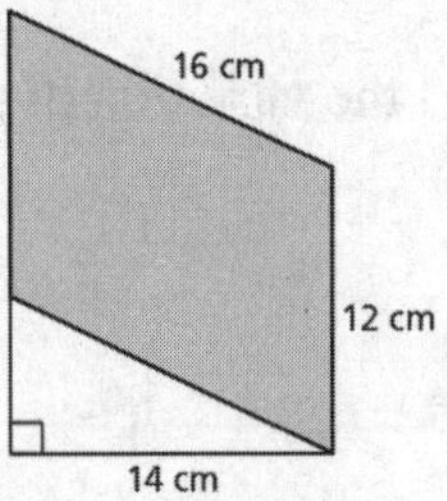

Determine whether you should survey the population or a sample. Explain.

4. You want to know the minutes driven to work by all workers in a town.

5. You want to know the favorite professional basketball team for all players on your basketball team.

6. A model contains a parallelogram with an area of 96 square inches. Find the height if the base is 12 inches.

Find the missing dimension of the parallelogram.

7.

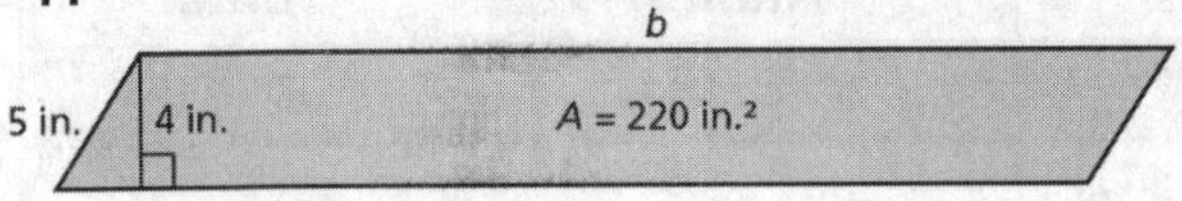

8.

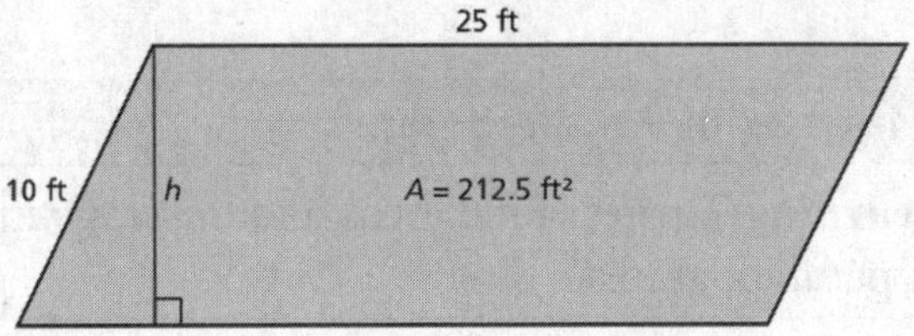

Determine whether the sample is *biased* or *unbiased*. Explain.

9. You want to estimate the number of people in a town that will vote in the next election. You survey every 20th registered voter.

Name ______________________________ Date ________

Lesson 8.1 Review & Refresh (continued)

10. Two data sets contain an equal number of values. The tables show the values.

Data Set A					
20	30	22	25	27	35
28	24	22	21	30	32

Data Set B					
25	35	34	33	26	27
28	31	33	30	32	35

a. Compare the data sets using the measures of center.

b. Compare the data sets using the measures of variation.

11. Describe the centers and the variation of the data set shown in the dot plot.

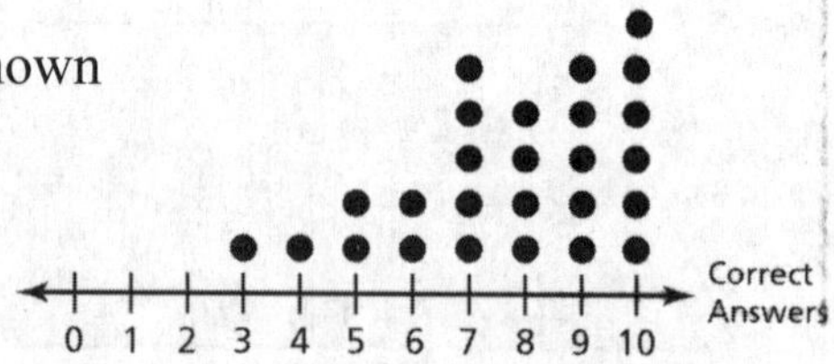

12. You randomly survey 200 students at school and ask them about their favorite subject. Of those students, 40 say math and 60 say English. You conclude that 50% of students favor math or English. Determine whether the conclusion is valid. Explain your reasoning.

Lesson 8.1 Self-Assessment

Use the scale to rate your understanding of the learning target and the success criteria.

1 I don't understand yet. 2 I can do it with help. 3 I can do it on my own. 4 I can teach someone else.

	Rating	Date
8.1 Areas of Parallelograms		
Learning Target: Find areas and missing dimensions of parallelograms.	1 2 3 4	
I can explain how the area of a rectangle is used to find the area of a parallelogram.	1 2 3 4	
I can use the base and the height of a parallelogram to find its area.	1 2 3 4	
I can use the area of a parallelogram and one of its dimensions to find the other dimension.	1 2 3 4	

Name______________________ Date__________

Lesson 8.2

Review & Refresh

Find the area of the trapezoid or parallelogram.

1.

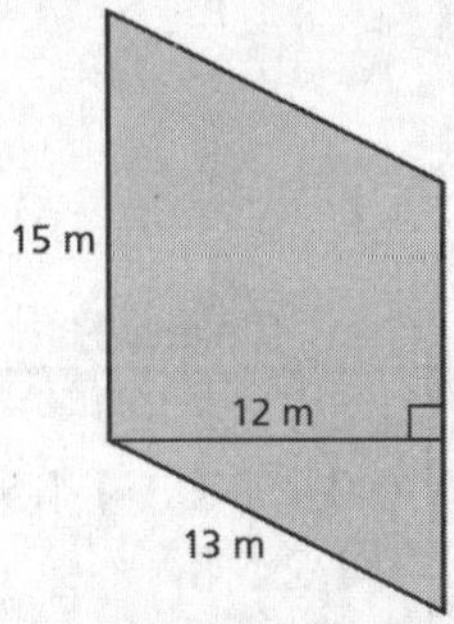

2.

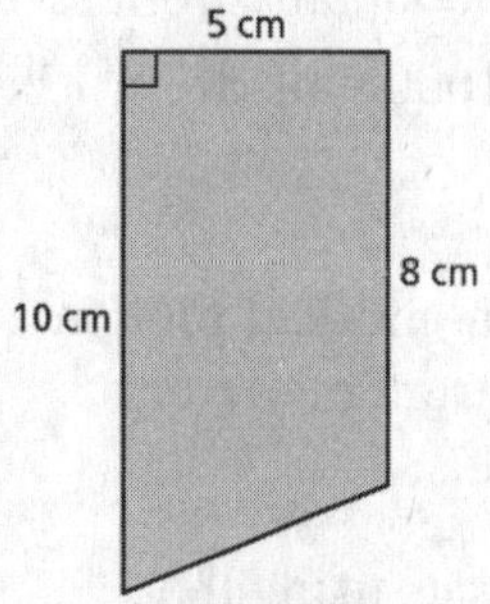

3.

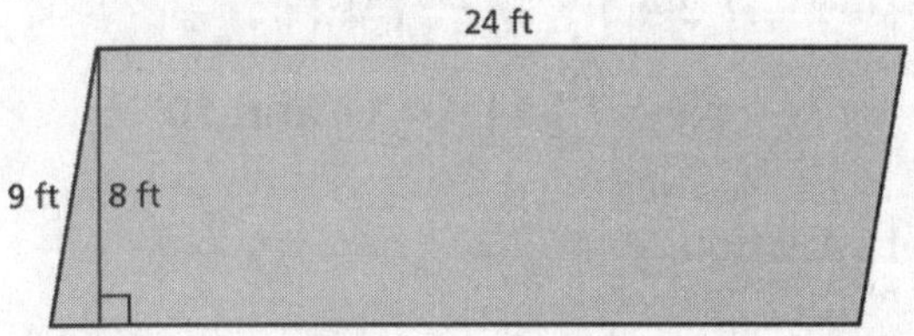

4.

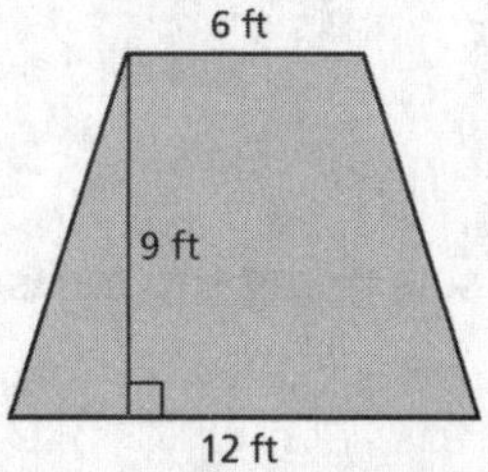

5. You ask 100 pet owners about their favorite animal. Seventy-five people say dogs are their favorite. You conclude that 75% of people like dogs. Determine whether the conclusion is valid. Explain your reasoning.

Find the area of the figure.

6.

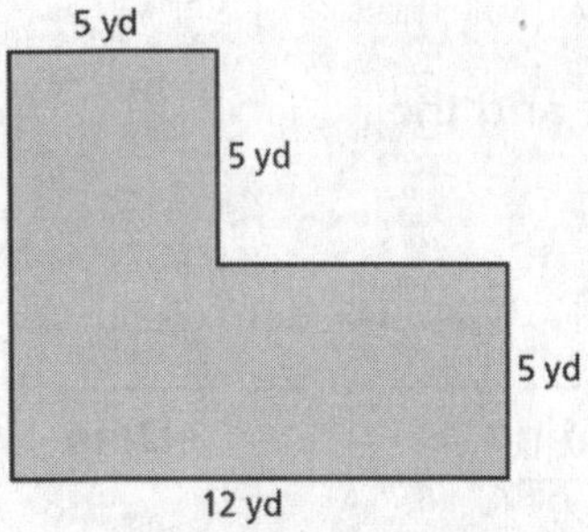

7.

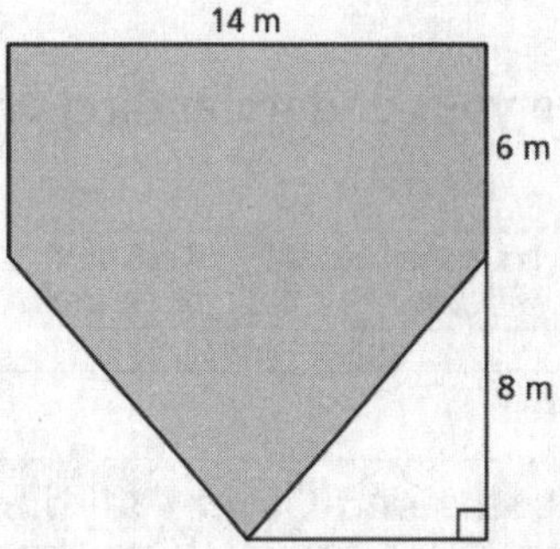

8. A tile shaped like a parallelogram has an area of 250 square centimeters. The base is 12.5 centimeters. Find the height.

Name ______________________________ Date __________

Lesson 8.2 Review & Refresh (continued)

9. Which sample is better for making an estimate? Explain.

A random sample of 1000 nails from 25 boxes.
A random sample of 1000 nails from 1 box.

10. The back-to-back stem-and-leaf plot on the right shows the margin of victory for two basketball teams.

Team A		Team B
3 4 5 7 9 9	0	1 5 7 7 8 8 9
0 0 1 5 7	1	0 0 1 1 2 3 4 4 5 6
0 2 4 5 6 6 8 8 9	2	0 1 2 5 8
1 2 4 5 5	3	0 2 4

Key: 7 | 1 | 0 = 17 and 10

a. Compare the data sets using the measures of center.

b. Compare the data sets using the measures of variation.

11. Find the missing dimension of the parallelogram.

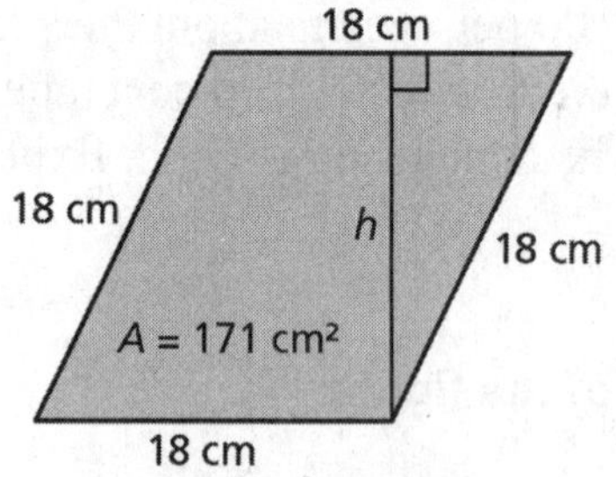

Lesson 8.2 Self-Assessment

Use the scale to rate your understanding of the learning target and the success criteria.

1 I don't understand yet. **2** I can do it with help. **3** I can do it on my own. **4** I can teach someone else.

	Rating	Date
8.2 Areas of Trapezoids and Other Polygons		
Learning Target: Find areas of trapezoids and other polygons.	1 2 3 4	
I can decompose trapezoids and other polygons into smaller shapes.	1 2 3 4	
I can use decomposition to find the area of a figure.	1 2 3 4	
I can use the bases and the height of a trapezoid to find its area.	1 2 3 4	
I can use the formula for the area of a trapezoid to find a missing dimension.	1 2 3 4	

Name____ Date__________

Lesson 8.3 Review & Refresh

Find the radius of the circle.

1.

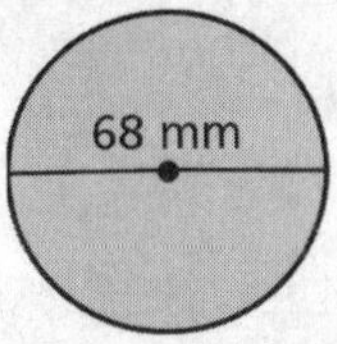

2.

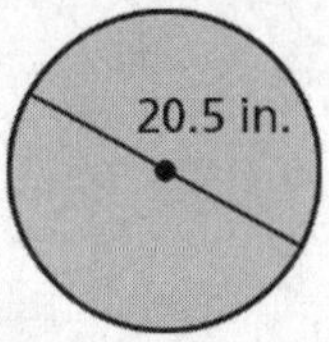

Find the area of the trapezoid or parallelogram.

3.

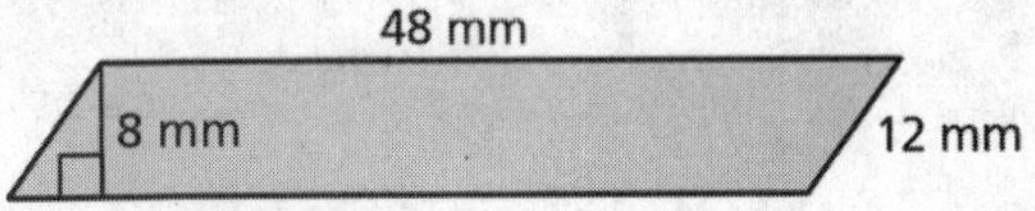

4.

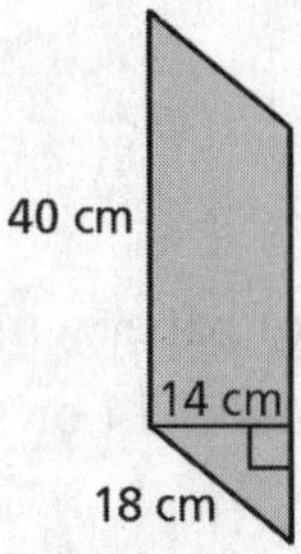

5.

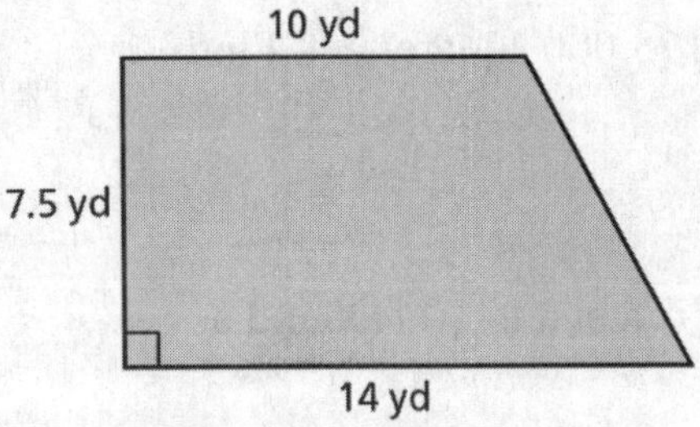

6.

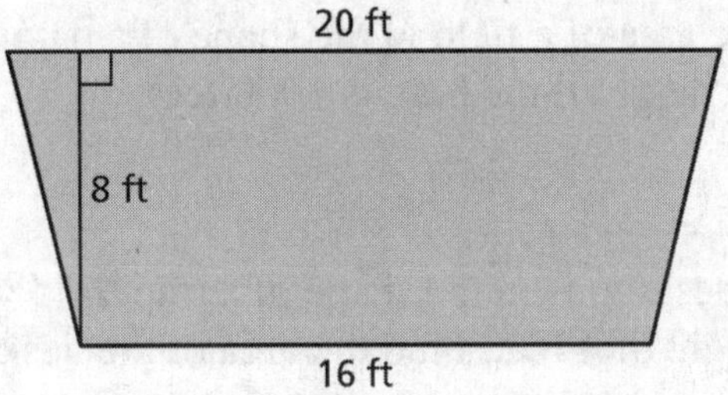

Find the circumference of the circle.

7.

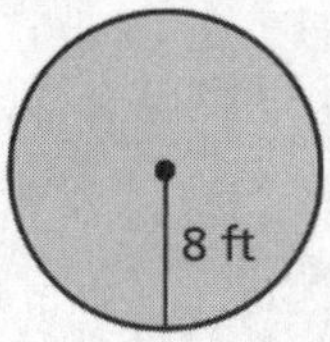

8.

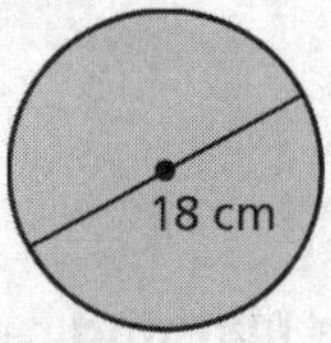

9.

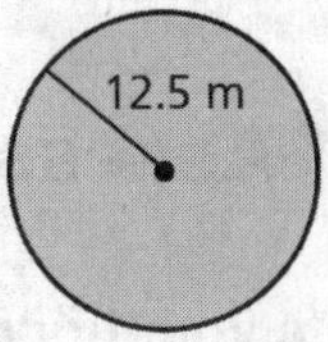

10. A plate has a circumference of 28.26 inches. Find the diameter of the plate.

Find the missing dimension of the trapezoid.

11.

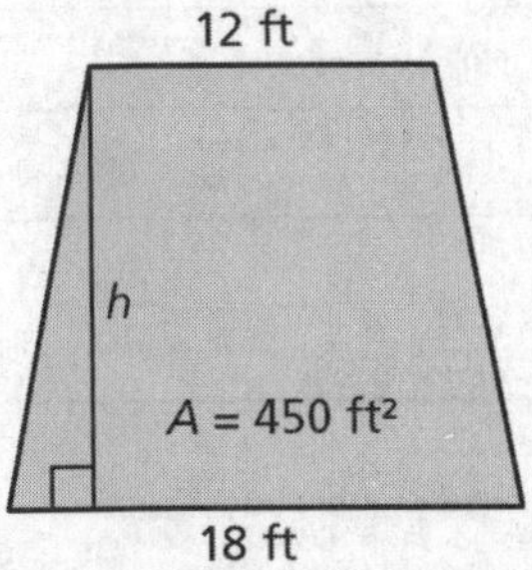

12.

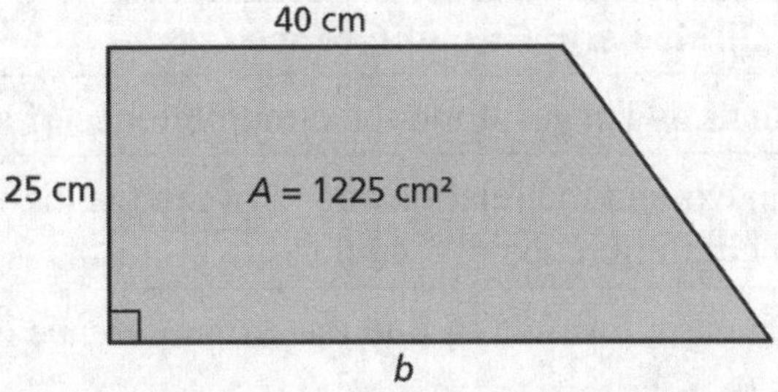

Name ______________________ Date ________

Lesson 8.3 Review & Refresh (continued)

Find the area of the figure.

13.

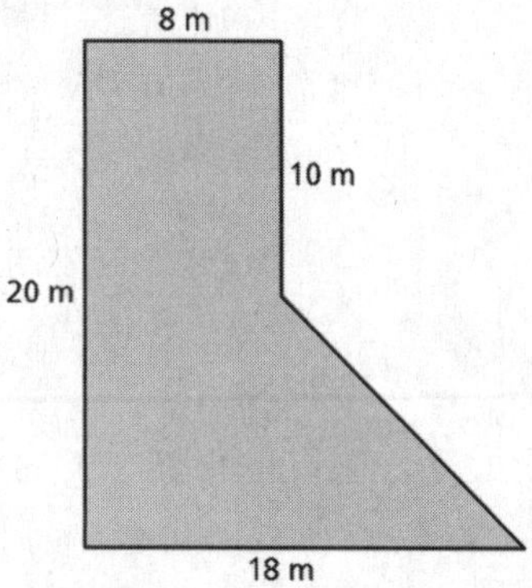

14.

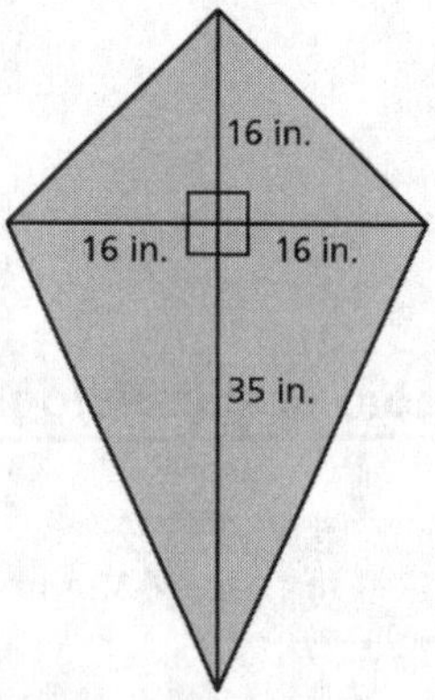

15. A circle is drawn on a piece of paper with a radius of 9.2 cm. Find the circumference of the circle. Use 3.14 or $\frac{22}{7}$ for π.

16. The area of a field in the shape of a parallelogram is 175,000 square feet. Find the height if the base is 1000 feet.

17. A desktop is in the shape of a trapezoid with bases of 6 feet and 10 feet and a height of 4 feet. Find the area of the desktop.

Lesson 8.3 Self-Assessment

Use the scale to rate your understanding of the learning target and the success criteria.

1 I don't understand yet. | 2 I can do it with help. | 3 I can do it on my own. | 4 I can teach someone else.

	Rating	Date
8.3 Circles and Circumference		
Learning Target: Find the circumference of a circle.	1 2 3 4	
I can explain the relationship between the diameter and circumference of a circle.	1 2 3 4	
I can use a formula to find the circumference of a circle.	1 2 3 4	

Name________________________________ Date__________

Lesson 8.4 Review & Refresh

Find the diameter of the circle.

1.

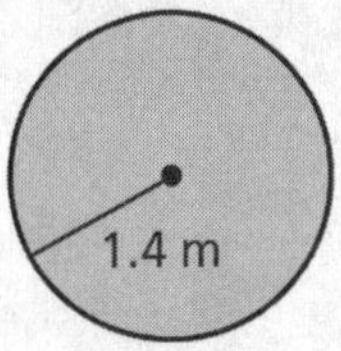

2.

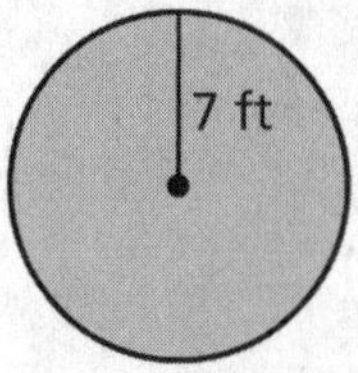

Find the area of the figure.

3.

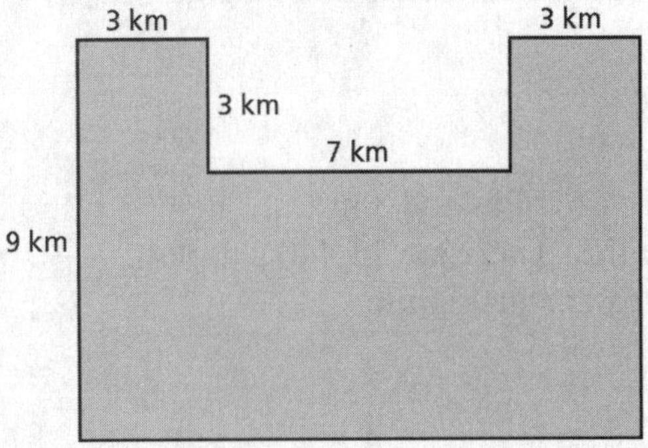

4.

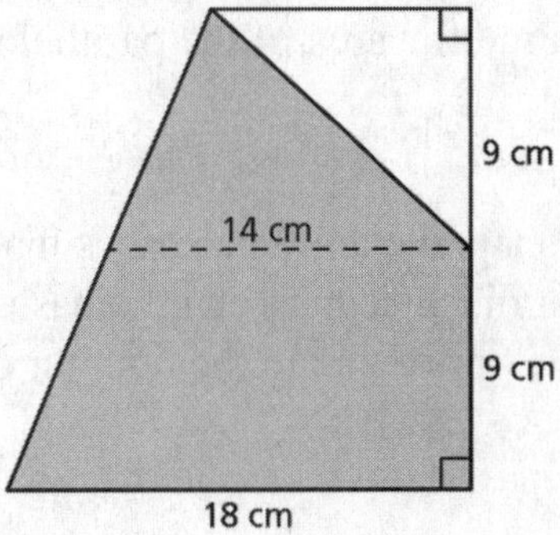

Find the area of the circle.

5.

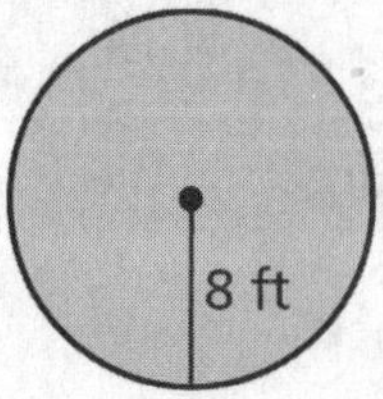

6.

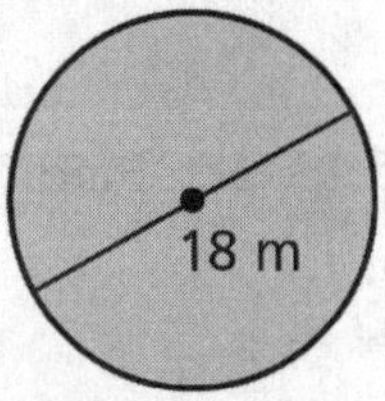

7.

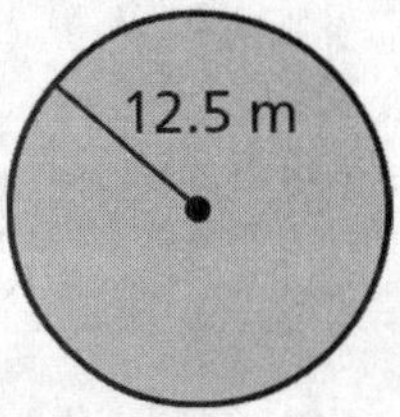

8. The top of a water bottle is a circle with a diameter of 5.5 cm.

a. Find the circumference.

b. Find the area.

Find the missing dimension of the parallelogram.

9.

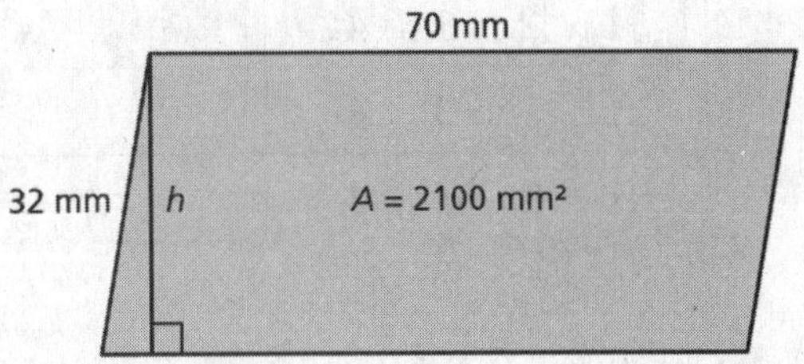

10.

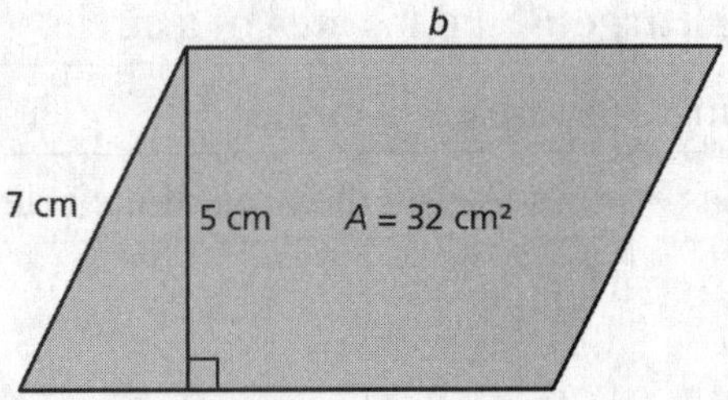

Name ______________________________ Date __________

Lesson 8.4 Review & Refresh (continued)

Given a semicircle, find (a) the perimeter and (b) the area.

11.

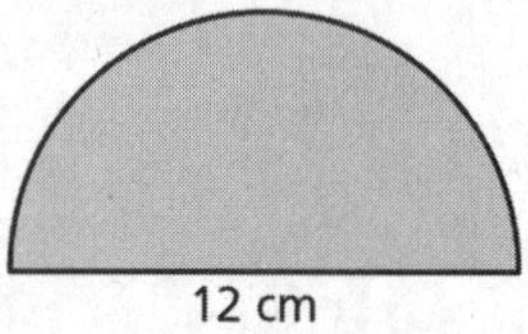

12.

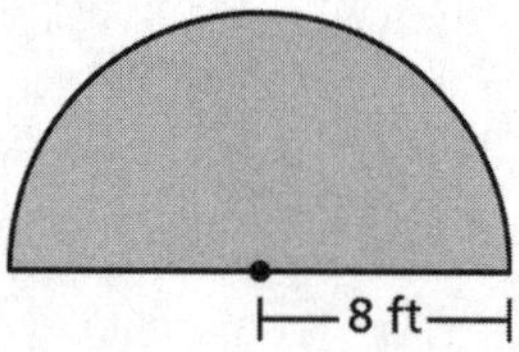

13. A parallelogram cut from a piece of paper has a base of 10 inches and a height of 6 inches. Find the area of the parallelogram.

14. A trapezoid-shaped county has bases that are about 6 miles and 8 miles. The perpendicular distance between the bases is 20 miles. There are 13,440 people in the county. Approximate the number of people per square mile.

15. A circular garden has a circumference of approximately 157 feet. Find the radius and the diameter.

16. A circular target has a circumference of 25.12 feet. Find the area of the target.

Lesson 8.4 Self-Assessment

Use the scale to rate your understanding of the learning target and the success criteria.

1 I don't understand yet. | 2 I can do it with help. | 3 I can do it on my own. | 4 I can teach someone else.

	Rating	Date
8.4 Areas of Circles		
Learning Target: Find the area of a circle.	1 2 3 4	
I can estimate the area of a circle.	1 2 3 4	
I can use a formula to find the area of a circle.	1 2 3 4	

Name________________________________ Date__________

Lesson 8.5

Review & Refresh

Find the perimeter and the area of the figure.

1.

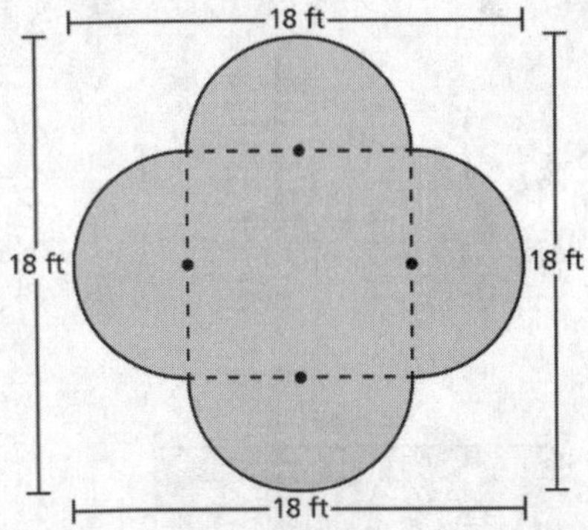

2.

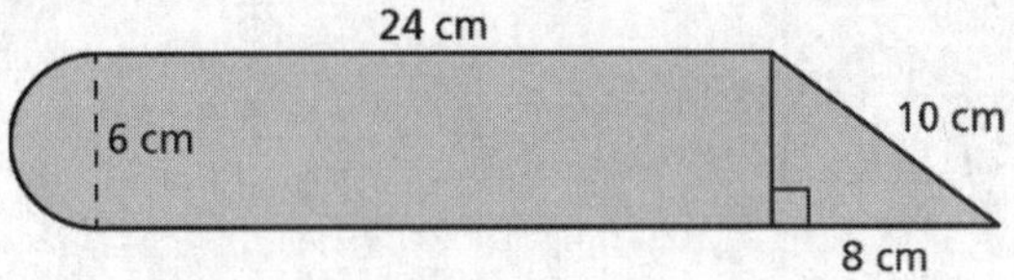

Find the circumferences of both circles.

3.

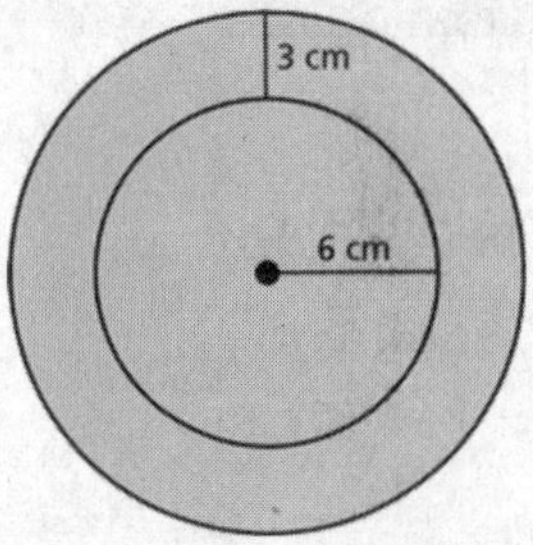

4.

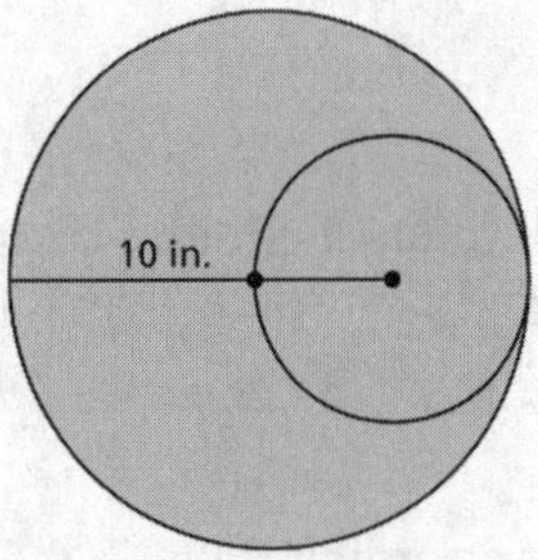

Find the missing dimension of the trapezoid.

5.

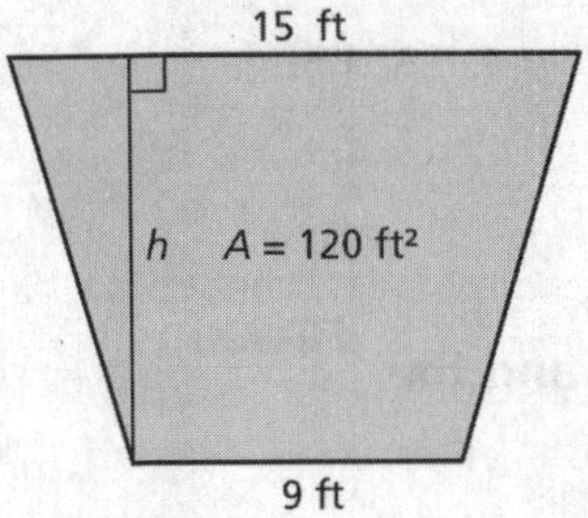

6.

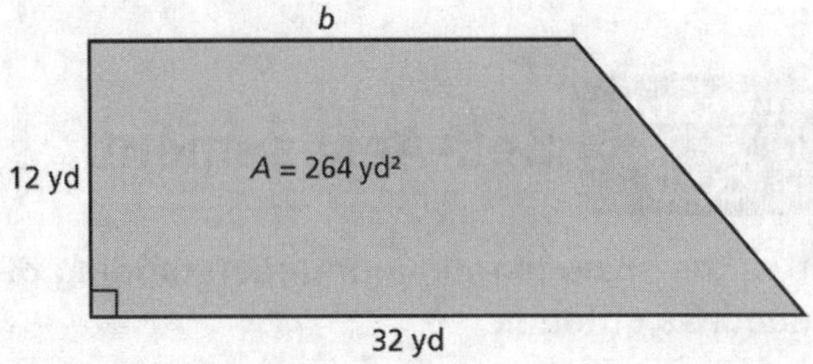

7. The free throw area on a basketball court is a rectangle with a half circle at one end of its width. The length of the lane is 19 feet and the width is 12 feet.

   a. Find the perimeter.

   b. Find the area.

Name ____ Date __________

Lesson 8.5 Review & Refresh (continued)

Find the area of the figure.

8.

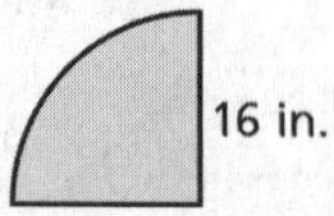

9.

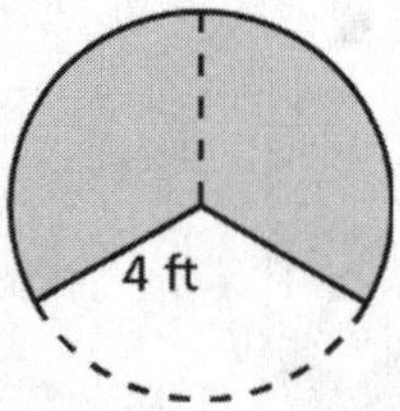

Find the area of the trapezoid.

10.

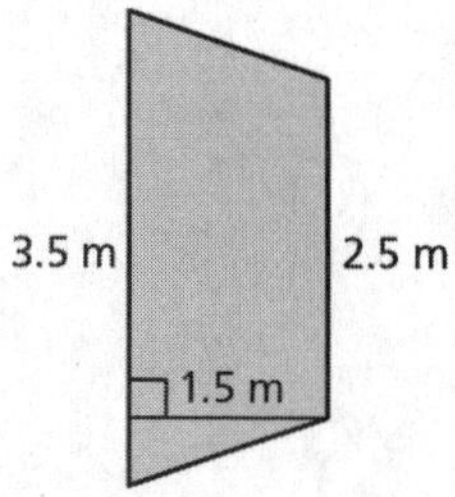

11.

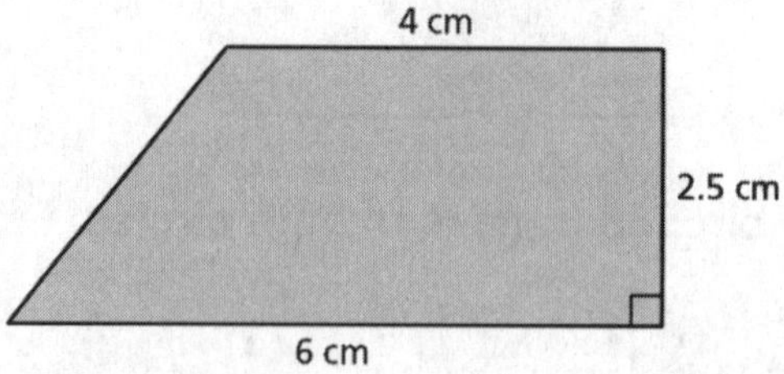

12. A sprinkler system waters a circular region with a radius of 150 feet. Find the area that is watered.

13. The top of a cake is a semicircle with a diameter of 20 inches. Find the circumference of the top of cake.

Lesson 8.5 Self-Assessment

Use the scale to rate your understanding of the learning target and the success criteria.

1 I don't understand yet. 2 I can do it with help. 3 I can do it on my own. 4 I can teach someone else.

	Rating	Date
8.5 Perimeters and Areas of Composite Figures		
Learning Target: Find perimeters and areas of composite figures.	1 2 3 4	
I can identify the shapes that make up a composite figure.	1 2 3 4	
I can find the perimeters and areas of shapes that make up composite figures.	1 2 3 4	

Name______________________________ Date__________

Lesson 8.6

Review & Refresh

Find the surface area of the cylinder.

1.

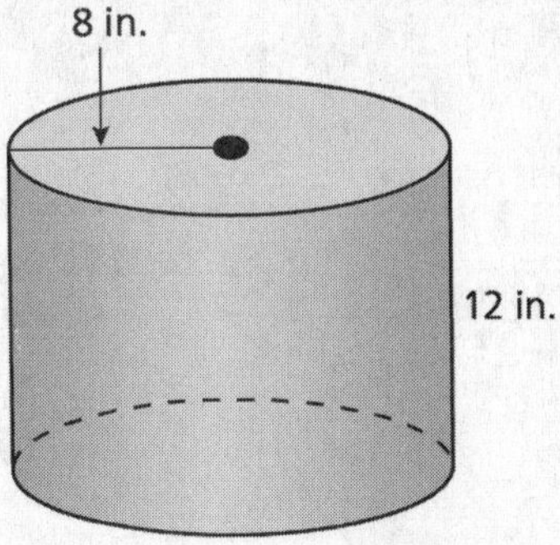

2.

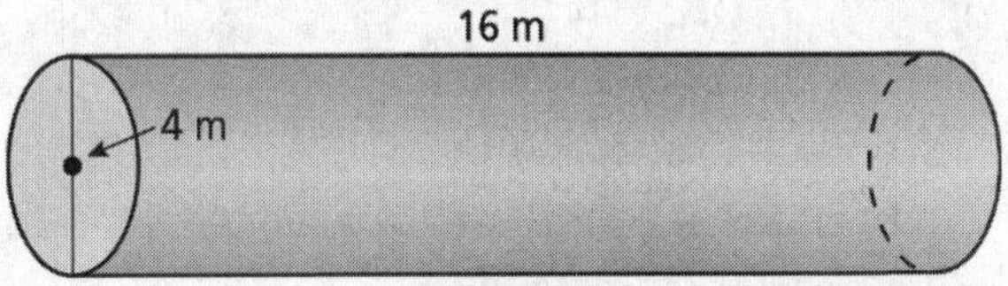

3. A baseball field is a quarter circle with a radius of 325 feet.

a. Find the perimeter.

b. Find the area.

4. A minute hand represents the radius of a clock. Find the following if the length of the minute hand is 4.25 centimeters.

a. Find the distance the minute hand travels in 1 hour.

b. Find the distance the minute hand travels in 1 day.

Given a semicircle, (a) find the perimeter and (b) find the area.

5.

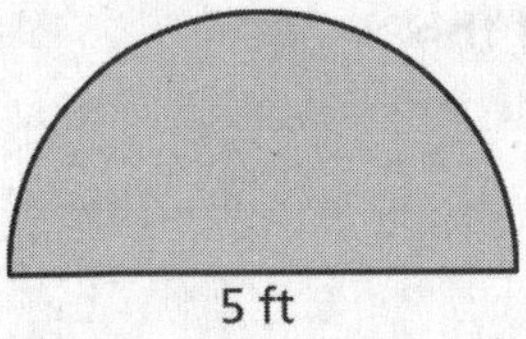

6.

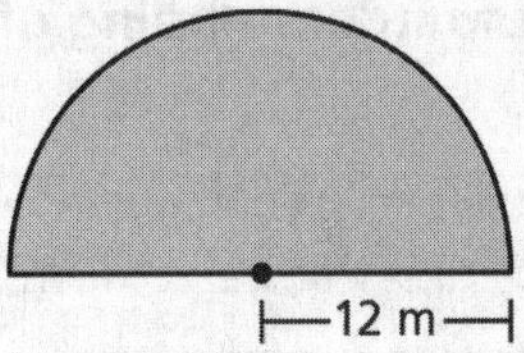

7. A circular tart has a diameter of 13 inches. Find the area of the top of the tart.

Name ______________________________ Date ________

Lesson 8.6 Review & Refresh (continued)

Find the lateral surface area of the cylinder.

8.

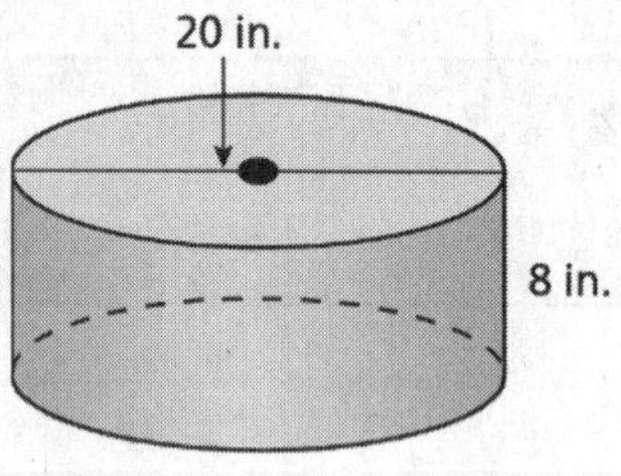

9.

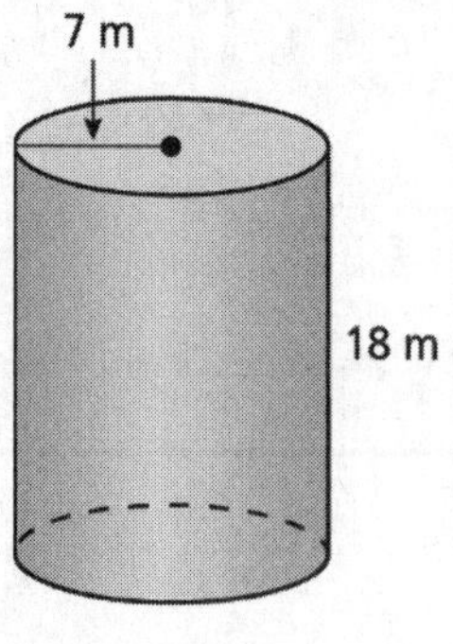

10. Find the area of the shaded region.

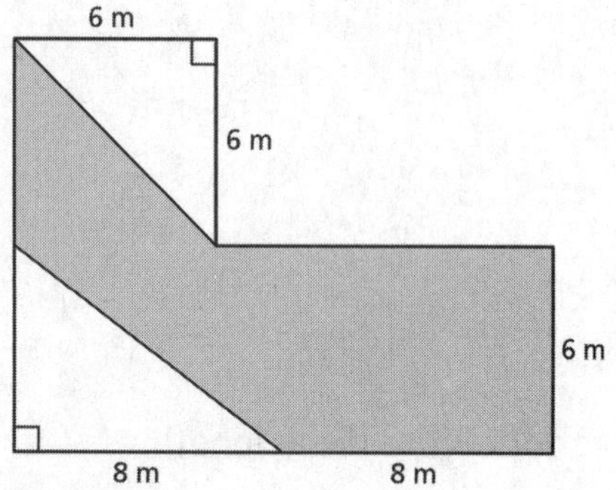

11. A small, circular hole in the road had a radius of 10 centimeters. After 2 weeks, the radius had increased to 14 centimeters. By how many square inches did the top of the hole increase in size?

Lesson 8.6 Self-Assessment

Use the scale to rate your understanding of the learning target and the success criteria.

1 I don't understand yet. 2 I can do it with help. 3 I can do it on my own. 4 I can teach someone else.

	Rating	Date
8.6 Surface Areas of Cylinders		
Learning Target: Find the surface area of a cylinder.	1 2 3 4	
I can use a net to find the surface area of a cylinder.	1 2 3 4	
I can find the lateral surface area of a cylinder.	1 2 3 4	

Name________________________________ Date__________

Lesson 8.7 Review & Refresh

Find the volume of the cylinder.

1.

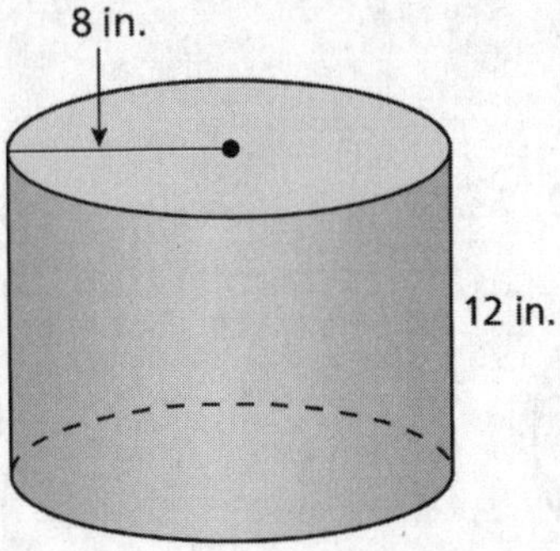

2.

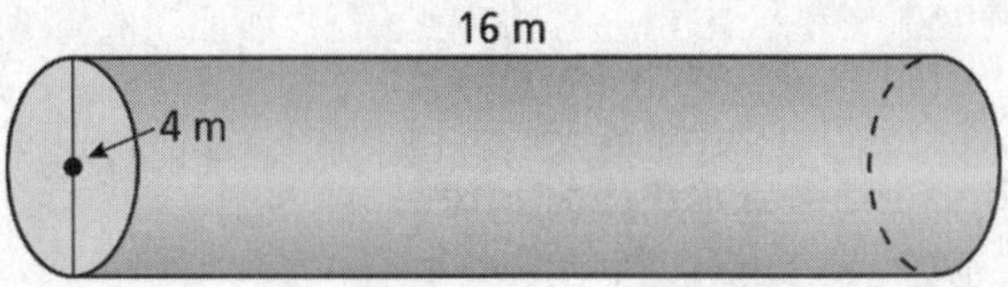

3. A cylindrical pool has a diameter of 30 feet and a depth of 5 feet.

a. Find the surface area of the top of the pool.

b. Find the volume of the pool.

Find the perimeter and the area of the figure.

4.

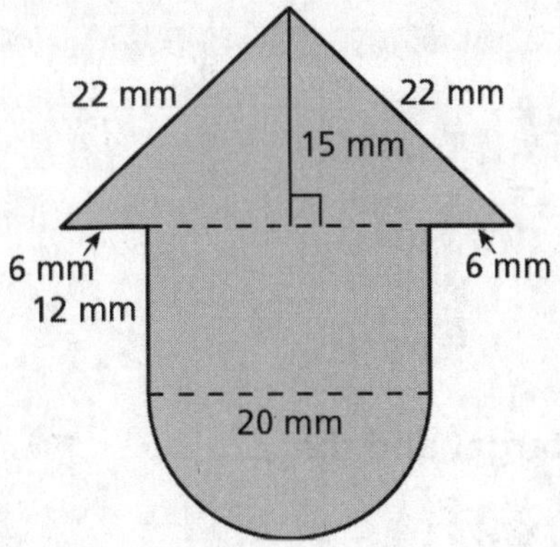

5.

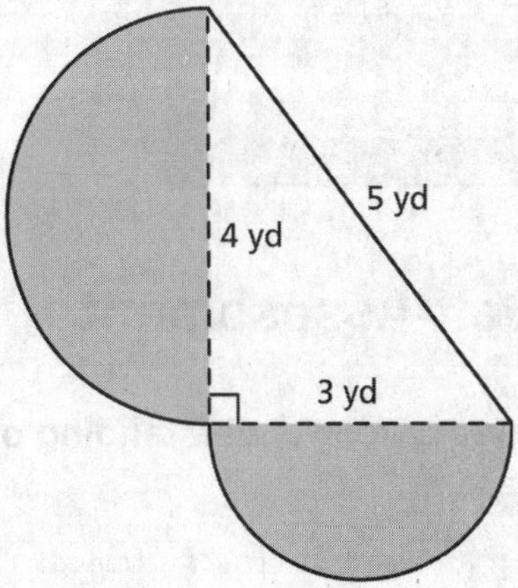

6. A room has two walls that are 10 feet tall and 14 feet long. The other two walls are 10 feet tall and 12 feet long. These walls will be painted. There are 2 windows measuring 2 feet by 3 feet and 1 door measuring 3 feet by 7 feet that will not be painted. Find the total area that will be painted.

Name ______________________________ Date __________

Lesson 8.7 Review & Refresh (continued)

7. A paper towel tube has a base with a diameter of 3 centimeters and a height of 15 centimeters. Find the lateral surface area that makes up the tube.

Find the area of the figure.

8.

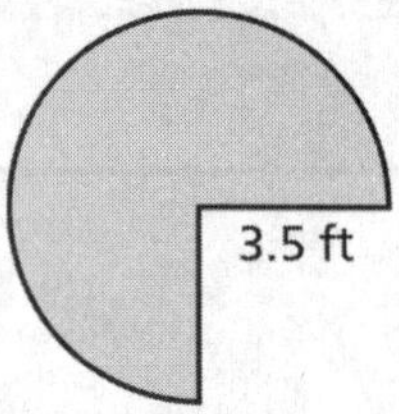

9.

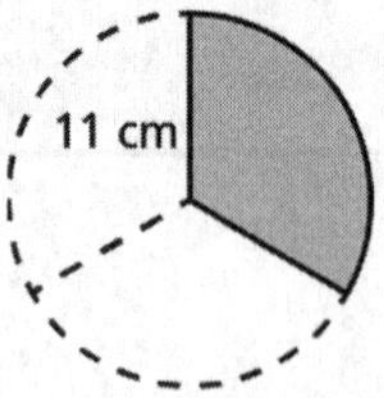

10. The circumference of the top of a circular sandbox is 78.5 centimeters. Find the surface area of the top of the sandbox.

Find the height of the cylinder.

11.

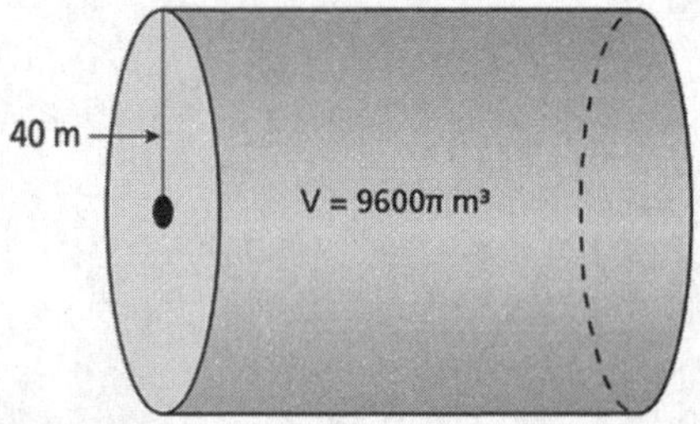

Lesson 8.7 Self-Assessment

Use the scale to rate your understanding of the learning target and the success criteria.

1 I don't understand yet. 2 I can do it with help. 3 I can do it on my own. 4 I can teach someone else.

	Rating	Date
8.7 Volumes of Cylinders		
Learning Target: Find the volume of a cylinder.	1 2 3 4	
I can use a formula to find the volume of a cylinder.	1 2 3 4	
I can use the volume of a cylinder and its radius to find the height.	1 2 3 4	

Name ____ Date __________

Chapter 8 Chapter Self-Assessment

Use the scale to rate your understanding of the learning target and the success criteria.

1 I don't understand yet. | 2 I can do it with help. | 3 I can do it on my own. | 4 I can teach someone else.

	Rating	Date
Chapter 8 Area, Surface Area, and Volume		
Learning Target: Understand measurements of figures and solids.	1 2 3 4	
I can use a formula.	1 2 3 4	
I can solve for a missing dimension.	1 2 3 4	
I can decompose figures to solve problems.	1 2 3 4	
I can find the surface area and volume of a cylinder.	1 2 3 4	
8.1 Areas of Parallelograms		
Learning Target: Find areas and missing dimensions of parallelograms.	1 2 3 4	
I can explain how the area of a rectangle is used to find the area of a parallelogram.	1 2 3 4	
I can use the base and the height of a parallelogram to find its area.	1 2 3 4	
I can use the area of a parallelogram and one of its dimensions to find the other dimension.	1 2 3 4	
8.2 Areas of Trapezoids and Other Polygons		
Learning Target: Find areas of trapezoids and other polygons.	1 2 3 4	
I can decompose trapezoids and other polygons into smaller shapes.	1 2 3 4	
I can use decomposition to find the area of a figure.	1 2 3 4	
I can use the bases and the height of a trapezoid to find its area.	1 2 3 4	
I can use the formula for the area of a trapezoid to find a missing dimension.	1 2 3 4	

Name ______________________________ Date __________

Chapter 8 Chapter Self-Assessment (continued)

	Rating	Date
8.3 Circles and Circumference		
Learning Target: Find the circumference of a circle.	1 2 3 4	
I can explain the relationship between the diameter and circumference of a circle.	1 2 3 4	
I can use a formula to find the circumference of a circle.	1 2 3 4	
8.4 Areas of Circles		
Learning Target: Find the area of a circle.	1 2 3 4	
I can estimate the area of a circle.	1 2 3 4	
I can use a formula to find the area of a circle.	1 2 3 4	
8.5 Perimeters and Areas of Composite Figures		
Learning Target: Find perimeters and areas of composite figures.	1 2 3 4	
I can identify the shapes that make up a composite figure.	1 2 3 4	
I can find the perimeters and areas of shapes that make up composite figures.	1 2 3 4	
8.6 Surface Areas of Cylinders		
Learning Target: Find the surface area of a cylinder.	1 2 3 4	
I can use a net to find the surface area of a cylinder.	1 2 3 4	
I can find the lateral surface area of a cylinder.	1 2 3 4	
8.7 Volumes of Cylinders		
Learning Target: Find the volume of a cylinder.	1 2 3 4	
I can use a formula to find the volume of a cylinder.	1 2 3 4	
I can use the volume of a cylinder and its radius to find the height.	1 2 3 4	

Name ______________________________ Date __________

Chapter 8 B.E.S.T. Test Prep

1. Which graph represents the proportional relationship in the table?

Minutes	8	16	24
Gallons	400	800	1200

Ⓐ
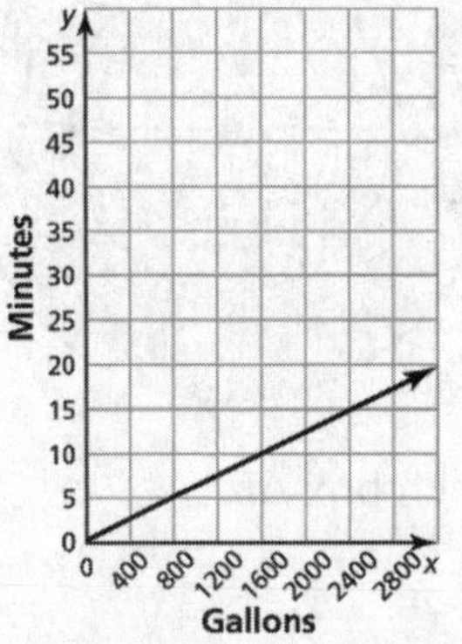

Ⓑ
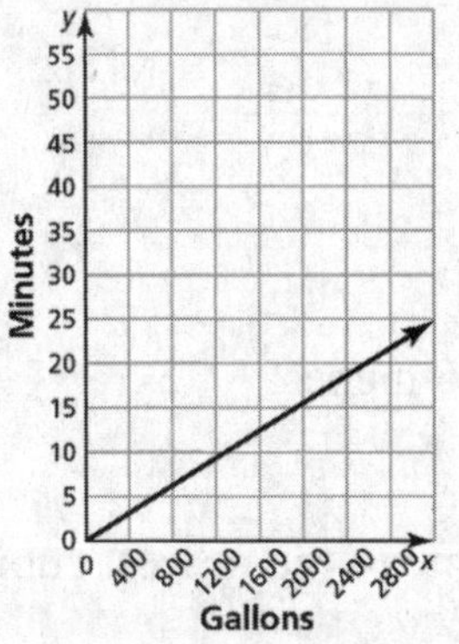

Ⓒ
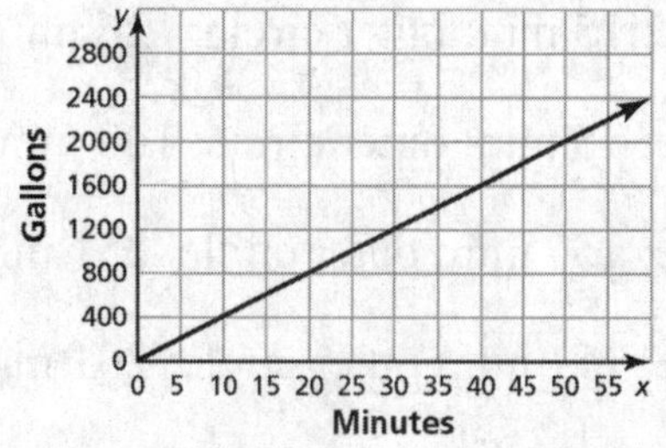

Ⓓ
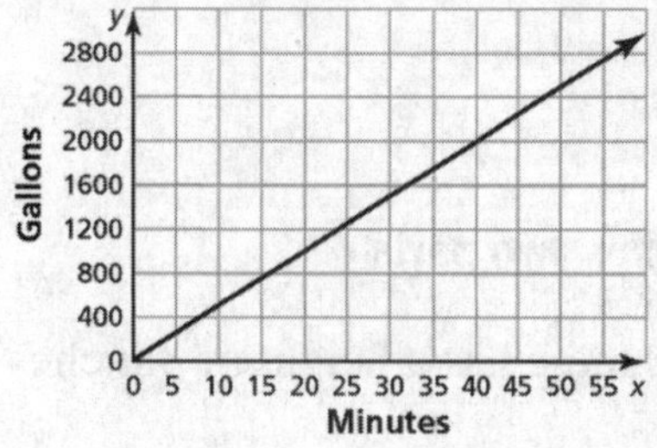

2. Solve $\frac{1}{4} = 2x - \frac{3}{8}$ for x.

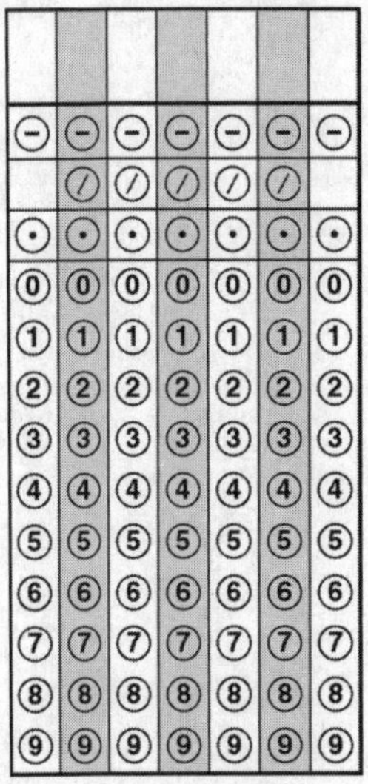

3. What is 160% of 110?

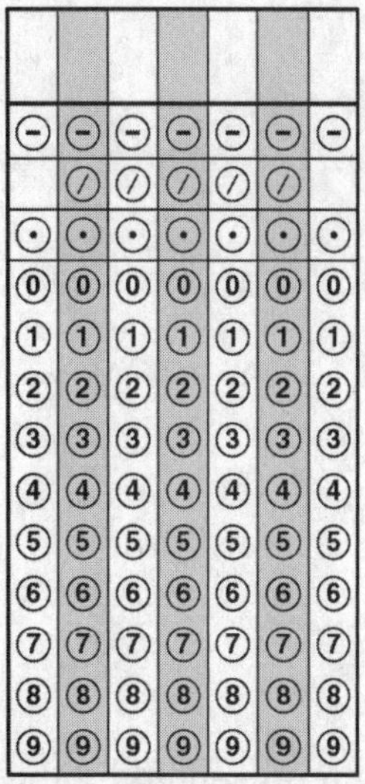

4. An extra-large, circular pizza has a diameter of 23 inches. What is the area of the pizza to the nearest square inch?

Ⓐ 144 in.^{2}

Ⓑ 415 in.^{2}

Ⓒ 831 in.^{2}

Ⓓ 1661 in.^{2}

Name ______________________________ Date __________

Chapter 8 B.E.S.T. Test Prep (continued)

5. What are the circumferences of both circles to the nearest millimeter?

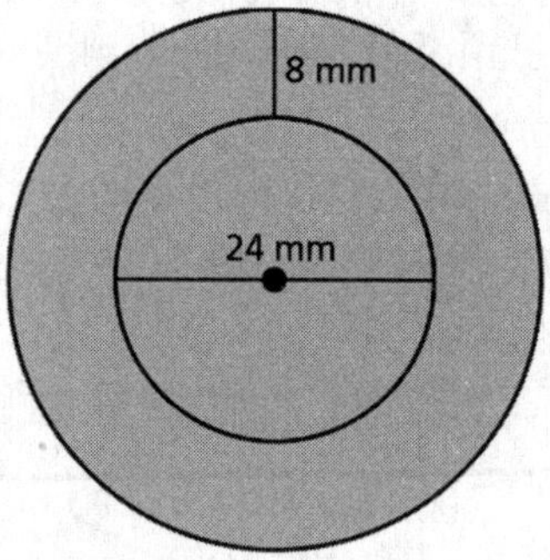

Ⓐ inner circle: 75 mm; outer circle: 126 mm

Ⓑ inner circle: 75 mm; outer circle: 100 mm

Ⓒ inner circle: 151 mm; outer circle: 251 mm

Ⓓ inner circle: 151 mm; outer circle: 201 mm

6. A bag of cereal is 32 ounces. The acceptable error is 2.5%. Which box of cereal has an acceptable weight?

Ⓐ 30 ounces

Ⓑ 30.5 ounces

Ⓒ 32.5 ounces

Ⓓ 33 ounces

7. This question has **two** parts.

A cylindrical candle has a height of 8 inches and a diameter of 6 inches.

Part A

What is the surface area to the nearest square inch?

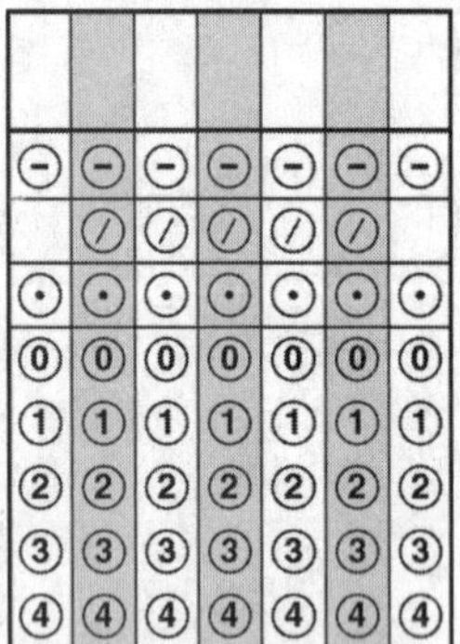

Part B

What is the volume to the nearest cubic inch?

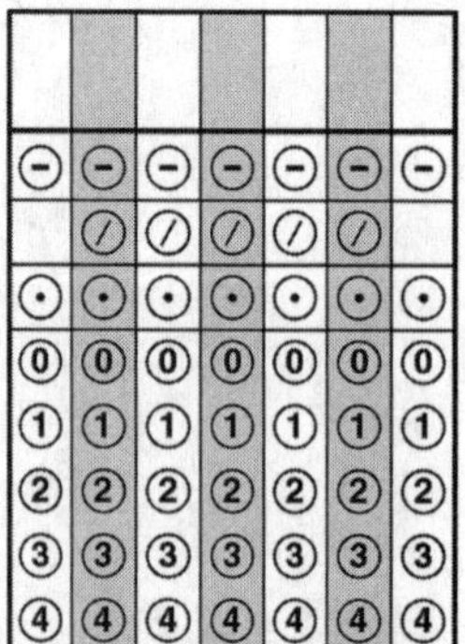

8. What is the inequality represented by the number line?

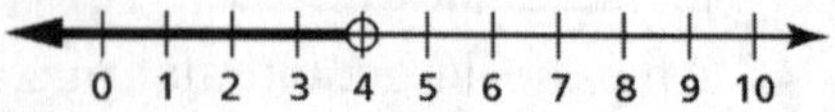

Ⓐ $x \geq 4$

Ⓑ $x \leq 4$

Ⓒ $x > 4$

Ⓓ $x < 4$

Name____ Date____________

B.E.S.T. Test Prep (continued)

9. What is the area, in square millimeters, of the trapezoid?

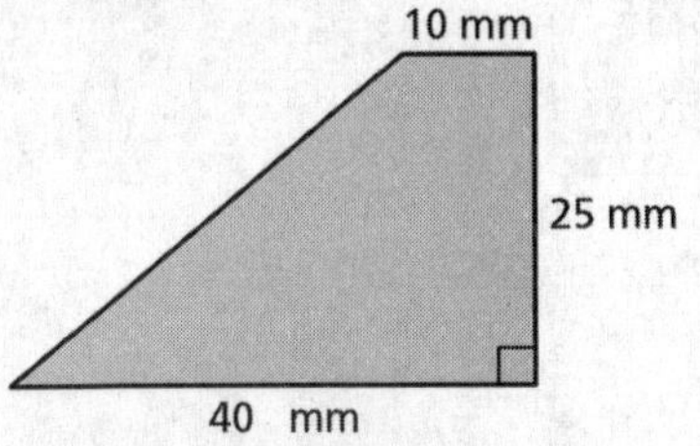

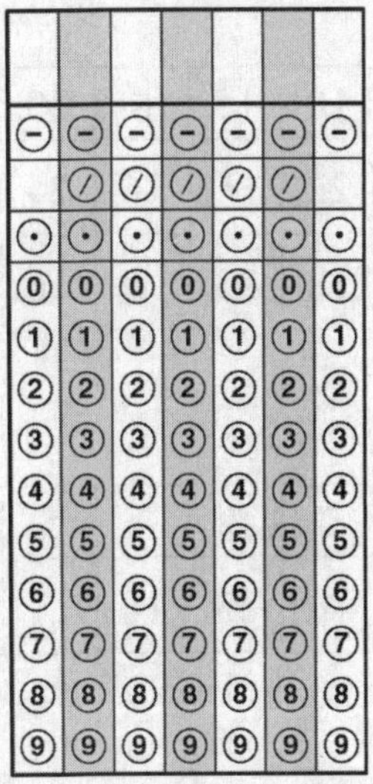

10. What is the height, in inches, of the parallelogram?

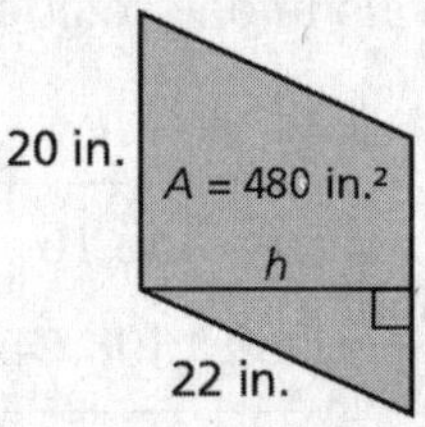

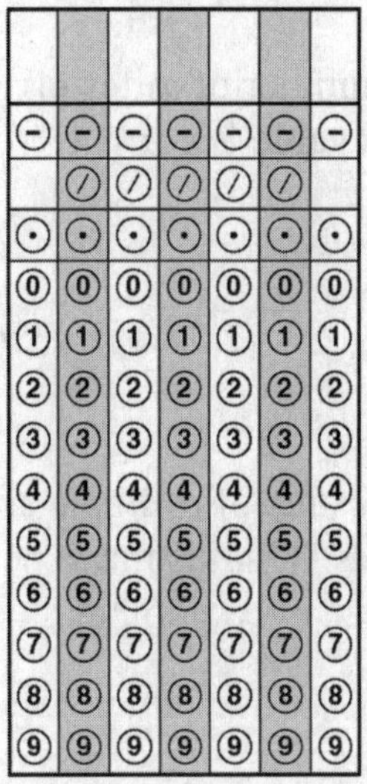

11. Which proportions are solved correctly?

Ⓐ $\frac{g}{9} = \frac{15}{3}; g = 30$

Ⓑ $\frac{10}{h} = \frac{25}{4}; h = 1.6$

Ⓒ $\frac{j}{12} = \frac{8}{1.5}; j = 96$

Ⓓ $\frac{6}{k} = \frac{39}{10}; k = 1.5$

Ⓔ $\frac{l}{20} = \frac{2.5}{50}; l = 1$

Ⓕ $\frac{4.5}{m} = \frac{22.5}{2}; m = 0.5$

12. Which sums or differences are negative?

Ⓐ 18.75 – 24.55

Ⓑ –16.5 – (–18.4)

Ⓒ 34.2 – 28.6

Ⓓ 19.5 + (–17.4)

Ⓔ –32.75 + 28.95

Ⓕ –21.3 + (–14.8)

13. Determine whether the expressions are equivalent.

	Yes	No
$4(x-1)+2(x+1); 6x-2$	Ⓐ	Ⓑ
$-3(2x-1)+4x+4; -2x+7$	Ⓒ	Ⓓ
$3x+4-2(1-x); 2x+2$	Ⓔ	Ⓕ

B.E.S.T. Test Prep (continued)

14. A tire has a diameter of 24 inches.

The distance the tire travels in one rotation is about [Ⓐ 37.68 / Ⓑ 75.36 / Ⓒ 150.72] inches.

The area of the tire is about [Ⓐ 452.16 / Ⓑ 1808.64] square inches.

15. The table shows the number of miles driven to work by 15 employees. Which value is correct?

10	15	8	20	17
22	9	16	24	25
18	23	7	16	30

Ⓐ mean: 16

Ⓑ median: 17

Ⓒ interquartile range: 7

Ⓓ range: 20

16. The table shows the results of rolling a six-sided number cube 100 times. What is the experimental probability of rolling an even number?

Number	1	2	3	4	5	6
Results	14	16	23	18	17	12

Ⓐ $\frac{27}{50}$

Ⓑ $\frac{1}{6}$

Ⓒ $\frac{1}{2}$

Ⓓ $\frac{23}{50}$

17. What is the amount of interest, in dollars, earned on an account with a deposit of $5000 earning 0.75% simple interest for 30 months?

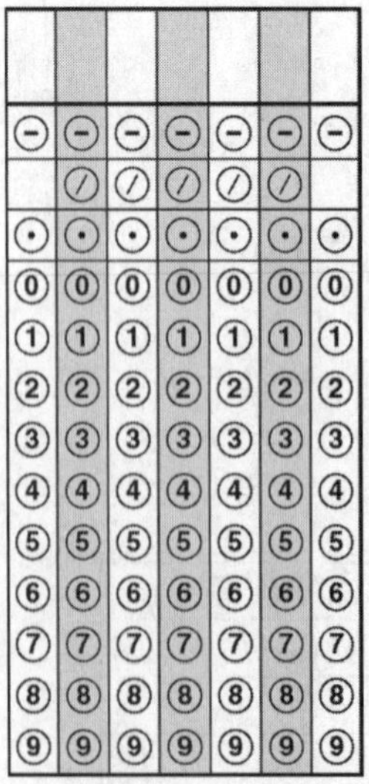

Name________________________________ Date__________

Grade 7

Post-Course Test

1. Match to show which rates are equivalent.

	Equivalent	Not Equivalent
80 inches in 4 years 45 inches in 30 months	Ⓐ	Ⓑ
12 revolutions in 5 minutes 72 revolutions in $\frac{1}{2}$ hour	Ⓒ	Ⓓ
\$1.47 for $1\frac{1}{2}$ pounds \$0.57 for $\frac{3}{5}$ pound	Ⓔ	Ⓕ

2. What is the value of -4^4?

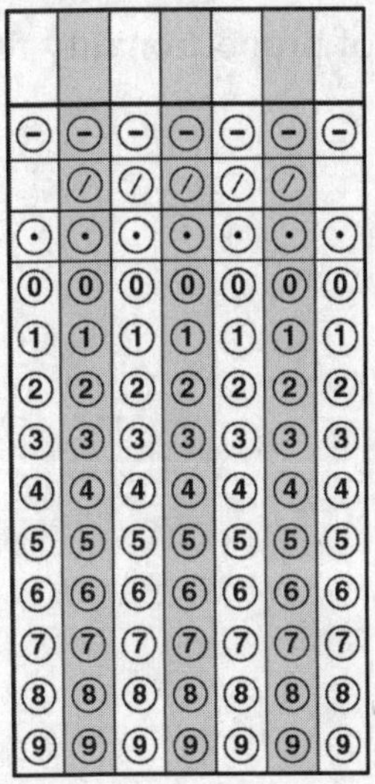

3. What number is 48% of 60?

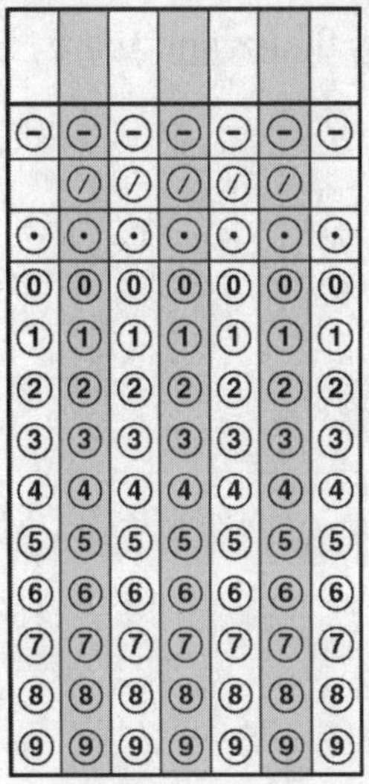

4. Which sums or differences are correct?

Ⓐ $-3\frac{2}{3} + 4\frac{1}{3} = \frac{1}{3}$

Ⓑ $-8.3 + (-7.4) = -15.7$

Ⓒ $-19.25 + 15.5 = 4.75$

Ⓓ $5\frac{1}{6} - 4\frac{1}{2} = \frac{2}{3}$

Ⓔ $-\frac{7}{8} - \left(-\frac{1}{4}\right) = -\frac{5}{8}$

Ⓕ $-7.8 - 9.2 = -14$

5. What is the sum of $\left(\frac{7}{10}a + 2\right) + (a - 3) + \left(\frac{9}{10}a - 4\right)$?

Ⓐ $\frac{13}{5}a - 5$

Ⓑ $\frac{13}{5}a - 3$

Ⓒ $\frac{8}{5}a - 5$

Ⓓ $\frac{8}{5}a - 3$

Name ______________________________ Date __________

Grade 7 Post-Course Test (continued)

6. The table shows the number of building permits approved by a city in the last five years. Which data display best represents the data?

Year	2016	2017	2018	2019	2020
Building Permits	75	140	98	115	126

Ⓐ circle graph

Ⓑ dot plot

Ⓒ histogram

Ⓓ bar graph

7. This question has **two** parts.

Part A

Which equation shows that x and y are proportional?

Ⓐ $x + y = 12$

Ⓑ $x - y = 14$

Ⓒ $\frac{y}{x} = 16$

Ⓓ $xy = 18$

Part B

What is the constant of proportionality for this equation?

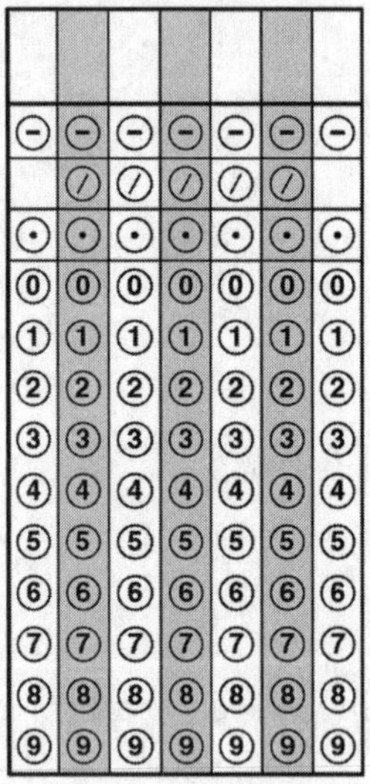

8. Which equation has a solution of −1?

Ⓐ $5(w - 2) = 10$

Ⓑ $4(2 - x) = 12$

Ⓒ $\frac{y}{8} = -8$

Ⓓ $-16z = -16$

9. A cube has a side length of $\frac{3}{5}$ feet. What is the volume of the box?

Ⓐ $\frac{27}{125}$ cubic feet

Ⓑ $\frac{9}{25}$ cubic feet

Ⓒ $\frac{6}{5}$ cubic feet

Ⓓ $\frac{9}{15}$ cubic feet

Name____ Date__________

Grade 7 Post-Course Test (continued)

10. There is a 68% chance your team will win the game. What is the likelihood of the event?

Ⓐ impossible

Ⓑ unlikely

Ⓒ likely

Ⓓ certain

11. What is the value of x that makes $\frac{2}{3}$ to 9 and x to 36 proportional?

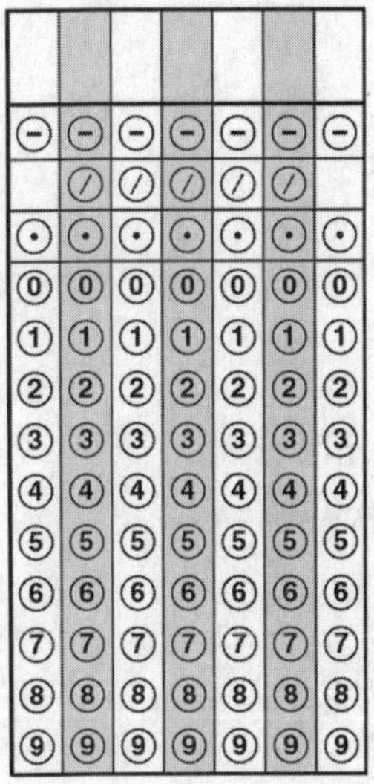

12. A pair of golf clubs cost \$250 and are marked up 40% at the store. What is the selling price?

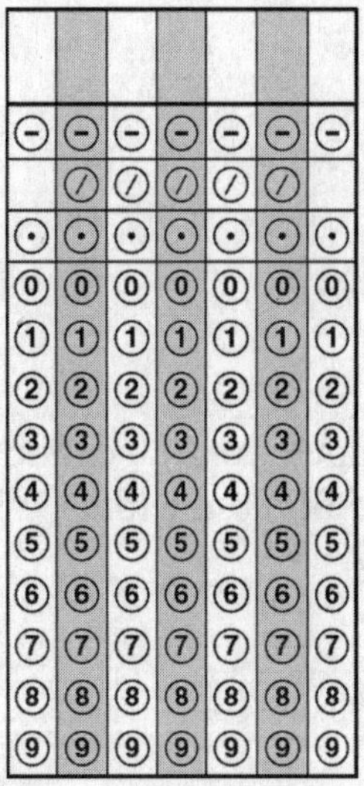

13. A window has the shape of a semicircle with a diameter of 3 feet.

The approximate perimeter of the window is [Ⓐ 3.71 / Ⓑ 7.71 / Ⓒ 11.71] feet. The approximate area of the window is [Ⓐ 3.53 / Ⓑ 7.07 / Ⓒ 14.13 / Ⓓ 28.26] square feet.

14. Which random sample is the better option to determine the students' favorite subject?

Ⓐ 20 students in math class

Ⓑ 100 students in math class

Ⓒ 20 students selected by a computer

Ⓓ 100 students selected by a computer

Name ______________________________ Date __________

Grade 7 Post-Course Test (continued)

15. What is the quotient of $-\frac{7}{12} \div \frac{7}{9}$?

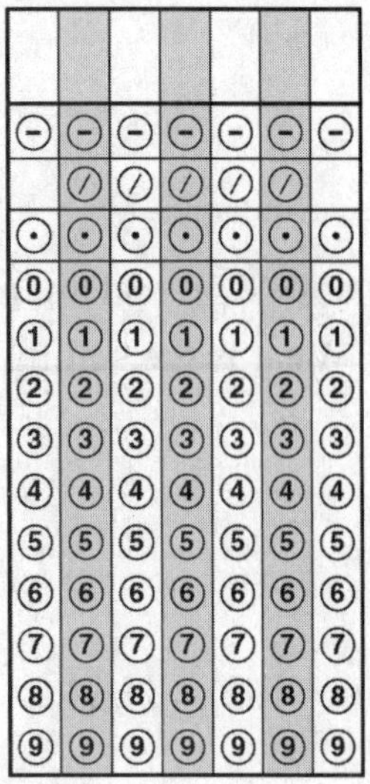

16. Which ratios form a proportion?

Ⓐ $\frac{1}{3}$ to 4 and $\frac{1}{6}$ to 2

Ⓑ 9 to 11 and 22 to 18

Ⓒ 3.2 to 1.4 and 4.8 to 3

Ⓓ 1.8 to 2.5 and 9 to 12.5

Ⓔ $\frac{2}{5}$ to 2 and $\frac{4}{5}$ to 5

Ⓕ 12 to 5 and 36 to 15

17. A rectangle has a perimeter of 120 centimeters. The length is 24 centimeters. What is an equation to find the width? What is the width of the rectangle?

Ⓐ $2w - 48 = 120$; 36 cm

Ⓑ $2w - 48 = 120$; 84 cm

Ⓒ $2w + 48 = 120$; 36 cm

Ⓓ $2w + 48 = 120$; 84 cm

18. In a class of 30 students, 16 are girls. What percent of students are boys?

Ⓐ 14%

Ⓑ 16%

Ⓒ $44\frac{2}{3}\%$

Ⓓ $46\frac{2}{3}\%$

19. What is the area of a trapezoid with a base of 5 and 7 centimeters and a height of 4 centimeters?

Ⓐ 24 cm^2

Ⓑ 48 cm^2

Ⓒ 70 cm^2

Ⓓ 140 cm^2

20. What is the expression $\frac{3}{4}(2x - y) - \frac{1}{4}(y - 2x)$ simplified?

Ⓐ $x - y$

Ⓑ $2x - y$

Ⓒ $x - 2y$

Ⓓ $2x - 2y$

Name ____________________ Date __________

21. The cost of a 12 ounce can of dog food is \$8.88. What is the cost, in dollars, of a 16 ounce can of dog food?

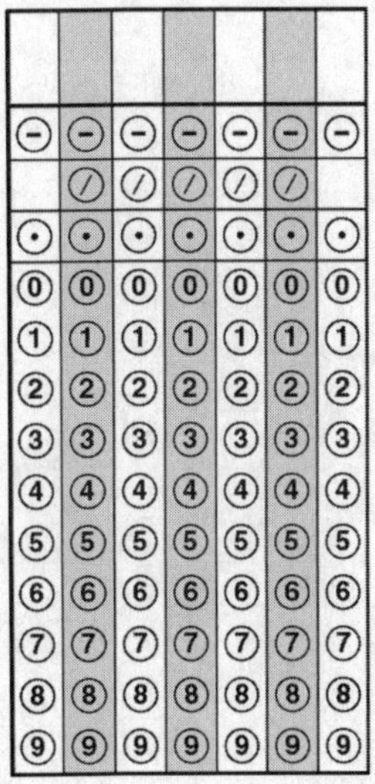

22. For a contest, there are 300 jellybeans in a container. You made a guess of 315 jellybeans. What is the percent error?

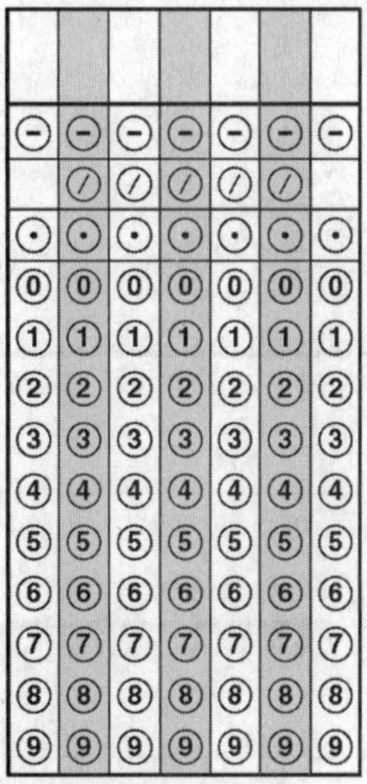

23. This question has **two** parts.

Use the figure shown.

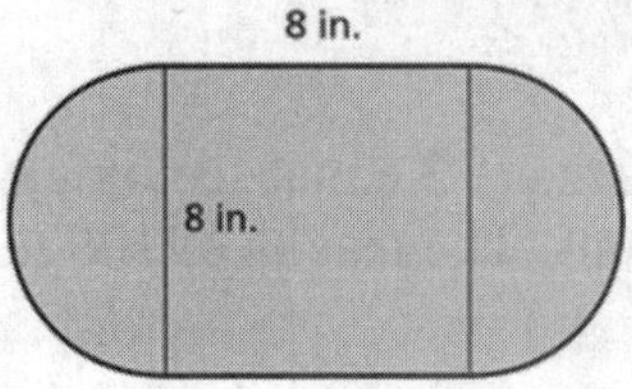

Part A

What is the perimeter of the figure to the nearest inch?

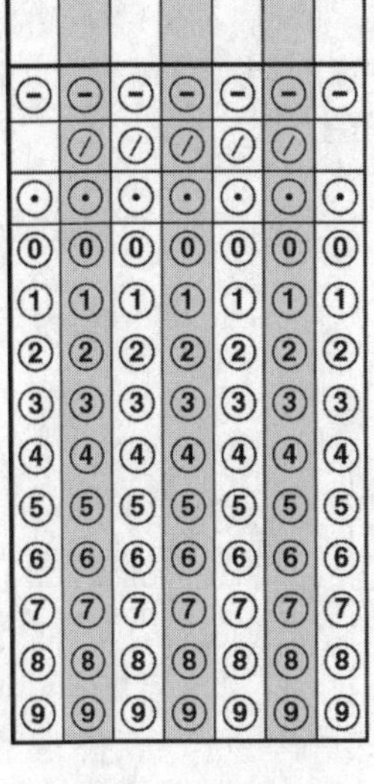

Part B

What is the area of the figure to the nearest whole square inch?

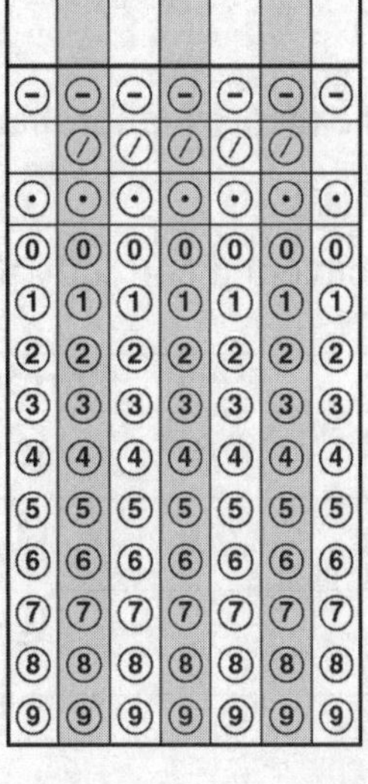

Name ____________________ Date ________

Grade 7

Post-Course Test (continued)

24. A fish is $37\frac{3}{8}$ inches below sea level. The fish swims to $21\frac{1}{2}$ inches below sea level. What is the change in height?

Ⓐ $15\frac{1}{6}$ inches

Ⓑ $16\frac{1}{4}$ inches

Ⓒ $15\frac{7}{8}$ inches

Ⓓ $16\frac{1}{3}$ inches

25. What is the solution to $-\frac{x}{4} < 2$?

Ⓐ 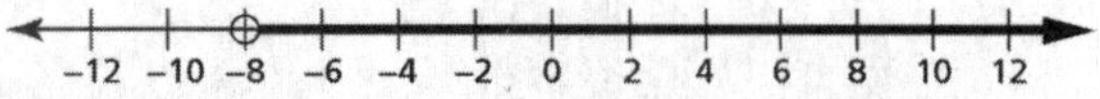

Ⓑ 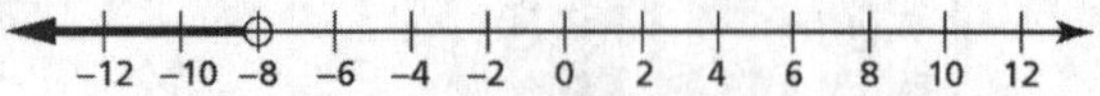

Ⓒ 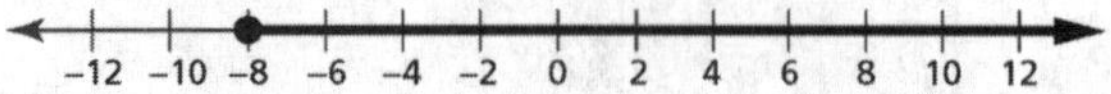

Ⓓ 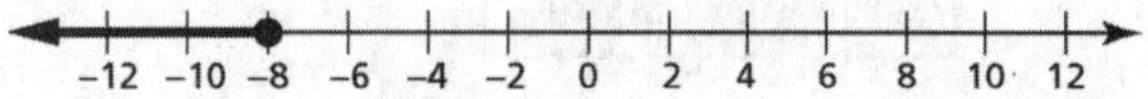

26. A game is played in which there are 3 equal sections where a player can score 1, 2, or 3 points. The results of 100 turns are shown in the table.

Points	1	2	3
Results	38	35	27

The theoretical probability for each turn is [Ⓐ $\frac{3}{10}$ / Ⓑ $\frac{1}{3}$ / Ⓒ $\frac{1}{2}$]. The experimental probability

is [Ⓐ less than / Ⓑ greater than] the theoretical probability for the score of 1 point.

27. Which fractions are converted correctly to decimals?

	Correctly	**Incorrectly**
$-\frac{7}{16} = -0.4375$	Ⓐ	Ⓑ
$1\frac{7}{9} = 1.777$	Ⓒ	Ⓓ
$\frac{29}{12} = 2.42$	Ⓔ	Ⓕ

Name____________________ Date__________

Grade 7

Post-Course Test (continued)

28. 32 is what percent of 20?

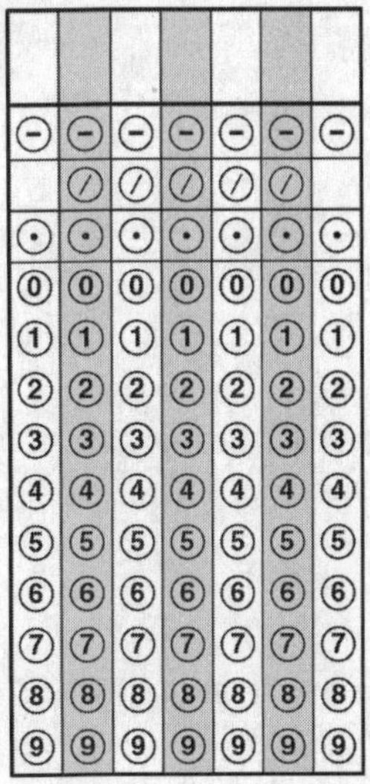

29. Solve $\frac{a}{3} + \frac{1}{2} = \frac{5}{6}$ for a.

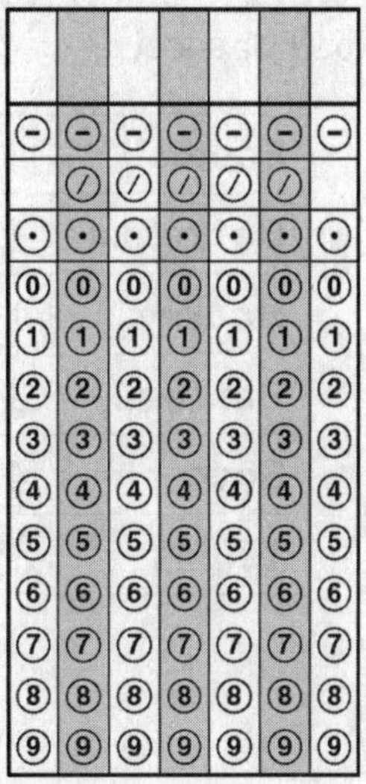

30. What is the value of $-|-4.5|$?

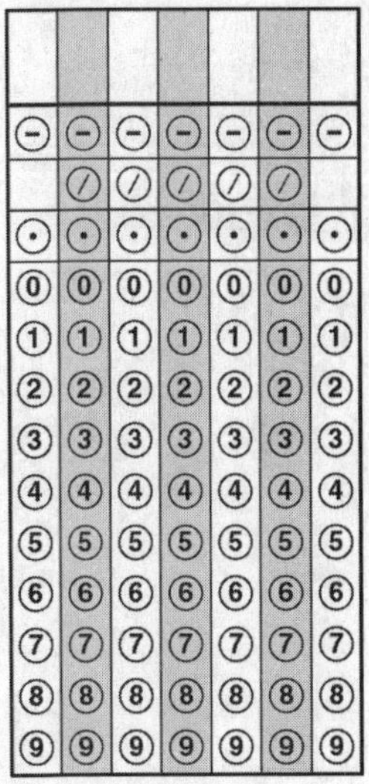

31. A square has a perimeter of 72 inches What equation represents the length of one side? What is the length of the side?

Ⓐ $6s^2 = 72$; 3.5 inches

Ⓑ $s^2 = 72$; 8.5 inches

Ⓒ $2s = 72$; 36 inches

Ⓓ $4s = 72$; 18 inches

32. Select all expressions that are written correctly as a power.

Ⓐ $(6^{12})^4 \stackrel{?}{=} 6^{48}$

Ⓑ $4^7 \cdot 4^3 \stackrel{?}{=} 4^{21}$

Ⓒ $(5 \cdot 8)^5 \stackrel{?}{=} 5 \cdot 8^5$

Ⓓ $\frac{7^{17}}{7^{11}} \stackrel{?}{=} 7^{28}$

Ⓔ $\frac{9^4 \cdot 9^6}{9^2} \stackrel{?}{=} 9^8$

Ⓕ $\frac{3^8}{3^2} \cdot \frac{3^6}{3^4} \stackrel{?}{=} 3^8$

Name ______________________________ Date __________

Grade 7 Post-Course Test (continued)

33. You surveyed 200 randomly selected students about their favorite sport. The results are in the table below. There are 2500 students in the school. What is the number of students whose favorite sport is basketball or soccer?

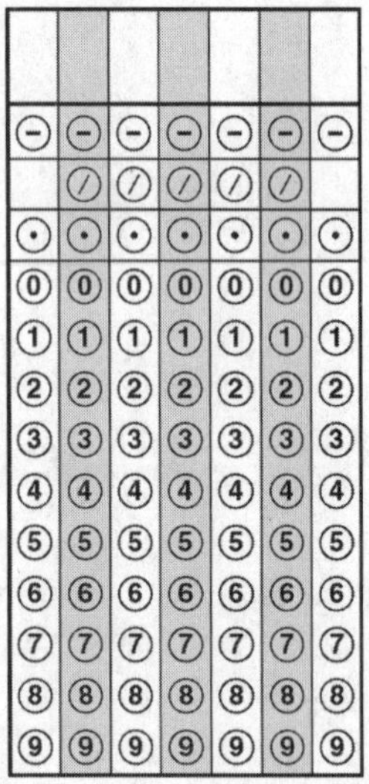

Football	47
Basketball	42
Hockey	19
Baseball	37
Soccer	40
Tennis	15

34. A small concert hall seats 1000 people. A total of 350 people bought tickets. What is an inequality that represents how many more people can be seated? What is the solution to the inequality?

Ⓐ $p + 350 \leq 1000; p \leq 1350$

Ⓑ $p - 350 \leq 1000; p \leq 1350$

Ⓒ $p + 350 \leq 1000; p \leq 650$

Ⓓ $p - 350 \leq 1000; p \leq 650$

35. What is $2.1(-3)(-4.5)$?

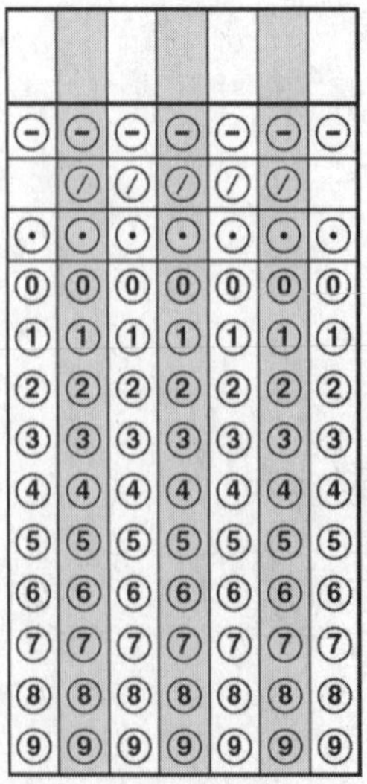

36. 65% of what number is 18.2?

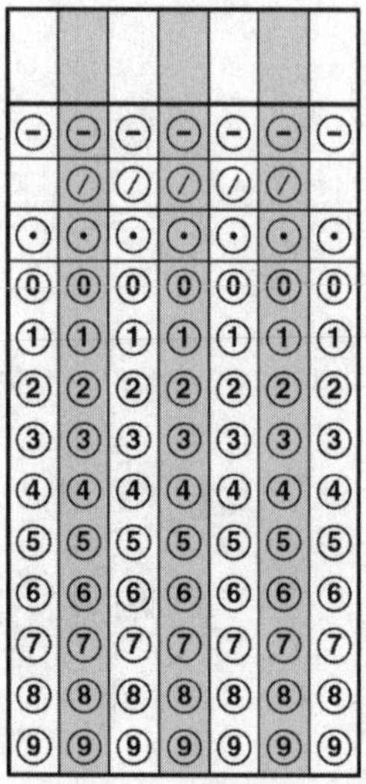

Name______________________________ Date__________

Grade 7 Post-Course Test (continued)

37. The number of pets for 15 households is listed $\{3, 2, 4, 1, 0, 2, 1, 3, 8, 2, 1, 1, 0, 2, 3\}$. Which statements related to the data set are true?

Ⓐ The mean and the median are the same value.

Ⓑ There is no mode for the data set.

Ⓒ The interquartile range is 2 pets.

Ⓓ The median number of pets is 3.

Ⓔ The range is 8 pets for the data set.

Ⓕ The outlier impacts the mean and the range of the data set.

38. The design of a logo is a parallelogram with an area of 192 square inches and a base of 12 inches. What is the height?

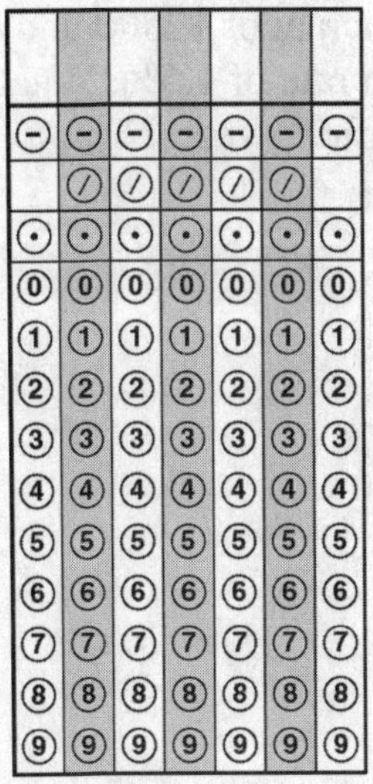

39. A plant grew $1\frac{2}{3}$ inches the first year, $1\frac{3}{4}$ inches the second year, and $2\frac{1}{12}$ inches the third year. What is the total amount of growth?

Ⓐ $4\frac{6}{19}$ inches

Ⓑ $4\frac{1}{2}$ inches

Ⓒ $5\frac{6}{19}$ inches

Ⓓ $5\frac{1}{2}$ inches

40. What is 88 kilometers per hour in feet per second?

Ⓐ about 17 feet per second

Ⓑ about 80 feet per second

Ⓒ about 1460 feet per second

Ⓓ about 4811 feet per second

41. What is the difference $(3 - 1.1b) - (2 - 2.2b) - (3b + 5)$?

Ⓐ $-1.9b - 4$

Ⓑ $1.9b - 4$

Ⓒ $-6.3b - 6$

Ⓓ $6.3b - 6$

Name ______________________________ Date __________

Grade 7 Post-Course Test (continued)

42. A scale model of a tower is 24 inches. The scale is 1.5 in. : 10 ft. What is the actual height, in feet, of the tower?

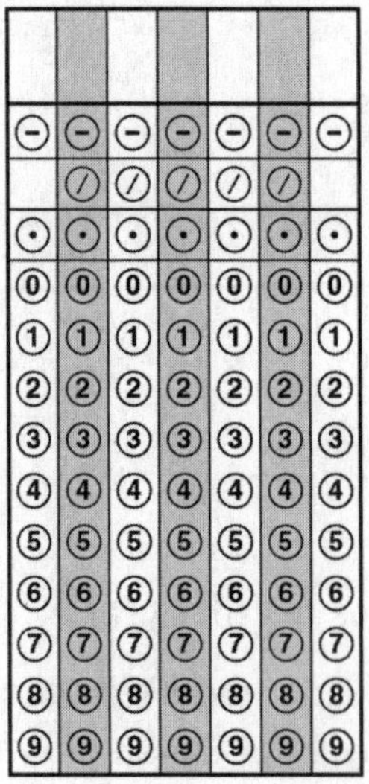

43. The original price of a book was \$48. It is now 70% off. What is the sale price of the book?

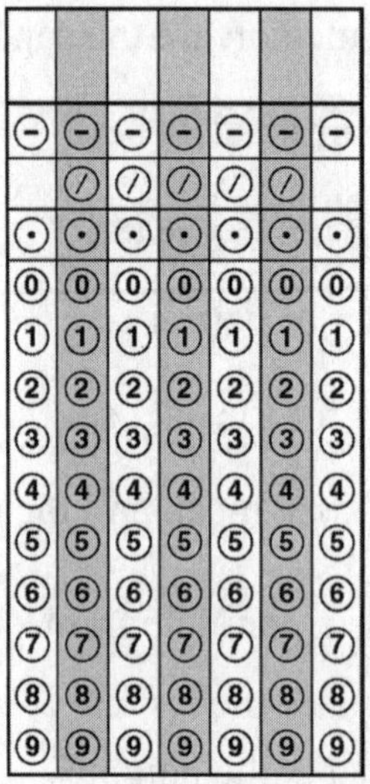

44. Which inequalities have a solution of 3?

Ⓐ $a - 4 < 7$

Ⓑ $\frac{b}{6} \geq \frac{1}{2}$

Ⓒ $c + \frac{1}{2} > 3\frac{1}{2}$

Ⓓ $4d < 12$

Ⓔ $2e \geq 3$

Ⓕ $f - 5 \geq 2$

45. An account has a principal of \$2500 and an annual simple interest rate of 1.5%. What is the account balance after 4 years?

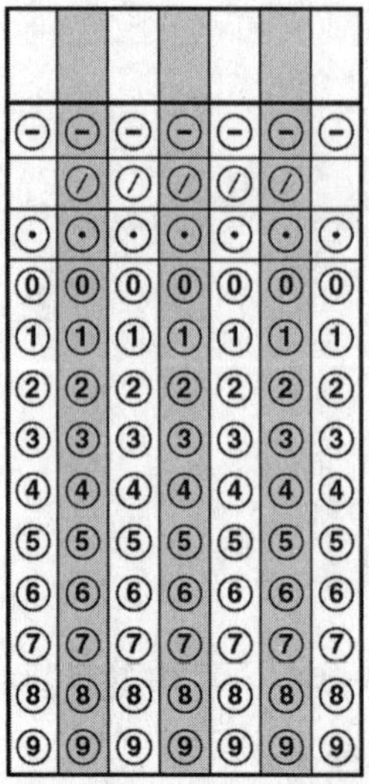

46. A can of sausage is a cylinder with a diameter of 4 centimeters and a height of 8 centimeters. What is the surface area of the can to the nearest square centimeter?

Ⓐ 126 cm^2

Ⓑ 201 cm^2

Ⓒ 301 cm^2

Ⓓ 402 cm^2

Correlation to Florida's B.E.S.T. Standards

Chapter 1 B.E.S.T. Test Prep

1. MA.7.NSO.1.1
2. MA.6.NSO.1.4
3. MA.6.NSO.2.3
4. MA.7.NSO.2.1
5. MA.7.NSO.2.1
6. MA.6.AR.1.3
7. MA.7.NSO.1.1
8. MA.7.NSO.1.1
9. MA.6.AR.3.4
10. MA.6.GR.2.3
11. MA.6.NSO.1.1, MA.6.NSO.1.4
12. MA.7.NSO.1.1
13. MA.7.NSO.1.1
14. MA.7.NSO.2.1
15. MA.7.NSO.2.1
16. MA.6.NSO.4.1, MA.6.NSO.4.2
17. MA.7.NSO.1.1
18. MA.6.NSO.1.3
19. MA.6.NSO.1.3, MA.6.NSO.1.4
20. MA.6.NSO.4.1

Chapter 2 B.E.S.T. Test Prep

1. MA.7.NSO.2.2
2. MA.7.NSO.1.1
3. MA.7.NSO.1.1, MA.7.NSO.2.3
4. MA.7.NSO.2.2
5. MA.7.NSO.1.1
6. MA.7.NSO.1.1, MA.7.NSO.2.3
7. MA.6.NSO.1.1, MA.6.NSO.1.4
8. MA.7.NSO.2.3
9. MA.7.NSO.2.3
10. MA.6.NSO.1.1
11. MA.6.AR.1.3
12. MA.6.DP.1.2, MA.6.DP.1.6
13. MA.7.NSO.1.1
14. MA.7.NSO.2.2
15. MA.6.NSO.1.3, MA.6.NSO.4.1
16. MA.7.NSO.2.3
17. MA.6.NSO.1.3
18. MA.6.NSO.4.1

Chapter 3 B.E.S.T. Test Prep

1. MA.7.AR.2.1
2. MA.7.NSO.2.1
3. MA.7.AR.2.2
4. MA.7.NSO.2.1, MA.7.NSO.2.2
5. MA.7.AR.2.1
6. MA.6.NSO.1.1
7. MA.7.NSO.2.1
8. MA.7.AR.1.2
9. MA.7.NSO.1.1
10. MA.7.NSO.2.1
11. MA.7.NSO.2.3
12. MA.7.AR.2.2
13. MA.7.NSO.2.3
14. MA.7.AR.1.1
15. MA.7.NSO.2.1
16. MA.7.NSO.2.3
17. preparing for MA.7.AR.2.2
18. preparing for MA.7.AR.1.1
19. MA.7.NSO.2.2

Chapter 4 B.E.S.T. Test Prep

1. MA.7.AR.4.1
2. MA.7.AR.2.2
3. MA.7.NSO.2.2
4. MA.7.NSO.1.2
5. MA.7.AR.3.3
6. preparing for MA.7.AR.2.2
7. MA.7.AR.1.1
8. MA.7.NSO.1.1
9. MA.7.NSO.3.3
10. MA.7.AR.1.1
11. MA.7.AR.4.5
12. MA.7.NSO.1.1
13. MA.7.AR.2.1
14. MA.7.AR.3.2
15. MA.7.NSO.2.2
16. MA.7.AR.4.4
17. MA.6.NSO.1.1
18. MA.7.AR.1.2
19. MA.7.GR.1.5

Chapter 5 B.E.S.T. Test Prep

1. MA.7.AR.2.2
2. MA.7.NSO.2.1
3. MA.7.NSO.1.1
4. MA.7.AR.4.5
5. MA.7.AR.3.1
6. MA.7.AR.4.1
7. preparing for MA.7.AR.2.2
8. MA.7.NSO.2.1
9. MA.7.AR.3.1
10. MA.7.AR.3.1
11. MA.7.NSO.2.3
12. MA.7.NSO.1.2
13. MA.7.AR.3.3
14. MA.7.AR.3.1
15. MA.7.NSO.2.3
16. MA.7.AR.4.2
17. MA.7.AR.1.1
18. MA.7.AR.3.1
19. MA.7.AR.3.1
20. MA.7.GR.1.5

Chapter 6 B.E.S.T. Test Prep

1. MA.7.AR.3.1
2. MA.7.AR.4.3
3. MA.7.DP.2.2
4. MA.7.AR.2.2
5. MA.7.DP.2.3
6. preparing for MA.7.AR.2.2
7. MA.7.DP.2.4
8. MA.7.AR.3.3
9. MA.7.DP.1.4
10. MA.7.AR.2.1
11. MA.7.NSO.2.2
12. MA.7.AR.3.2

Correlation to Florida's B.E.S.T. Standards (continued)

13. MA.7.DP.1.5

14. MA.7.AR.3.1

Chapter 7 B.E.S.T. Test Prep

1. MA.7.DP.2.2

2. MA.7.AR.3.1

3. MA.7.AR.3.1

4. MA.7.DP.1.1

5. MA.7.AR.3.3

6. MA.7.DP.1.3

7. MA.7.NSO.1.2

8. MA.7.DP.1.2

9. MA.7.DP.1.1

10. MA.7.DP.1.3

11. MA.7.NSO.1.2

12. MA.7.AR.3.1

13. MA.7.AR.4.1

14. MA.7.AR.3.2

15. MA.7.NSO.1.1

Chapter 8 B.E.S.T. Test Prep

1. MA.7.AR.4.3

2. MA.7.AR.2.2

3. MA.7.AR.3.1

4. MA.7.GR.1.4

5. MA.7.GR.1.3

6. MA.7.AR.3.1

7. MA.7.GR.2.2, MA.7.GR.2.3

8. MA.7.AR.2.1

9. MA.7.GR.1.1

10. MA.7.GR.1.1

11. MA.7.AR.3.2

12. MA.7.NSO.2.2

13. MA.7.AR.1.2

14. MA.7.GR.1.3, MA.7.GR.1.4

15. MA.7.DP.1.1

16. MA.7.DP.2.4

17. MA.7.AR.3.1

Post-Course Test

1. MA.7.AR.3.3

2. MA.7.NSO.1.1

3. MA.7.AR.3.1

4. MA.7.NSO.2.2

5. MA.7.AR.1.1

6. MA.7.DP.1.5

7. MA.7.AR.4.1, MA.7.AR.4.2

8. MA.7.AR.2.2

9. MA.7.NSO.1.1

10. MA.7.DP.2.2

11. MA.7.AR.3.2

12. MA.7.AR.3.1

13. MA.7.GR.1.3, MA.7.GR.1.4

14. MA.7.DP.1.3

15. MA.7.NSO.2.2

16. MA.7.AR.4.1

17. MA.7.AR.2.2

18. MA.7.AR.3.1

19. MA.7.GR.1.1

20. MA.7.AR.1.1

21. MA.7.AR.3.2

22. MA.7.AR.3.1

23. MA.7.GR.1.3, MA.7.GR.1.4

24. MA.7.NSO.2.3

25. MA.7.AR.2.1

26. MA.7.DP.2.3, MA.7.DP.2.4

27. MA.7.NSO.1.2

28. MA.7.AR.3.1

29. MA.7.AR.2.2

30. MA.7.NSO.2.1

31. preparing for MA.7.AR.2.2

32. MA.7.NSO.1.1

33. MA.7.DP.1.3

34. MA.7.AR.2.1

35. MA.7.NSO.2.2

36. MA.7.AR.3.1

37. MA.7.DP.1.1

38. MA.7.GR.1.1

39. MA.7.NSO.2.3

40. MA.7.AR.3.3

41. MA.7.AR.1.1

42. MA.7.GR.1.5

43. MA.7.AR.3.1

44. MA.7.AR.2.1

45. MA.7.AR.3.1

46. MA.7.GR.2.2

Name ______________________________ Date ________

Evidence-Based Scale Worksheets

Number Sense and Operations
MA.7.NSO.1.1 Know and apply the Laws of Exponents to evaluate numerical expressions and generate equivalent numerical expressions, limited to whole-number exponents and rational number bases.

Circle the scale that best demonstrates your knowledge of the standard.

	Description	Evidence
4	**I can go beyond the standard.** • Demonstrate to other students the rules for Power of a Power, Power of a Product, and Power of a Quotient by using different examples.	
3	**I understand the entire standard.** • Apply the laws of exponents to rewrite the expression as a power.	Simplify each expression. Write your answer as a power. **a.** $\left(\left(\frac{5}{8}\right)^4\right)^9$ **b.** $\frac{(-1.7)^8}{(-1.7)^3}$ **c.** $(0.2)^5 \cdot (0.2)^7$

Name ____ Date ________

MA.7.NSO.1.1 (continued)

	Description	Evidence
2	**I understand some parts, but not the entire standard.** • Evaluate numerical expressions with whole-number exponents and rational number bases.	Evaluate each expression. **a.** 0.6^3 **b.** $\left(-\frac{1}{9}\right)^2$ **c.** $-\left(\frac{2}{5}\right)^4$
1	**I understand the basic skills needed to begin learning this standard.** • Evaluate numerical expressions with whole-number exponents and whole number bases.	Evaluate each expression. **a.** 3^4 **b.** 1^5 **c.** 4^3

Name ______________________________ Date ________

Evidence-Based Scale Worksheets

Number Sense and Operations
MA.7.NSO.1.2 Rewrite rational numbers in different but equivalent forms including fractions, mixed numbers, repeating decimals and percentages to solve mathematical and real-world problems.

Circle the scale that best demonstrates your knowledge of the standard.

	Description	Evidence
4	**I can go beyond the standard.** • Write a real-world problem that requires rewriting rational numbers in different, but equivalent forms.	
3	**I understand the entire standard.** • Solve a real-world problem that requires rewriting rational numbers.	The home team misses 7 out of 30 free throws in a basketball game. The road team misses 6 out of 24 free throws. What team had the greater percentage of free throws made? Explain your reasoning.

Name ____________________ Date ________

MA.7.NSO.1.2 (continued)

	Description	Evidence
2	**I understand some parts, but not the entire standard.** • Rewrite rational numbers in different forms.	Write the repeating decimal as a fraction. **a.** $1.\overline{1}$ Write the mixed number as a decimal. **b.** $2\frac{3}{11}$ Write the percent as a fraction. **c.** $16\frac{2}{3}\%$
1	**I understand the basic skills needed to begin learning this standard.** • Write fractions as decimals and percents.	Write each fraction as a decimal and a percent. **a.** $\frac{7}{10}$ **b.** $\frac{81}{100}$ **c.** $\frac{829}{1000}$

Name ____________________ Date ________

Evidence-Based Scale Worksheets

Number Sense and Operations
MA.7.NSO.2.1 Solve mathematical problems using multi-step order of operations with rational numbers including grouping symbols, whole-number exponents and absolute value.

Circle the scale that best demonstrates your knowledge of the standard.

	Description	Evidence
4	**I can go beyond the standard.** • Write an expression that includes all four operations with rational numbers and exponents. Teach someone else how to evaluate the expression.	
3	**I understand the entire standard.** • Evaluate expressions involving rational numbers.	Evaluate each expression. **a.** $-10\|5-12\|-95$ **b.** $4.92 - 9.5 \div 2^2$ **c.** $1\frac{5}{12} + \frac{1}{2} - \frac{5}{3} \div \left(-\frac{1}{2}\right)$

Name________________________________ Date ________

MA.7.NSO.2.1 (continued)

	Description	Evidence
2	**I understand some parts, but not the entire standard.** • Evaluate expressions with positive rational numbers.	Evaluate each expression. **a.** $2(8 - 5) + 3$ **b.** $3.5 \div 0.5 - 2^2$ **c.** $\frac{7}{6} \div 2 \times 3$
1	**I understand the basic skills needed to begin learning this standard.** • Evaluate expressions with whole numbers.	Evaluate the expression. **a.** $8 \times 7 - 4 \times 5$ **b.** $27 \div 3 + 9$ **c.** $3^2 + 12 - 2^3$

Name ______________________________ Date __________

Evidence-Based Scale Worksheets

Number Sense and Operations
MA.7.NSO.2.2 Add, subtract, multiply and divide rational numbers with procedural fluency.

Circle the scale that best demonstrates your knowledge of the standard.

	Description	Evidence
4	**I can go beyond the standard.** • Demonstrate to other students the rules for when an answer is positive or negative when adding, subtracting, multiplying, or dividing two rational numbers.	
3	**I understand the entire standard.** • Add, subtract, multiply, and divide rational numbers with procedural fluency.	Find the sum, difference, product, or quotient. Write fractions in simplest form. **a.** $-4.7 + (-3.8) - 5.9$ **b.** $-2\frac{1}{4} - \left(-\frac{3}{2}\right) + \frac{7}{8}$ **c.** $(-4.6)(0.7)$ **d.** $-9\frac{3}{4} \div 3\frac{2}{5}$

Name ______________________________ Date ________

MA.7.NSO.2.2 (continued)

	Description	Evidence
2	**I understand some parts, but not the entire standard.** • Add, subtract, multiply, and divide integers with procedural fluency.	Find the sum, difference, product, or quotient. **a.** $-12 + 8$ **b.** $-11 - 14$ **c.** $(-1)(15)(-3)(-4)$ **d.** $(-150) \div 25$
1	**I understand the basic skills needed to begin learning this standard.** • Add, subtract, multiply, and divide whole numbers with procedural fluency.	Find the sum, difference, product, or quotient. **a.** $348 + 236$ **b.** $178 - 93$ **c.** $(16)(17)$ **d.** $2701 \div 37$

Name ______________________________ Date ________

Evidence-Based Scale Worksheets

Number Sense and Operations
MA.7.NSO.2.3 Solve real-world problems involving any of the four operations with rational numbers.

Circle the scale that best demonstrates your knowledge of the standard.

	Description	Evidence
4	**I can go beyond the standard.** • Write a real-world problem with rational numbers that requires the use of multiple operations to solve.	
3	**I understand the entire standard.** • Solve a real-life problem involving operations with rational numbers.	You have $100 in your bank account. You make 1 deposit of $118.47 during the week. You also make 2 withdrawals for $49.95 and 1 additional withdrawal of $135.79. What is the balance on the account?

Name_______________________________________ Date ________

MA.7.NSO.2.3 (continued)

	Description	Evidence
2	**I understand some parts, but not the entire standard.** • Solve a real-life problem involving operations with integers.	Customers rate their experience at a restaurant on a scale from −2 to 2. The ratings are shown in the table. Find the mean rating.
1	**I understand the basic skills needed to begin learning this standard.** • Solve a real-life problem involving operations with whole numbers.	There are 4,500 fans in the lower section and 2,250 fans in the upper section for a concert. Lower section tickets cost \$65 and upper section tickets cost \$40. How much money was bought in for the concert?

Rating	Number of Customers
−2	3
−1	0
0	2
1	9
2	11

Name ______________________________ Date ________

Evidence-Based Scale Worksheets

Algebraic Reasoning
MA.7.AR.1.1 Apply properties of operations to add and subtract linear expressions with rational coefficients.

Circle the scale that best demonstrates your knowledge of the standard.

	Description	Evidence
4	**I can go beyond the standard.** • Simplify complex linear expressions with rational coefficients that require the use of the Distributive Property.	**a.** Simplify $-2\left(\frac{3}{4}a - \frac{5}{2}\right) + \frac{1}{2}(3a + 8)$. **b.** Simplify $\frac{1}{5}\left(5 - \frac{2}{3}y\right) - 4\left(-\frac{1}{2} - \frac{1}{9}y\right)$.
3	**I understand the entire standard.** • Add and subtract linear expressions with rational coefficients.	**a.** Simplify $\left(-\frac{4}{3}x - 5\right) + \left(2x - \frac{1}{2}\right)$. **b.** Simplify $\left(4 + \frac{1}{2}y\right) - \left(-3 + \frac{1}{4}y\right)$. **c.** Simplify $\left(\frac{1}{2}z + 4\right) - \left(z + \frac{3}{2}\right)$.

Name____________________ Date ________

MA.7.AR.1.1 (continued)

	Description	Evidence
2	**I understand some parts, but not the entire standard.** • Add and subtract linear expressions with integer coefficients.	**a.** Simplify $(2f + 5) - (3f + 4)$. **b.** Simplify $(6 - g) - (4 + 2g)$. **c.** Simplify $(8h - 3) - (5h - 2)$.
1	**I understand the basic skills needed to begin learning this standard.** • Add and subtract integers.	Find the sum or the difference. **a.** $24 + (-35)$ **b.** $(-27) + 44$ **c.** $-18 - 36$ **d.** $-16 - (-48)$

Name ______________________________ Date ________

Evidence-Based Scale Worksheets

Algebraic Reasoning
MA.7.AR.1.2 Determine whether two linear expressions are equivalent.

Circle the scale that best demonstrates your knowledge of the standard.

	Description	Evidence
4	**I can go beyond the standard.** • Rewrite real-life expressions in different equivalent forms.	After *x* months, you have $(20x + 50)$ dollars in your savings account and $(25x + 100)$ dollars in your checking account. Write and simplify an expression that represents the total amount, in dollars, in the accounts after *x* months.
3	**I understand the entire standard.** • Determine whether two linear expressions are equivalent.	Determine whether the expressions are equivalent. **a.** $\frac{2}{3}(9 - x) + 4x$ and $6 + 3x$ **b.** $-5x + \frac{3}{4}(2x - 6)$ and $-\frac{7}{2}x - \frac{9}{2}$

Name ______________________________ Date __________

MA.7.AR.1.2 (continued)

	Description	Evidence
2	**I understand some parts, but not the entire standard.** • Apply the Distributive Property to expressions.	**a.** Simplify $3(x-7)$. **b.** Simplify $\frac{1}{2}(4y+16)$. **c.** Simplify $-5(2-3z)$.
1	**I understand the basic skills needed to begin learning this standard.** • Add, subtract, and multiply rational numbers.	Find the sum, the difference, or the product. **a.** $1\frac{3}{4}-\frac{2}{5}$ **b.** $1\frac{3}{4}+\frac{2}{5}$ **c.** $1\frac{3}{4}\left(\frac{2}{5}\right)$

Name ____ Date ________

Evidence-Based Scale Worksheets

Algebraic Reasoning
MA.7.AR.2.1 Write and solve one-step inequalities in one variable within a mathematical context and represent solutions algebraically or graphically.

Circle the scale that best demonstrates your knowledge of the standard.

	Description	Evidence
4	**I can go beyond the standard.** • Write and solve a real-world problem that involves a one-step inequality.	
3	**I understand the entire standard.** • Solve a word problem leading to a one-step inequality. • Graph and interpret an inequality.	Tickets to a fundraiser cost $10. **a.** Write and solve an inequality that represents the number x of additional tickets that must be sold to make at least $1000 on ticket sales. **b.** Graph and interpret the solution.

Name ______________________________ Date __________

MA.7.AR.2.1 (continued)

	Description	Evidence
2	**I understand some parts, but not the entire standard.** • Solve one-step inequalities.	Solve each inequality. **a.** $a - 6 < 1$ **b.** $y + 4 \leq -1$ **c.** $-2.5x \leq 10$ **d.** $\frac{2}{3}t > -\frac{1}{2}$
1	**I understand the basic skills needed to begin learning this standard.** • Graph inequalities on a number line.	Graph the inequality on a number line. **a.** $a > 4$ 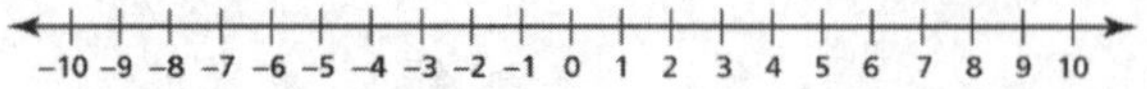 **b.** $b \leq -3$ 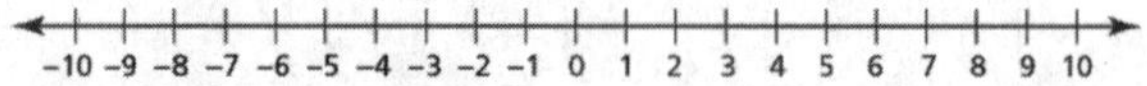 **c.** $6 > c$ 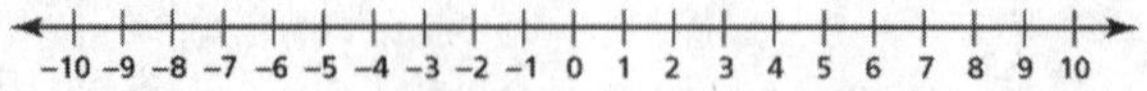

Name ______________________________ Date ________

Evidence-Based Scale Worksheets

Algebraic Reasoning

MA.7.AR.2.2 Write and solve two-step equations in one variable within a mathematical or real-world context, where all terms are rational numbers.

Circle the scale that best demonstrates your knowledge of the standard.

	Description	Evidence
4	**I can go beyond the standard.** • Write a word problem that requires writing a two-step equation where all terms are rational numbers.	
3	**I understand the entire standard.** • Solve a word problem leading to a two-step equation with rational numbers.	You install $86\frac{3}{8}$ feet of fencing around a rectangular vegetable garden that has a length of $24\frac{1}{2}$ feet. Write and solve an equation to find the width of the garden.

Name________________________________ Date ________

MA.7.AR.2.2 (continued)

	Description	Evidence
2	**I understand some parts, but not the entire standard.** • Solve two-step equations with rational numbers for all terms.	Solve each equation. **a.** $\frac{2}{3}x + \frac{7}{3} = \frac{1}{6}$ **b.** $\frac{1}{2}y - \frac{3}{4} = \frac{7}{8}$ **c.** $\frac{7}{2} - \frac{3}{10}x = -\frac{4}{5}$
1	**I understand the basic skills needed to begin learning this standard.** • Solve one-step equations.	Solve each equation. **a.** $x - 5 = -2$ **b.** $y + 1.5 = 1$ **c.** $3z = 12$ **d.** $\frac{m}{2} = -6$

Name____ Date ________

Evidence-Based Scale Worksheets

Algebraic Reasoning
MA.7.AR.3.1 Apply previous understanding of percentages and ratios to solve multi-step real-world percent problems.

Circle the scale that best demonstrates your knowledge of the standard.

	Description	Evidence
4	**I can go beyond the standard.** • Write and solve a real-world percent problem that requires multiple steps to solve.	
3	**I understand the entire standard.** • Solve a multi-step real-world percent problem.	**a.** Your food total for dinner is \$32.50. Sales tax is an additional \$1.95. You leave a 20% tip on the food total. Find the percent of sales tax on the food total and the total amount you pay for dinner. **b.** The ratio of wins to losses for a baseball team is 4 : 5. What is the team's winning percentage?

Name ______________________________ Date __________

MA.7.AR.3.1 (continued)

	Description	Evidence
2	**I understand some parts, but not the entire standard.** • Solve percent problems.	Solve each problem. **a.** What percent of 60 is 27? **b.** What number is 40% of 250? **c.** 150% of what number is 21?
1	**I understand the basic skills needed to begin learning this standard.** • Understand how to write percents as decimals.	Write each percent as a decimal. **a.** 10% **b.** 79% **c.** 100% **d.** 150%

Name ______________________________ Date __________

Evidence-Based Scale Worksheets

Algebraic Reasoning
MA.7.AR.3.2 Apply previous understanding of ratios to solve real-world problems involving proportions.

Circle the scale that best demonstrates your knowledge of the standard.

	Description	Evidence
4	**I can go beyond the standard.** • Write and solve a real-world problem that requires a proportion.	
3	**I understand the entire standard.** • Solve real-world problems involving proportions.	A factory can assemble 1500 phones during an 8-hour shift. Write and solve a proportion to find the number of phones that can be assembled in one day and in one week.

Name ______________________________ Date ________

MA.7.AR.3.2 (continued)

	Description	Evidence
2	**I understand some parts, but not the entire standard.** • Make a plan for how to solve real-world problems involving proportions.	Make a plan on how to write and solve the problem. A car drives 137 miles on 5 gallons of gas. How far can the car travel on a full 12.5-gallon tank of gas?
1	**I understand the basic skills needed to begin learning this standard.** • Solve proportions.	Solve each proportion. **a.** $\frac{x}{8} = \frac{42}{48}$ **b.** $\frac{y+1}{2} = \frac{24}{36}$ **c.** $\frac{4.5}{12.5} = \frac{2z}{15}$

Name ____________________ Date ________

Evidence-Based Scale Worksheets

Algebraic Reasoning
MA.7.AR.3.3 Solve mathematical and real-world problems involving the conversion of units across different measurement systems.

Circle the scale that best demonstrates your knowledge of the standard.

	Description	Evidence
4	**I can go beyond the standard.** • Write and solve a real-world problem that requires a conversion of units across different measurement systems.	
3	**I understand the entire standard.** • Solve real-world problems involving conversion of units across different measurement systems.	**a.** The average cost of gasoline in Canada is 1.15 Canadian dollars per liter. If 1 Canadian dollar is approximately 0.77 United States dollars, what is the cost in United States dollars per gallon? **b.** The speed of light is approximately 300,000,000 meters per second. What is the approximate speed in miles per hour?

Name ______________________________ Date ________

MA.7.AR.3.3 (continued)

	Description	Evidence
2	**I understand some parts, but not the entire standard.** • Solve mathematical problems involving conversion of units across different measurement systems.	Convert the unit of measure. Round to the nearest hundredth where applicable. **a.** Convert 8 kilograms to pounds. **b.** Convert 28 pints to liters. **c.** Convert 120 yards to meters.
1	**I understand the basic skills needed to begin learning this standard.** • Solve mathematical problems involving conversion of units across same measurement systems.	Convert the unit of measure. **a.** Convert 64 pounds to ounces. **b.** Convert 7.25 kilometers to meters. **c.** Convert 6 feet to inches. **d.** Convert 45,000 milliliters to liters.

Name ____________________ Date ________

Evidence-Based Scale Worksheets

Algebraic Reasoning

MA.7.AR.4.1 Determine whether two quantities have a proportional relationship by examining a table, graph or written description.

Circle the scale that best demonstrates your knowledge of the standard.

	Description	Evidence
4	**I can go beyond the standard.** • Describe two quantities in real life that are in a proportional relationship.	
3	**I understand the entire standard.** • Determine whether two quantities are in a proportional relationship.	Tell whether *x* and *y* are proportional. Explain your reasoning. **a.** (table a) **b.** (table b)

a.

x	0	1	2	3
y	0	3	6	9

b.

x	2	4	6	8
y	0	1	2	3

Name____ Date ________

MA.7.AR.4.1 (continued)

<table>
<tr><th></th><th>Description</th><th>Evidence</th></tr>
<tr><td>2</td><td>I understand some parts, but not the entire standard.
• Use a graph to represent the relationship between two quantities.</td><td>Represent the relationship between the quantities using a graph.
<table><tr><td>x</td><td>1</td><td>2</td><td>3</td><td>4</td></tr><tr><td>y</td><td>2</td><td>4</td><td>6</td><td>8</td></tr></table></td></tr>
<tr><td>1</td><td>I understand the basic skills needed to begin learning this standard.
• Determine whether ratios are equivalent.</td><td>Determine whether each pair of ratios are equivalent.
a. 6 : 3 and 2 : 4
b. 4 : 12 and 3 : 9
c. 5 : 10 and 10 : 5</td></tr>
</table>

Name ______________________________ Date ________

Evidence-Based Scale Worksheets

Algebraic Reasoning
MA.7.AR.4.2 Determine the constant of proportionality within a mathematical or real-world context given a table, graph or written description of a proportional relationship.

Circle the scale that best demonstrates your knowledge of the standard.

	Description	Evidence
4	**I can go beyond the standard.** • Teach someone else to find the constant of proportionality between different relationships.	
3	**I understand the entire standard.** • Determine the constant of proportionality with a real-world context from a table, graph, or written description.	Identify the constant of proportionality in each proportional relationship.

a.

Hours, *x*	1	2	3	4
Miles, *y*	35	70	105	140

b.

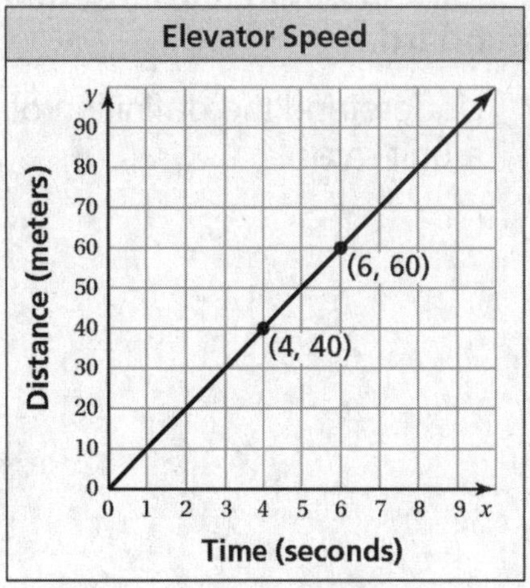

c. A lava flow travels 20 feet every 10 minutes.

Name ______________________________ Date __________

MA.7.AR.4.2 (continued)

Description | **Evidence**

2

I understand some parts, but not the entire standard.

- Determine the constant of proportionality with a mathematical context from a table or a graph.

Identify the constant of proportionality in each proportional relationship.

a.

x	1	2	3	4
y	2.5	5	75	10

b.

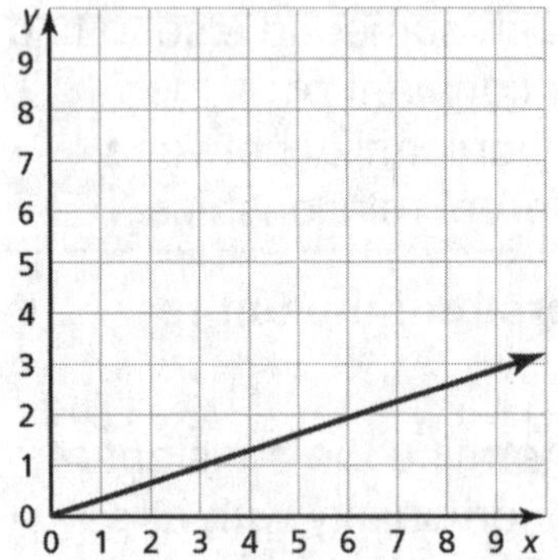

1

I understand the basic skills needed to begin learning this standard.

- Understand the definition of a unit rate.

Determine whether each rate is a unit rate.

a. 5 cups : 2 cups

b. 65 miles per hour

c. $6 for every pound

Name ______________________________ Date ________

Evidence-Based Scale Worksheets

Algebraic Reasoning
MA.7.AR.4.3 Given a mathematical or real-world context, graph proportional relationships from a table, equation or a written description.

Circle the scale that best demonstrates your knowledge of the standard.

	Description	Evidence
4	**I can go beyond the standard.** • Create a real-world context to graph a proportional relationship given a written description.	
3	**I understand the entire standard.** • Given a real-world context, graph proportional relationships based on the given information.	Graph the relationship. Label each axis. **a.** The equation $y = 10x$ represents the number of points scored *y* for answering *x* questions correctly in a game. **b.** Ten horses need 2 bales of hay, while 20 horses need 4 bales of hay.

Name ______________________________ Date ________

MA.7.AR.4.3 (continued)

	Description	Evidence
2	**I understand some parts, but not the entire standard.** • Given a mathematical context, graph proportional relationships based on the given information.	Graph the relationship. **a.** <table><tr><td>*x*</td><td>1</td><td>2</td><td>3</td><td>4</td></tr><tr><td>*y*</td><td>2</td><td>4</td><td>6</td><td>8</td></tr></table> **b.** $y = \frac{1}{4}x$
1	**I understand the basic skills needed to begin learning this standard.** • Determine whether two quantities are in a proportional relationship. • Identify the constant of proportionality in a proportional relationship.	Tell whether *x* and *y* are proportional. If so, identify the constant of proportionality. **a.** $y = 3x$ **b.** <table><tr><td>*x*</td><td>4</td><td>5</td><td>6</td><td>7</td></tr><tr><td>*y*</td><td>3</td><td>5</td><td>7</td><td>9</td></tr></table>

Name ______________________________ Date ________

Evidence-Based Scale Worksheets

Algebraic Reasoning
MA.7.AR.4.4 Given any representation of a proportional relationship, translate the representation to a written description, table or equation.

Circle the scale that best demonstrates your knowledge of the standard.

	Description	Evidence
4	**I can go beyond the standard.** • Explain the process of translating a proportional relationship to different forms.	Explain how to translate a proportional relationship to the following forms. **a.** Equation to table **b.** Written description to graph **c.** Graph to equation
3	**I understand the entire standard.** • Translate the representation of a proportional relationship to another form.	**a.** John earns \$116 for 8 hours of work and \$217.50 for 15 hours of work. Write an equation that represents the amount John earns, y, for working x hours. **b.** The table shows the number of points scored for correct answers in a game show. Write an equation that shows the relationship.

Correct questions, *x*	3	6	9	12
Points, *y*	24	48	72	96

Name ______________________________ Date __________

MA.7.AR.4.4 (continued)

	Description	Evidence
2	**I understand some parts, but not the entire standard.** • Make a plan for how to translate the representation of a proportional relationship to another form.	The graph shows the number of miles a child rides a bike. Explain how to translate the representation to a written description, table, or equation. 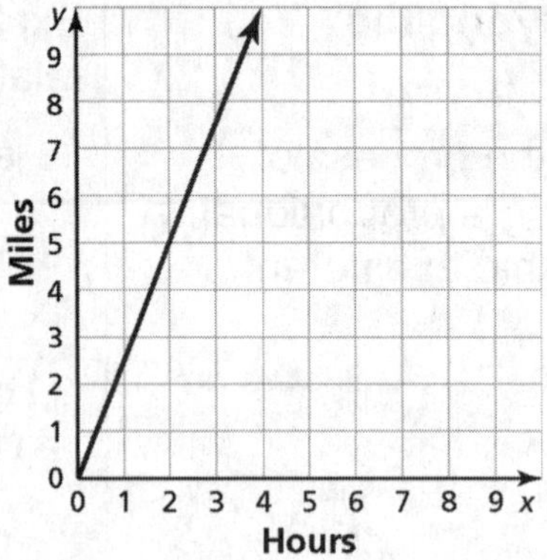
1	**I understand the basic skills needed to begin learning this standard.** • Find the constant of proportionality.	Find the constant of proportionality for each proportional relationship. **a.** $y = \frac{1}{5}x$ **b.** x: 2, 5, 8, 11; y: 6, 15, 24, 33 **c.** When $x = 8$, $y = 12$ and when $x = 2$, $y = 3$.

Table for b.:

x	2	5	8	11
y	6	15	24	33

Name ______________________________ Date __________

Evidence-Based Scale Worksheets

Algebraic Reasoning
MA.7.AR.4.5 Solve real-world problems involving proportional relationships.

Circle the scale that best demonstrates your knowledge of the standard.

	Description	Evidence
4	**I can go beyond the standard.** • Create a real-world problem involving proportional relationships.	
3	**I understand the entire standard.** • Solve real-world problems involving proportional relationships.	**a.** The lockers in a school are blue and gold. There are 8 blue lockers for every 5 gold lockers. There are 200 gold lockers. How many blue lockers are there? **b.** Three bags of fertilizer cover 22,500 square feet. How many square feet are covered with 8 bags of fertilizer?

Name ______________________________ Date ________

MA.7.AR.4.5 (continued)

	Description	Evidence
2	**I understand some parts, but not the entire standard.** • Make a plan for how to solve a real-world proportional problem.	The ratio of boys to girls at a school is $4:5$. If there are 810 students in the school, then how many boys and girls are there in the school? Explain how to translate the representation to a written description, table, or equation.
1	**I understand the basic skills needed to begin learning this standard.** • Solve proportions.	Solve the proportion. **a.** $\frac{4}{5} = \frac{a}{25}$ **b.** $\frac{36}{15} = \frac{12}{b}$ **c.** $\frac{c}{48} = \frac{9}{32}$

Name ______________________________ Date __________

Evidence-Based Scale Worksheets

Geometric Reasoning
MA.7.GR.1.1 Apply formulas to find the areas of trapezoids, parallelograms and rhombi.

Circle the scale that best demonstrates your knowledge of the standard.

	Description	Evidence
4	**I can go beyond the standard.** • Find an unknown dimension of a trapezoid given the area.	Find the unknown dimension of the figure with an area of 114 square centimeters. 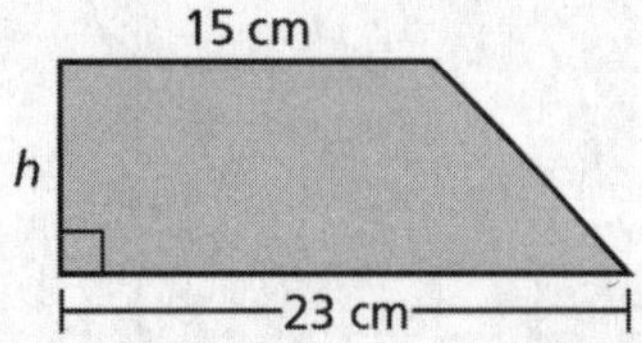
3	**I understand the entire standard.** • Find the areas of trapezoids, parallelograms, and rhombi.	Find the area of each figure. **a.** 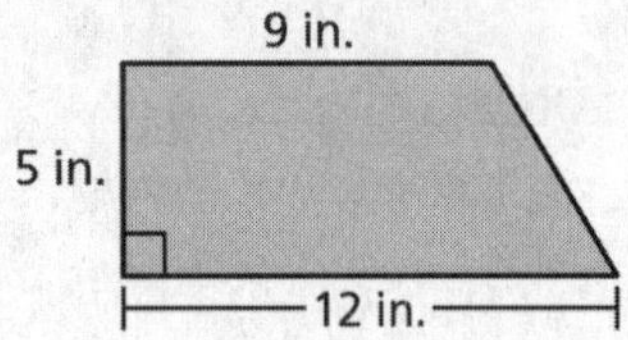 **b.** 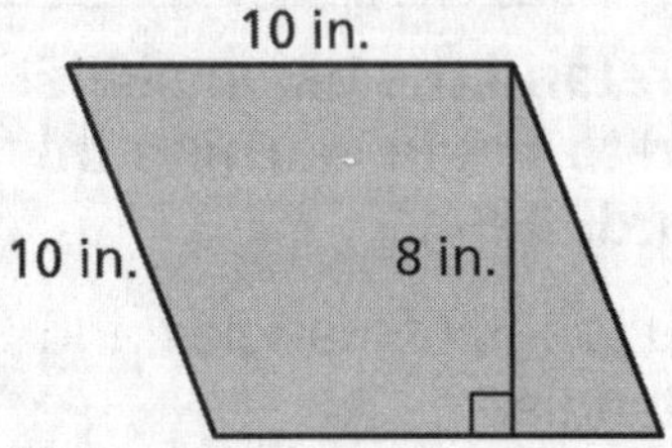 **c.** 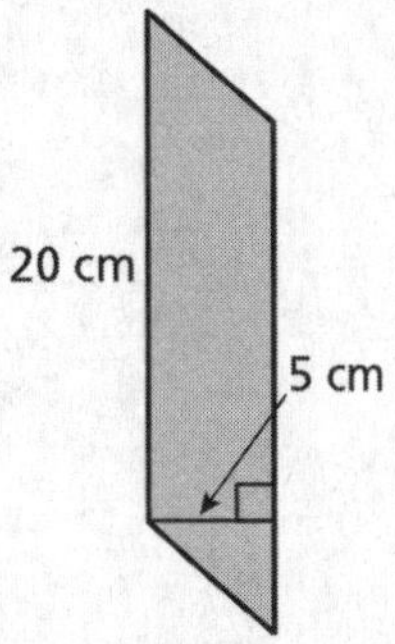

MA.7.GR.1.1 (continued)

	Description	**Evidence**
2	**I understand some parts, but not the entire standard.** • Find the area of a quadrilateral made up of squares, rectangles, and triangles.	Find the area of each figure. **a.** 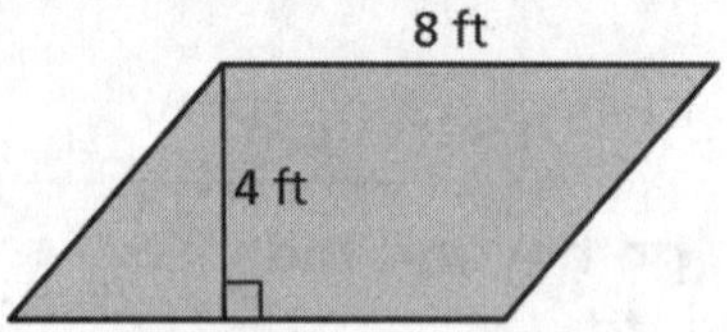 **b.** 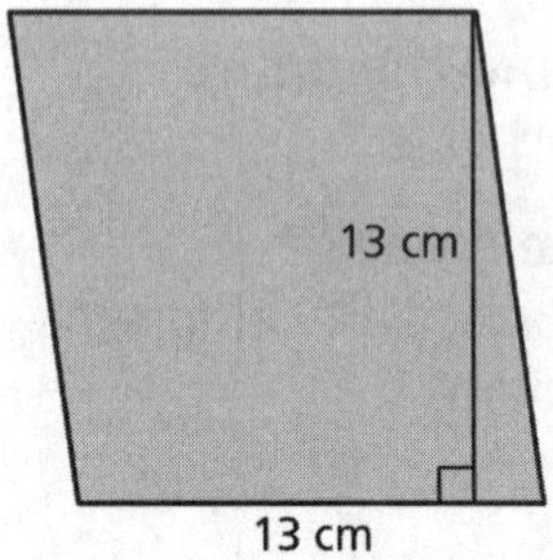
1	**I understand the basic skills needed to begin learning this standard.** • Find areas of triangles and rectangles.	Find the area of each figure. **a.** 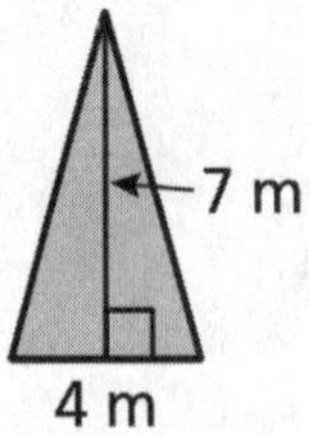 **b.** 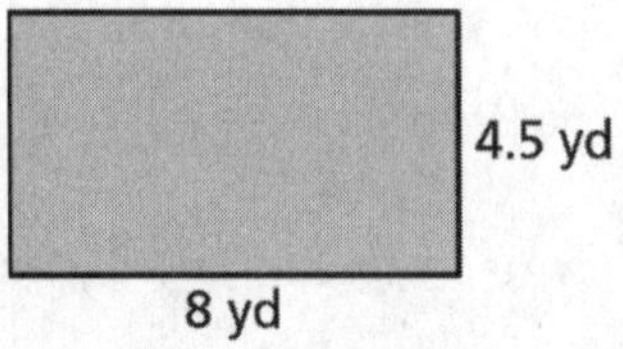

Name ______________________________ Date ________

Evidence-Based Scale Worksheets

Geometric Reasoning
MA.7.GR.1.2 Solve mathematical or real-world problems involving the area of polygons or composite figures by decomposing them into triangles or quadrilaterals.

Circle the scale that best demonstrates your knowledge of the standard.

	Description	Evidence
4	**I can go beyond the standard.** • Write and solve a real-world problem that involves finding areas of composite figures.	
3	**I understand the entire standard.** • Solve a real-world problem involving areas of polygons or composite figures by decomposing them into triangles or quadrilaterals.	A room is to be painted with 2 coats of paint. All walls have a height of 10 feet. Two walls have a length of 18 feet, and the other two walls have a length of 14 feet. There are two windows that are 4 feet by 4 feet and one door that is 3 feet by 7 feet that is not painted. If one quart of paint covers 100 square feet, how many quarts are needed?

Name ______________________________ Date __________

MA.7.GR.1.2 (continued)

	Description	Evidence
2	**I understand some parts, but not the entire standard.** • Solve mathematical problems involving areas of polygons or composite figures by decomposing them into triangles or quadrilaterals.	Find the area of each figure. **a.** 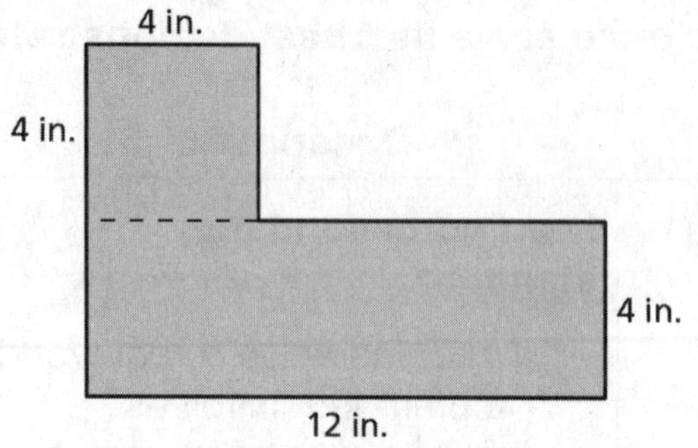 **b.** 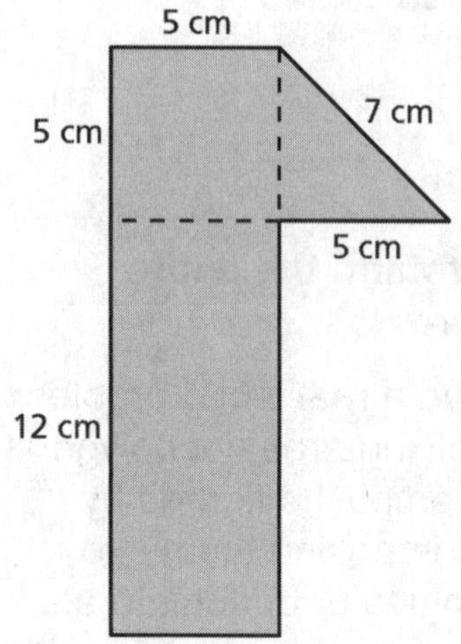
1	**I understand the basic skills needed to begin learning this standard.** • Find areas of quadrilaterals.	Find the area of each figure. **a.** 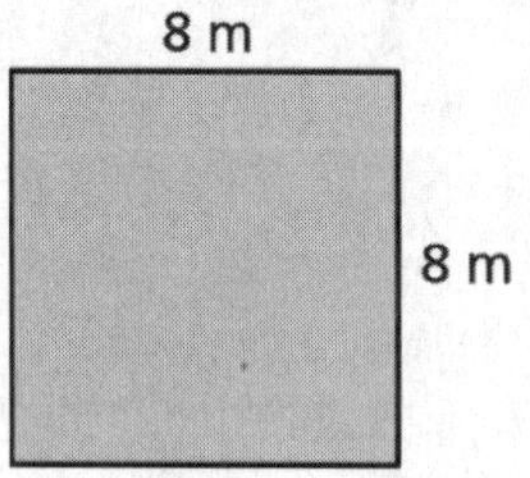 **b.** 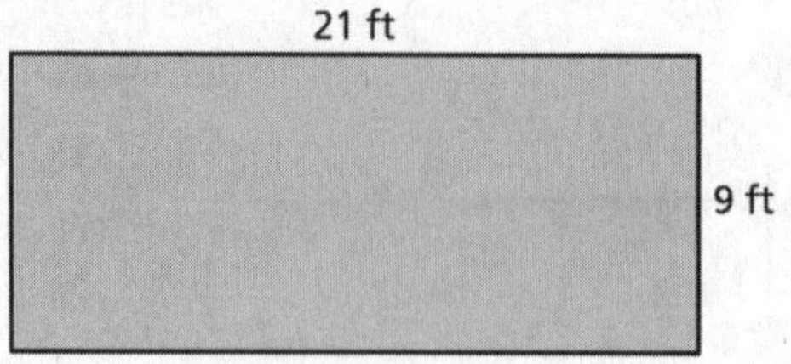

Name ______________________________ Date ________

Evidence-Based Scale Worksheets

Geometric Reasoning
MA.7.GR.1.3 Explore the proportional relationship between circumferences and diameters of circles. Apply a formula for the circumference of a circle to solve mathematical and real-world problems.

Circle the scale that best demonstrates your knowledge of the standard.

	Description	Evidence
4	**I can go beyond the standard.** • Teach someone the proportional relationships between the circumference and the diameter of a circle.	
3	**I understand the entire standard.** • Solve a real-world problem involving the circumference of a circle.	You install a circular pool. The radius of a circular pool cover is 12 feet. You install a fence around the pool so that there is 5 feet between the pool and the fence. The fence costs $3.75 per foot. About how much do you pay for the fence?

MA.7.GR.1.3 (continued)

	Description	Evidence
2	**I understand some parts, but not the entire standard.** • Find circumferences of circles.	Find the circumference of each circle. **a.** 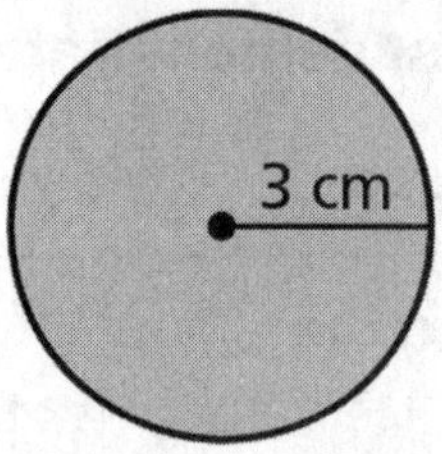 **b.** 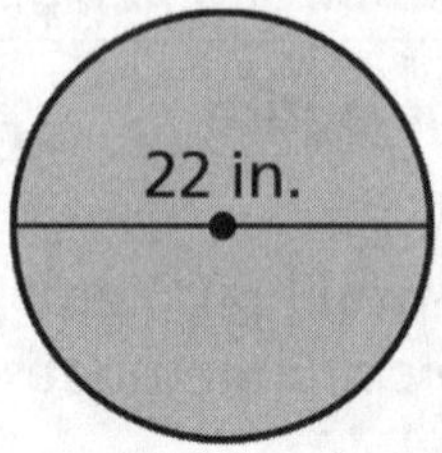
1	**I understand the basic skills needed to begin learning this standard.** • Find the radius of a circle.	Find the radius of each circle. **a.** 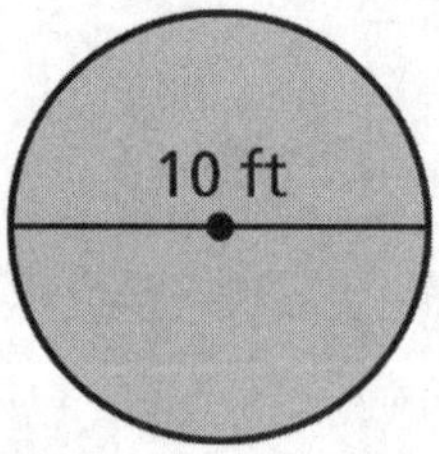 **b.** 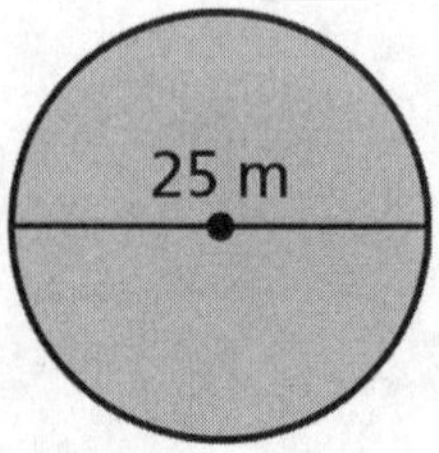

Name ____________________ Date ________

Evidence-Based Scale Worksheets

Geometric Reasoning
MA.7.GR.1.4 Explore and apply a formula to find the area of a circle to solve mathematical and real-world problems.

Circle the scale that best demonstrates your knowledge of the standard.

	Description	Evidence
4	**I can go beyond the standard.** • Solve a real-world problem involving the circumference and the area of a circle.	A circular garden is to be dug with a diameter of 16 feet. There is to be a 1-foot border around the garden. **a.** What is the circumference of the garden? **b.** What is the area of the garden?
3	**I understand the entire standard.** • Solve a real-world problem involving the area of a circle.	A target for a game is shown. 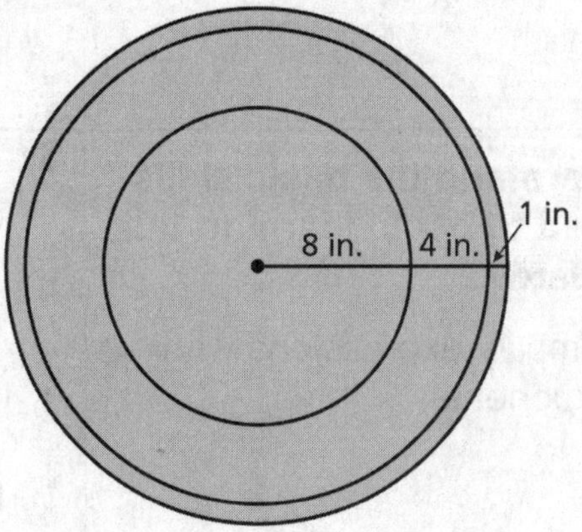 **a.** What is the area of the outer ring? **b.** What is the area of the middle ring?

Name ______________________________ Date ________

MA.7.GR.1.4 (continued)

	Description	Evidence
2	**I understand some parts, but not the entire standard.** • Find areas of circles.	Find the area of each circle. **a.** 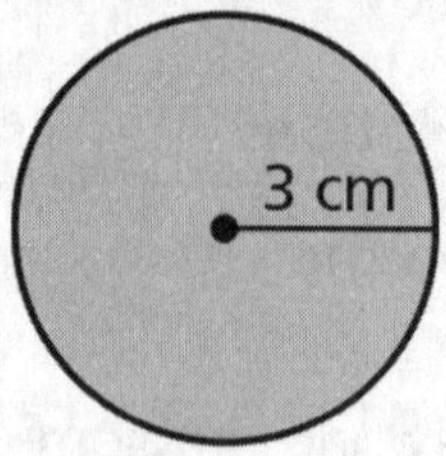 **b.** 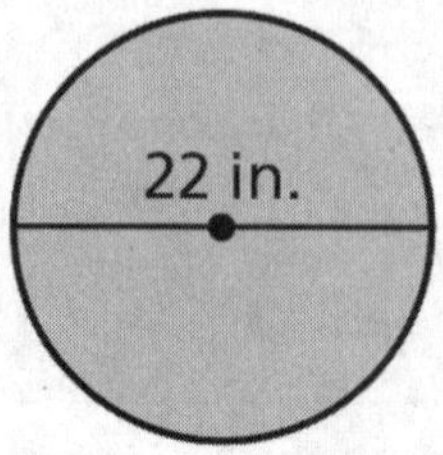
1	**I understand the basic skills needed to begin learning this standard.** • Simplify expressions with exponents.	Simplify each expression. **a.** $3(4)^2$ **b.** $3.1(5)^2$ **c.** $3.14(10)^2$

Name ______________________________ Date ________

Evidence-Based Scale Worksheets

Geometric Reasoning

MA.7.GR.1.5 Solve mathematical and real-world problems involving dimensions and areas of geometric figures, including scale drawings and scale factors.

Circle the scale that best demonstrates your knowledge of the standard.

	Description	Evidence
4	**I can go beyond the standard.** • Create a blueprint of a room in a house on graph paper. Write a problem to find the dimensions and the area of the room.	
3	**I understand the entire standard.** • Solve a real-world problem involving dimensions and areas of geometric figures, including scale drawings.	A scale drawing of the bottom of a rectangular pool has a scale of 2 cm : 5 m. The dimensions of the scale drawing are 10 centimeters by 5 centimeters. **a.** What is the area of the scale drawing? **b.** What is the area of the bottom of the pool?

Name ____________________ Date ________

MA.7.GR.1.5 (continued)

	Description	Evidence
2	**I understand some parts, but not the entire standard.** • Solve a mathematical problem involving dimensions of geometric figures, including scale drawings.	A map has a scale of 1 in. : 80 mi. **a.** On the map, two cities are 3.5 inches apart. What is the actual distance between the two cities? **b.** Two cities are 500 miles apart. What is the distance between the two cities on a map?
1	**I understand the basic skills needed to begin learning this standard.** • Solve proportions.	Solve each proportion. **a.** $\frac{x}{2} = \frac{1}{4}$ **b.** $\frac{4}{5} = \frac{x}{15}$ **c.** $\frac{8}{x} = \frac{2}{5}$

Name ______________________________ Date __________

Evidence-Based Scale Worksheets

Geometric Reasoning

MA.7.GR.2.1 Given a mathematical or real-world context, find the surface area of a right circular cylinder using the figure's net.

Circle the scale that best demonstrates your knowledge of the standard.

	Description	Evidence
4	**I can go beyond the standard.** • Write a real-world problem to find the surface area of a cylinder using the figure's net.	
3	**I understand the entire standard.** • Find the surface area of a cylinder using the figure's net in a real-world context.	A cylindrical water bottle is shown. Find the surface area of the water bottle. 

Name ______________________ Date ________

MA.7.GR.2.1 (continued)

	Description	Evidence
2	**I understand some parts, but not the entire standard.** • Find the surface area of a cylinder using the figure's net in a mathematical context.	Use the net to find the surface area of the cylinder. 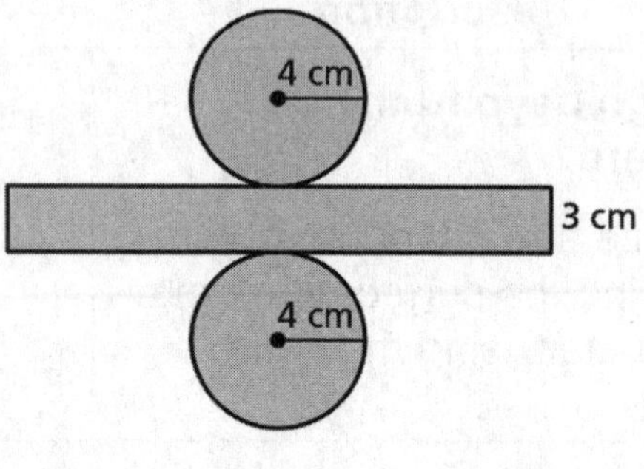
1	**I understand the basic skills needed to begin learning this standard.** • Simplify algebraic expressions that involve π.	Simplify each expression. **a.** $2\pi(12)^2 + 2\pi(12)(3)$ **b.** $2\pi(7.5)^2 + 2\pi(7.5)(20)$

Name ______________________________ Date __________

Evidence-Based Scale Worksheets

Geometric Reasoning
MA.7.GR.2.2 Solve real-world problems involving surface area of right circular cylinders.

Circle the scale that best demonstrates your knowledge of the standard.

	Description	Evidence
4	**I can go beyond the standard.** • Given the surface area of a cylinder, find the height and the radius of the cylinder.	The surface area of a cylinder is 1000π square centimeters. The height is 4 times the radius. Find the height and the radius.
3	**I understand the entire standard.** • Solve a real-world problem involving the surface areas of cylinders.	**a.** The diameter of a cylindrical soup can is 8 inches and has a height of 6 inches. Find the amount of material needed to make the can. **b.** A large cylindrical container has a diameter of 5 feet and a height of 3.5 feet. Find the amount of material needed to make the container.

Name ______________________________ Date ________

MA.7.GR.2.2 (continued)

	Description	Evidence
2	**I understand some parts, but not the entire standard.** • Make a plan for how to find the surface area of a cylinder in a real-world problem.	Make a plan for how to find the surface area of a cylinder. A wheel of cheese is in the shape of a cylinder. The height of the wheel is 2.5 centimeters and the diameter is 18 centimeters.
1	**I understand the basic skills needed to begin learning this standard.** • Find the surface area of a cylinder given the radius and the height.	Find the surface area of a cylinder with the given dimensions. **a.** radius = 8 feet, height = 20 feet **b.** radius = 6 inches, height = 5 inches

Name ______________________________ Date __________

Evidence-Based Scale Worksheets

Geometric Reasoning
MA.7.GR.2.3 Solve mathematical and real-world problems involving volume of right circular cylinders.

Circle the scale that best demonstrates your knowledge of the standard.

	Description	Evidence
4	**I can go beyond the standard.** • Given the surface area and the radius of a cylinder, find the volume of the cylinder.	The surface area of a cylinder is approximately 2034.72 square centimeters. Find the volume of the cylinder if the radius is 12 centimeters.
3	**I understand the entire standard.** • Solve a real-world problem involving the volume of a cylinder.	**a.** The diameter of a cylindrical soup can is 8 inches and has a height of 6 inches. The can is 90% full. Find the amount of soup that the can holds. **b.** A large cylindrical container has a diameter of 5 feet and a height of 3.5 feet. Find the number of gallons the container holds. (1 ft^3 is approximately 7.5 gallons)

Name ______________________________ Date ________

MA.7.GR.2.3 (continued)

	Description	Evidence
2	**I understand some parts, but not the entire standard.** • Solve a mathematical problem involving the volume of a cylinder.	Find the volume of a cylinder with the given dimensions. **a.** radius = 8 feet, height = 20 feet **b.** diameter = 12 inches, height = 5 inches
1	**I understand the basic skills needed to begin learning this standard.** • Evaluate expressions.	Evaluate each expression. **a.** $(6^2)9$ **b.** $3(4^2)5.5$ **c.** $3.14(10^2)8$

Name ____ Date ________

Evidence-Based Scale Worksheets

Data Analysis and Probability
MA.7.DP.1.1 Determine an appropriate measure of center or measure of variation to summarize numerical data, represented numerically or graphically, taking into consideration the context and any outliers.

Circle the scale that best demonstrates your knowledge of the standard.

	Description	Evidence
4	**I can go beyond the standard.** • Explain which measures of center and variation can be determined when using different graphical representations.	Explain which measures of center and spread can be identified for a histogram, line plot, box plot, and stem-and-leaf plots.
3	**I understand the entire standard.** • Determine an appropriate measure of center to summarize numerical data. • Determine an appropriate measure of variation to summarize numerical data.	The stem and leaf plot shows the leading scorer in the last 15 basketball games. (See plot below.) **a.** Determine an appropriate measure of center to summarize the numerical data. Explain your reasoning. **b.** Determine an appropriate measure of variation to summarize the numerical data. Explain your reasoning.

Stem	Leaf
1	5
2	4 5 5 7 7 8 9
3	0 0 1 2 3 5 8

Key: 1|5 = 15

Name ______________________________ Date ________

MA.7.DP.1.1 (continued)

	Description	Evidence
2	**I understand some parts, but not the entire standard.** • Make a plan to determine the appropriate measures of center and variation from numerical data.	Make a plan to determine the appropriate measures of center and variation for the data set. 100, 110, 150, 140, 130, 170, 160, 180, 190
1	**I understand the basic skills needed to begin learning this standard.** • Find the mean, median, range, and interquartile range of numerical data.	Find the mean, median, range, and interquartile range of the data set. 18, 24, 15, 25, 24, 23, 22, 19, 21, 20

Name ______________________________ Date ________

Evidence-Based Scale Worksheets

Data Analysis and Probability
MA.7.DP.1.2 Given two numerical or graphical representations of data, use the measure(s) of center and measure(s) of variability to make comparisons, interpret results and draw conclusions about the two populations.

Circle the scale that best demonstrates your knowledge of the standard.

	Description	Evidence
4	**I can go beyond the standard.** • Write a real-world problem involving two populations with similar measures of center but greatly different measures of variation.	
3	**I understand the entire standard.** • Determine appropriate measures of center and variation to summarize numerical data of two population and draw conclusions.	Two bags each contain 500 numbered tiles. The double box-and-whisker plot represents a random sample of 10 numbers from each bag. 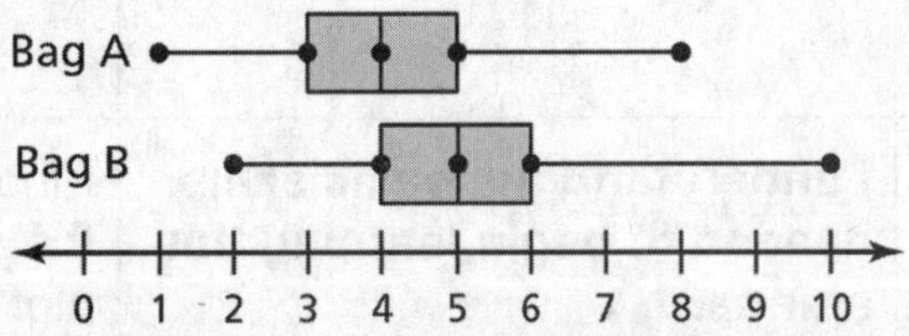 Compare the samples using measures of center and variability. Can you determine which bag contains tiles with greater numbers? Explain.

Name ______________________________ Date __________

MA.7.DP.1.2 (continued)

	Description	Evidence
2	**I understand some parts, but not the entire standard.** • Make a plan to summarize two sets of numerical data when given data values graphically.	Make a plan to determine the appropriate measures of center and variation from the double dot plot. 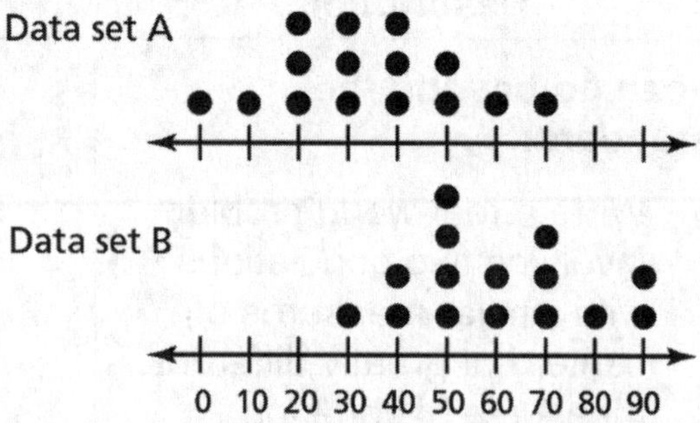
1	**I understand the basic skills needed to begin learning this standard.** • Read a box-and-whisker plot.	Find the median and interquartile range of the data represented by the box-and-whisker plot. 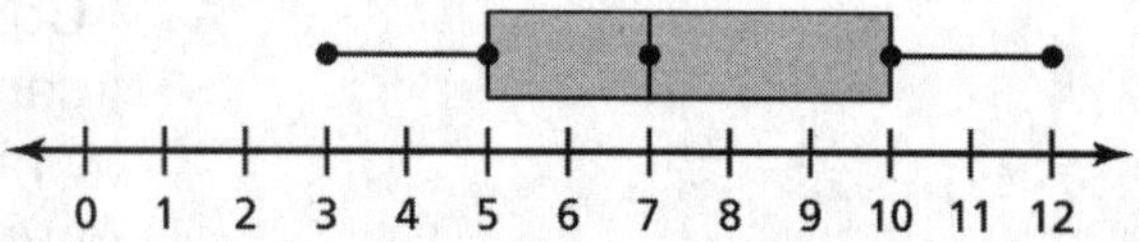

Name ______________________________ Date ________

Evidence-Based Scale Worksheets

Data Analysis and Probability
MA.7.DP.1.3 Given categorical data from a random sample, use proportional relationships to make predictions about a population.

Circle the scale that best demonstrates your knowledge of the standard.

	Description	Evidence
4	**I can go beyond the standard.** • Create a short survey and ask a random sample of 7th graders. Then draw conclusions about the populations using the total number of students in the 7th grade.	
3	**I understand the entire standard.** • Given categorical data from a random sample, use proportional relationships to make predictions about a population.	**a.** You ask 50 randomly chosen students at a school whether they can swim the length of a pool. Thirty-eight students say they can. There are 900 students in the school. Estimate the number of students in the school that can swim the length of a pool. **b.** You ask 40 randomly chosen employees at a company whether they use public transportation to get to work. Twelve people say yes. The company has 220 employees. Estimate the number of employees that use public transportation to get to work.

Name____ Date __________

MA.7.DP.1.3 (continued)

	Description	Evidence
2	**I understand some parts, but not the entire standard.** • Given categorical data from a random sample, find a percent of the sample.	**a.** You randomly select 2000 screws and find that 12 were defective. Find the percent of screws that are defective. **b.** You ask 150 students about their favorite sports. Eighty students say basketball. Find the percent of students that say basketball.
1	**I understand the basic skills needed to begin learning this standard.** • Find missing values in equivalent ratios.	Find the value of x so that each pair of ratios is equivalent. **a.** 2 : 4 and x : 8 **b.** 12 : 50 and x : 600

Name ______________________________ Date ________

Evidence-Based Scale Worksheets

Data Analysis and Probability
MA.7.DP.1.4 Use proportional reasoning to construct, display and interpret data in circle graphs.

Circle the scale that best demonstrates your knowledge of the standard.

	Description	Evidence
4	**I can go beyond the standard.** • Ask students in class a questions about a topic. Then create a circle graph from the data presented in class.	
3	**I understand the entire standard.** • Use proportional reasoning to interpret data in circle graphs.	The data in the circle graph shows the favorite animals of 7th graders. There are 10 students who favor cats. 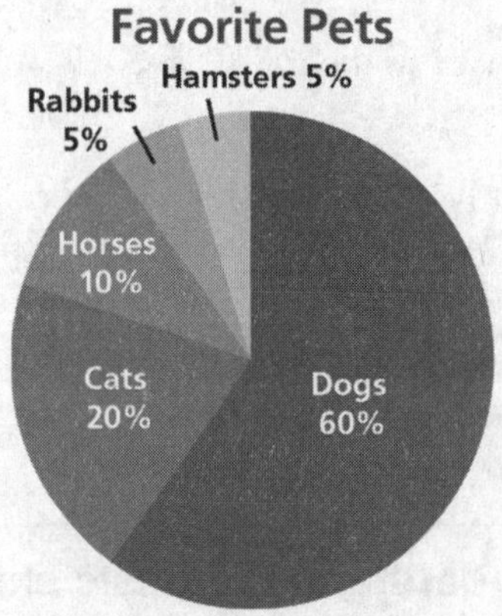 **a.** How many 7th-grade students are there? **b.** What is the probability that a randomly chosen 7th-grade student likes dogs?

Name____ Date ________

MA.7.DP.1.4 (continued)

<table>
<tr><th></th><th>Description</th><th>Evidence</th></tr>
<tr><td>2</td><td>I understand some parts, but not the entire standard.
• Construct a circle graph for the data.</td><td>Construct a circle graph for the data set.
<table><tr><th>Favorite Vegetable</th><th>Respondents</th></tr><tr><td>Carrots</td><td>40</td></tr><tr><td>Peas</td><td>16</td></tr><tr><td>Corn</td><td>20</td></tr><tr><td>Potatoes</td><td>9</td></tr><tr><td>Green Beans</td><td>15</td></tr></table>
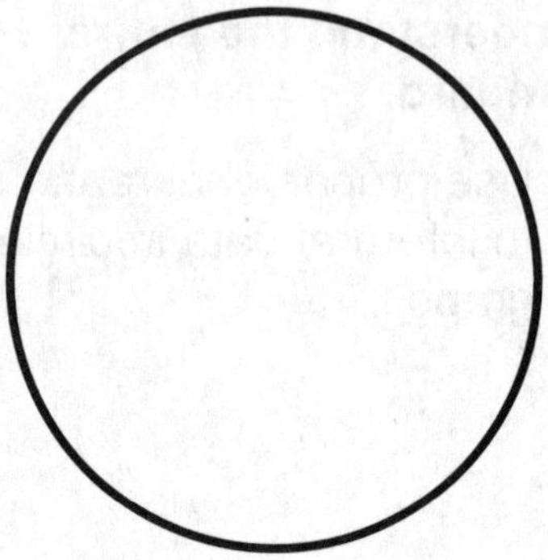</td></tr>
<tr><td>1</td><td>I understand the basic skills needed to begin learning this standard.
• Solve proportions.</td><td>Solve the proportions for x.
a. $\frac{20}{200} = \frac{x}{360}$
b. $\frac{75}{100} = \frac{x}{360}$
c. $\frac{120}{500} = \frac{x}{360}$</td></tr>
</table>

Name ______________________________ Date ________

Evidence-Based Scale Worksheets

Data Analysis and Probability
MA.7.DP.1.5 Given a real-world numerical or categorical data set, choose and create an appropriate graphical representation.

Circle the scale that best demonstrates your knowledge of the standard.

	Description	Evidence
4	**I can go beyond the standard.** • Explain what a histogram, bar graph, circle graph, line plot, box plot, and stem-and-leaf plot show in a data set.	Explain what a histogram, bar graph, circle graph, line plot, box plot, and stem-and-leaf plot show in a data set.
3	**I understand the entire standard.** • Given a real-world numerical or categorical data set, create an appropriate data display to represent the data.	Create an appropriate data display to represent the data. **a.** (see table below) **b.** (see table below)

a.

Birthday Months of Employees			
Jan.	4	Jul.	5
Feb.	3	Aug.	3
Mar.	5	Sept.	3
Apr.	7	Oct.	7
May	8	Nov.	6
Jun.	2	Dec.	8

b.

Number of Vacation Days for Employees			
8	10	12	9
16	14	15	17
19	20	25	7
21	22	23	16
24	11	5	6

Name ______________________________ Date __________

MA.7.DP.1.5 (continued)

	Description	Evidence
2	**I understand some parts, but not the entire standard.** • Given a real-world numerical or categorical data set, make a plan for how to create an appropriate data display to represent the data.	Make a plan for how to create an appropriate data display to represent the data. **a.** (Quiz Scores table below) **b.** (Books Read by a Class table below)
1	**I understand the basic skills needed to begin learning this standard.** • Identify the type of data display.	Identify the type of data display. **a.** 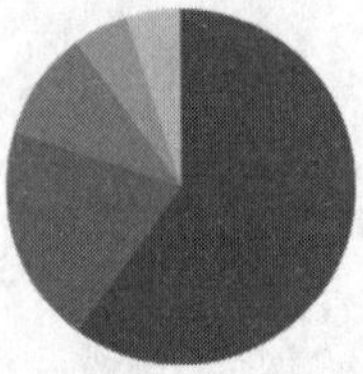 **b.** 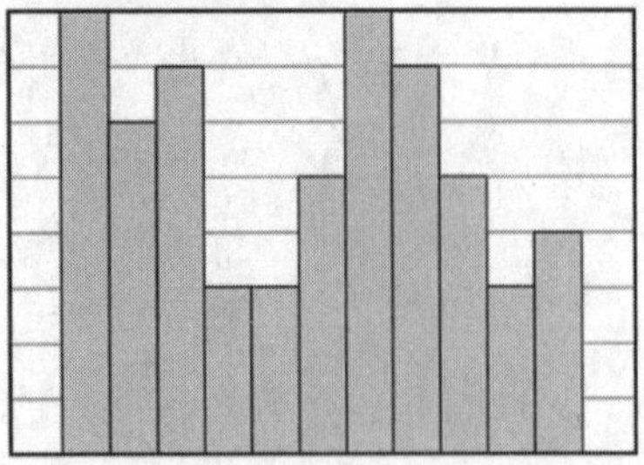

a.

Quiz Scores			
20	15	17	18
16	14	15	17
18	12	13	15
16	20	20	19
19	20	18	15

b.

Books Read by a Class			
30	18	9	16
34	15	25	8
11	16	19	22
33	31	7	11
22	24	25	21

Name ______________________________ Date ________

Evidence-Based Scale Worksheets

Data Analysis and Probability
MA.7.DP.2.1 Determine the sample space for a simple experiment.

Circle the scale that best demonstrates your knowledge of the standard.

	Description	Evidence
4	**I can go beyond the standard.** • Create a simple experiment where the sample space needs to be determined.	
3	**I understand the entire standard.** • Determine the sample space for an experiment.	**a.** You roll one six-sided number cube. Find the sample space. **b.** You roll two six-sided number cubes. Find the sample space.

Name ____ Date __________

MA.7.DP.2.1 (continued)

	Description	**Evidence**
2	**I understand some parts, but not the entire standard.** • Determine the sample space for a simple experiment.	**a.** You flip one coin. Find the sample space. **b.** You flip two coins. Find the sample space.
1	**I understand the basic skills needed to begin learning this standard.** • Define sample space.	Define sample space.

Name ______________________________ Date ________

Evidence-Based Scale Worksheets

Data Analysis and Probability
MA.7.DP.2.2 Given the probability of a chance event, interpret the likelihood of it occurring. Compare the probabilities of chance events.

Circle the scale that best demonstrates your knowledge of the standard.

	Description	Evidence
4	**I can go beyond the standard.** • Describe real-life events with a given likelihood.	Describe a real-life event that is impossible, a real-life event that is neither unlikely nor likely, and a real-life event that is certain.
3	**I understand the entire standard.** • Understand probability and describe the likelihood of an event.	There is a 90% chance a team wins their last game, a 50% chance they win their division, and a 10% chance they win the championship. Describe the likelihood of each event. **a.** The team wins their last game. **b.** The team wins their division. **c.** The team wins the championship.

Name ____ Date __________

MA.7.DP.2.2 (continued)

	Description	Evidence
2	**I understand some parts, but not the entire standard.** • Understand that the probability of an event is a number between 0 and 1 that expresses the likelihood of the event.	A meteorologist includes the probability that it will rain tomorrow in her weather forecast. Decide which numbers represent possible probabilities. 50% 0 150% –20% $1\frac{1}{2}$ 0.01 –0.8 1.25 $\frac{49}{100}$
1	**I understand the basic skills needed to begin learning this standard.** • Write decimals as fractions and percents.	Write each decimal as a fraction and a percent. **a.** 0.6 **b.** 0.38 **c.** 0.07

Name ______________________ Date ________

Evidence-Based Scale Worksheets

Data Analysis and Probability
MA.7.DP.2.3 Find the theoretical probability of an event related to a simple experiment.

Circle the scale that best demonstrates your knowledge of the standard.

	Description	Evidence
4	**I can go beyond the standard.** • Create a simple experiment problem and write problems to find the theoretical probability.	
3	**I understand the entire standard.** • Find the theoretical probability of an event related to a simple experiment.	There are 10 blue marbles, 6 red marbles, 12 green marbles, and 2 orange marbles. One marble is selected and replaced. Find the following theoretical probabilities. **a.** blue marble **b.** not a green marble. **c.** orange marble two times in a row

Name ______________________________ Date ________

MA.7.DP.2.3 (continued)

	Description	Evidence
2	**I understand some parts, but not the entire standard.** • Make a plan to find the theoretical probability of an event related to a simple experiment.	There are red, green, yellow, and orange cards in a deck. For each color, there is a number card from 0 to 9. Make a plan to find the theoretical probability of an event related to a simple experiment.
1	**I understand the basic skills needed to begin learning this standard.** • Write fractions as decimals and percents.	Write each fraction as a decimal and a percent. **a.** $\frac{2}{5}$ **b.** $\frac{2}{3}$ **c.** $\frac{11}{16}$

Name ______________________________ Date ________

Evidence-Based Scale Worksheets

Data Analysis and Probability
MA.7.DP.2.4 Use a simulation of a simple experiment to find experimental probabilities and compare them to theoretical probabilities.

Circle the scale that best demonstrates your knowledge of the standard.

<table>
<tr><th></th><th>Description</th><th>Evidence</th></tr>
<tr><td>4</td><td>I can go beyond the standard.
• Use collected data from a chance event to approximate the probability of the event.</td><td></td></tr>
<tr><td>3</td><td>I understand the entire standard.
• Use a simulation of a simple experiment to find experimental probabilities and compare them to theoretical probabilities.</td><td>You flip a coin 20 times and record the number of times it lands on heads and tails.
<table><tr><td>Heads</td><td>𝍸 𝍸 ||</td></tr><tr><td>Tails</td><td>𝍸 |||</td></tr></table>
a. What is the experimental probability that the coin lands on heads? Compare the probability to the theoretical probability.

b. How many times would you expect the coin to land on heads in 200 flips, based on the experiment?</td></tr>
</table>

Name ______________________________ Date __________

MA.7.DP.2.4 (continued)

	Description	Evidence
2	**I understand some parts, but not the entire standard.** • Find the probability of an event.	**a.** A student is selected at random in a class that has 13 girls and 12 boys. What is the probability that a girl is chosen? **b.** There are 15 red marbles, 10 blue marbles, and 5 green marbles in a bag. What is the probability of selecting a green marble?
1	**I understand the basic skills needed to begin learning this standard.** • Find products of rational numbers.	Find each product. **a.** 0.75(100) **b.** $\frac{1}{2} \cdot 80$ **c.** $\frac{3}{10} \times 150$